INTERNATIONAL LAW AND TRANSNATIONAL ORGANIZED CRIME

INTERNATIONAL LAW AND TRANSNATIONAL ORGANIZED CRIME

Anne Wade

SOCIETY Publishing

www.societypublishing.com

International Law and Transnational Organized Crime

Anne Wade

Society Publishing

2010 Winston Park Drive,

2nd Floor

Oakville, ON L6H 5R7

Canada

www.societypublishing.com

Tel: 001-289-291-7705
001-905-616-2116
Fax: 001-289-291-7601
Email: orders@arclereducation.com

ISBN: 978-1-77407-206-6 (Hardcover)

ABOUT THE AUTHOR

Dr. Anne Wade has been a researcher and an instruction in the Criminal Justice field for 27 years. She is currently an Associate Professor at a Community College in North Carolina. She holds an Ed.D. in Educational Leadership and a Ph.D. in Public Safety Leadership/Criminal Justice. Her research interests are in Criminology, Victimology, and the Human Services. She is married to Wesley Wade. She is an artist, writer, research, teacher, and trainer.

TABLE OF CONTENTS

LIST OF FIGURES

LIST OF ABBREVIATIONS

ACI	Andean counterdrug initiative
AID	Agency for International Development
AML	anti-money laundering
BIS	Bureau of industry and security
CATOC	convention against transnational organized crime
CBP	Customs and Border Protection
CC	control of corruption
CPI	corruption perception index
DBTCA	Deutsche Bank Trust Company of the Americas
DDR	disarmament, demobilization, and reintegration
DEA	Drug Enforcement Agency
DFS	Department of Financial Services
DOJ	Department of Justice
EXBS	Export Control and Related Border Security Assistance Program
FATF	financial action task force
FTA	free trade agreements
GTD	global terrorism database
HBMX	HSBC in Mexico
IACP	International Association of Chiefs of Police
ICC	International Criminal Court
ICE	immigration and customs enforcement
ICI	International Cocoa Initiative
ICTY	International Criminal Tribunal for the former Yugoslavia
IDP	internally displaced persons
IHL	International humanitarian law

ILEAs	International Law Enforcement Academies
ILO	International Labor Organization
INL	International Narcotics and Law
IP	intellectual property
ITERATE	International Terrorism: Attributes of Terrorist Events
KYC	Know Your Customer
MIPT	Memorial Institute for the Prevention of Terrorism
NIA	National Interest Analysis
OCCRP	organized crime and corruption reporting project
PFC	priority foreign country
START	Study of Terrorism and Responses to Terrorism
STOP!	Strategy Targeting Organized Piracy
SWBI	southwest border initiative
TFI	terrorism and financial intelligence
TOC	transnational organized crime
TWEED	Terrorism in Western Europe: Event Data
UNODC	United Nations Office on Drugs and Crime
UNTOC	United Nations Convention against Transnational Organized Crime
USTR	United States Trade Representative
VAR	vector autoregression
WMD	Weapon of Mass Destruction
WTO	World Trade Organization
WWF	World Wildlife Fund

PREFACE

The end of the Cold War gave rise to various forms of Transnational Organized Crime (TOC) in various States. These are organized crimes that happen to coordinate across different national borders which involve people of several groups along with some big networks and institutions working closely for implementing an illegal crime or activity. Such crimes are a threat to the growing international security which at the same time adversely affects public safety and the freedom to enjoy the rights provided by their nation's constitution. Thus, to eradicate the growing threat at an international level, it is important to have "International Law" which would help in acknowledging all organized crimes.

TOC and its impact are devastating. The corruptive practices make the public lose trust in their State and the policies of the State. This further erodes the integrity of government officials who work in saving the rights of the public. Therefore, it is necessary to examine a reduction of damage by taking a detailed look at various approaches, especially the "UN Conventions" and how they assist in controlling organized crimes.

This book will trace the meaning of TOC and the importance of International Law in handling issues related to it. It will also provide a concise insight into the challenges of prosecuting TOC. There is a plethora of information out there on various organized crimes that have been taking place in various nations all around the world. The existing UN conventions act as the global response to all those international challenges that emerged due to the penetration of organized crimes in various nations.

As defined in this book, "*Transnational organized crime happens through a web of homogeneous groups which are associated to one another sometimes across borders by several forms of complicity, solidarity, and a hierarchical order.*" It indicates how TOC has its own dynamic characteristic having no ordinary definition available in criminal theories. This book will offer clear insights and perceptions that can be worked upon for change, which will eventually help in lessening the impacts of organized crimes over the States and societies.

The subject matter of this book starts from establishing a clear picture of what exactly International Law is. Education will continue to widen the understanding of improving the effectiveness of those UN conventions that have been formulated to safeguard the common rights of the public and would help in understanding that how its protocols demonstrates the necessity to comprehend this subject in a systematic way. The next focus will be a list of various crimes that are related to TOC. For instance, terrorism, money laundering, corruption, etc. This section will also present the existing areas of improvement and challenges included under the various segments aimed at improving the complex situations of nations. Towards the end, an international perspective on policing TOC will be covered.

1

Introduction to International Law: History and Evolution

CONTENTS

The main role of International Law is to help in determining the obligations and the responsibilities of each State, individuals, organizations, and enterprises. During the past 50 years interconnection has become more popular across the world. In part, the popularity is because of the advances in the information and technology, and the increasing reliance on the various other countries for services as well as the resources. The terminology of International Law tends to include the various distinct subsets related to the law, possessing an inclusion of the private international law, supranational or regional agreements, foreign policy law, and public international law. This chapter talks about the history as well as the evolution of the International Law and how it helped the various domains in the world.

1.1. INTRODUCTION

The law promulgated on the global level or the law of the Nations, being the body of the various rules, generally tends to govern the association of the states which are independent. These laws are considered to be ancient similar to independent states themselves.

Unpretentious at the time of establishing and accepting the restricted provided rules which all are generally being interpreted by the pertaining states within the association, the law being made at a global level has been developed to a significant degree within each specific community.

These laws are based on the regions of the ancients that are related to the various nations across the globe, along with their performing or practiced the treaties. The presentation or the representation of these laws is diplomatic, negotiation at an international level and possessing the language, which is both- diplomatic as well as commonly used.

Laws were promulgated in Greek times in relation to the state where the nucleus of the law was about institutions rather than people. These laws expanded when nations needed to interact with each other. In the middle ages to current day, the laws made were binding on other states as well as the participating state. This mutually added accountability. These laws started inside the world of the Christians, and afterward, it carried onto the various communities belonging to the civilized nations.

The various treaties made were acknowledged as the major landmarks within the growth or the development of the scope of the law, which was made at an international level, common to all. As territories were created, they too possessed an acceptance of all the existing countries across the globe.

During this charter of history the various countries and the organizations and the agencies which have been connected or associated along with all of the power they possess and executing the novel rules which have just been established. These laws are binding upon the pertaining states in the name of the global peace, and providing justice as well as protection or security. These laws are recognized as legitimate due to the introduction of the novel epoch in the relations at an international level and are based on the legal, political, and the economic aspect.

The process of the associating various rules related to that of the international laws has been successful in making up a far greater process. During the past 14 years and just after the end of the Second World War, various peace treaties have included more international law than ever before.

This specific progress of creating more international laws became necessary with the growth of technology, ease of transportation across country borders and more sophistical methods of military destruction.

Despite having such great growth or development of international law, those reporting on the laws needed to feel the laws were legitimate in order to be able to defend their implementation. There have been concerns raised over the legitimacy of the laws and critical attacks being made by the jurists or the philosophers related to the law. Those attacking the laws are various writers as well as the many of the people who are educated and still feel that the international law is being related to the sphere of the morality at an international level.

Many of the writers share their outdated perceptions or the point of views, and therefore have caused much of the concern related to the points given below:

- The absenteeism of the authority, which is being superior, to the various independent states;
- The non- appearance of the legislator;
- The non- attendance of the pertaining sanctions;
- The inefficacy in the process of aversion of the war and also the uncountable violations of the rules related to the international law.

Thus, it becomes quite interesting to do the review of the various definitions as well as the description of the international law which has already been given by the several authorities within this field, as the existing definitions or the descriptions.

The description or the definition which has been provided within various groups, does not tend to differ significantly from each other but it has been said by the various writers that the definitions or the description being provided by many writers are considered to be much more similar as compared to that of the expectations one might be possessing regarding the distinctive opinions or the perceptions, which all the writers tend to exhibit.

The classical definition regarding the international law, which has been provided by the many of the scholars of the law two centuries. It might be available in the leading textbooks written by many of the writers and for whom, the law which has been made at a global level is still being the body of the various existing rules as well as the regulations, which generally helps in determining the rights and the duties of the various states in respect of their mutual connections.

1.2. INTERNATIONAL LAW

When there are concerns related to global issues, it is the International Law that helps in determining the responsibilities and obligations of each State, organization or individual. During the last 50 years, there has been a connection between different countries with huge leaps in communication and technology.

Countries are now dependent on each other for various resources and also services during times of need. However, countries are always cooperative with each other, and a lot of friction has been observed between the governments of various countries. In such circumstances, international law plays an important role for achieving international cooperation at every level.

International Law, at a day-to-day level, performs various functions effectively with little or no awareness by those affected and done so seamlessly. People of different countries now have the flexibility to travel from one country to another without cause for concern. There are also various television programs that are broadcasted at a global level. With international agreements, postal, and electronic mail are now easily delivered across borders (Figure 1.1).

Figure 1.1: Various subsets of international law.

The term "international law" is basically used to cover different subsets of law, which also includes private international law, public international law, supranational or regional agreements, and foreign policy law. When the term "international law" is used in the media or in everyday discussion, it is then referred to public international law. Below, private international law and public international have been described in detail:

1.2.1. Private International Law

"Private international law" (according to civil law countries such as France, Italy, and Spain) and for common law countries like the United Kingdom, the United States, Australia, and Canada, the term Private International Law is referred to as "conflict of laws." So, private international law is that body of law that has been developed to resolve issues related to private, non-state disputes which comprise more than one jurisdiction or one foreign law element.

According to the term, conflict of laws, it can also be stated as that body of law, where more than one jurisdiction is a part of a legal action, and there are chances that a conflict might arise between laws of the different jurisdictions that are inter-related with each other. Conflict of laws is generally applicable in situations such as marriage, birthrights, divorce, settlement of property, and commercial disputes when more than one jurisdiction is involved. But, there are two questions that are required to be answered while getting involved in such situations of conflict of laws. Those two questions are: Does the proposed court or tribunal in a certain nation-state (State) have the jurisdiction to hear and decide this case? and

- Which of the competing States' laws should be applied to resolve this case?

An example which demands for the conflict of laws would be the situation:

A couple residing in New York City decides to file for divorce. In this case, the wife is a Sri Lankan national and the husband is an American national. The couple owns a property together in the New York City and in England. If the wife believes she would get better treatment in a Sri Lankan court than an American court, she may want to bring divorce proceedings in Sri Lanka rather than in New York City. The husband may decide to bring his own court action in New York City, if he believes this court would give him a better result than a Sri Lankan court would.

Each State has its own laws related to divorce, each court to which an action is brought must decide if it has the jurisdiction to hear and rule on the underlying case before it. It must also decide if it is the appropriate forum for deciding the dispute. Here, the appropriate court in Sri Lanka and in the United States are first required to resolve the conflict of laws questions before the particulars of the divorce case can proceed.

If a court decides it has the jurisdiction to hear the case, it will then decide which law should apply to the case. This may mean that a Sri Lankan court applies American law to the divorce case. Generally, the more foreign law elements that are present in a conflict of laws situation, the more complex is the analysis to reach a resolution.

1.2.2. Public International Law

- **In general terminology:** Previously, International Law was known as Law of Nations, and it consisted of various rules and regulations along with few principles that would help in providing governance and achieving cordial relations between different states. This would further help in binding all the international actors together. At the core of international law, it is believed that all commitments are supposed to be made publicly, formally, and voluntarily by a State, and they all should be honored by the general public of each state ("agreements are to be kept").

In practice, international law is based on reciprocity of treatment, which states that one State is required to treat other States as it wants to be treated. The development of international law has occurred over time. At an early stage, international law was exclusively applied only to international diplomatic situations and to the conduct of war. Until the last half of the twentieth century, international law only applied to and between States. Now it has been expanded to cover international organizations such as the United Nations and the International Committee of the Red Cross, and certain individuals (such as war criminals).

One important factor to understand about international law is that international law is implemented and is practiced quite differently, when compared with other domestic laws or municipal laws. International law implies a consensual basis between countries, rather than being imposed by a single ruling world-body or government. These laws are practiced horizontally, across the spectrum, as opposed to domestic law, which works vertically. States consent to the international legal obligations and responsibilities either implicitly through custom or explicitly through treaties and agreements.

Once an international law is promulgated there is no other way to get that law unilaterally changed at will by a State. For example, despite the U.S. government's proclamation that the crime of "conspiracy" is to be an international crime, however, the rest of the international community disagreed with the United States Conspiracy will only become an international crime if other States agree with the United States, in a treaty, that it is a crime.

But, there is always a negative point attached to any law, and same goes for the international laws as well. The true picture of international law is that it does work, but it is highly dependent on the participants to make it work successfully by following each law effectively. Just like any other domestic law, there are situations when international law gets broken by the participants.

However, this is a very expected situation, as many of the issues that arise on the international stage are political ones. While international law does not have the same strong enforcement measures a State has under its domestic law, there are different options available that can be used against a State which refuses to fulfill its international obligations and responsibilities.

When any international law gets violated, there are chances that any other State or an international organization might get into a diplomatic debate to have control over that situation. Because reciprocity is an important part of international law, the threat of condemnation by other States can be a powerful tool against some, but not all States. Sanctions involving economic or financial threats or promises can be used by one or more States against the State in violation of international law. Treaties with the violating State can be suspended.

- **In specific terminology:** There are several norms related to International law, and these norms are formulated with the consent of States. Consent by States is given either by following certain international practices over a long period of time, under a belief that there is a legal requirement to do so (customary law), or is given expressly by entering into written agreements with one or more States (treaty law).

To frame international law, various other sources are considered such as judicial decisions, peremptory norms (jus cogens), and articles written by scholars of international law. These sources of international law are also listed in Article 38 of the Statute of the International Court of Justice.

1.2.3. Customary Law

The customary law which has been made at an international level has been written down initially as the law similar to that of the express law being related to the various treaties as well as the convention at an international level, but tends to grow or develop into the law by doing much of practice over the specified period of time.

Thus, the two pertaining components or the elements are required to be presented prior to making up of something into law by the custom which is:

- There has to be a general practice by the various states belonging to a particular norm, which are generally present to either provide with the assistance or forbid a specific action, over a longer period of time; and
- There has to be a general belief by the various states that this particular context or norm has to get accepted, being a law.

The component or the element which has been mentioned possesses the requirement regarding the belief that something is being legitimately obligated and this basically makes it unique from the various other behaviors amongst the different states which are actually based on merely the tradition, the courtesy or as per the convenience.

In the case both of the elements are in existence then, the novel law related to the customer will be getting applied to and are being bounded on all of the pertaining states in the world. Thus, not all the states are supposed to follow the practice belonging to a custom, so that it could become the customary law.

The practice of shipping and also the customs which are being followed by each of the States faring the sea will surely become the customary law even in the case of the state being landlocked and not owning any of the ships, and thus, they are not able to follow up with the practice of the custom.

At that particular time, this particular customary law for shipping will be applied to the State, which is landlocked, even in the case of shipping.

Therefore, in the process of determining if there pertains a general or common practice related to the factors of custom, for instance, the number of the present States, their comparative size and also the importance possessed by the States, after having a consideration of the customs. Also, the amount of time taken by the States to follow up with the custom is considered as an important factor.

In case, the state does not second with the following up of the novel customs; then they are being supposed to object regularly whilst the formation of the law. None of the objections can be made to the law of the custom after it being wholly identified or recognized and have been practiced upon.

Having an inclusion of the international court related to the decision of the Justice, possess the belief that in case, the state tends to make up a timely as well as consistent declaration against the novel customary law, this law will not get applied to it.

Various scholars possess the belief that because of the nature of the customary law which has been made at the global level, once the law gets formed, it will be applicable to all the pertaining States all across the world, even all those who did not provide with their consent.

Since the law of the customary has been applied to all the States; thus, any part belonging to the treaty or the convention which helps in mirroring up the customary law will get applied to all the pertaining States by its righteousness as being the law of customary. It provides the meaning that at the time when the treaty provides with the restating of the customary law, the State which is not the basic party to the treaty will be possessing the same legitimate obligations as well as the rendered responsibilities as all those States which are legitimate parties in respect of the treaty.

1.2.4. Treaty Law

The Vienna Convention on the law related to treaties provides the description regarding the several treaties being international, all the agreements being present in the written form and are made amongst the various States that all are governed by the law, which has been made at an international level.

The terminology 'treaty' generally tends to possess the inclusion of the various arrangements, the protocols, agreements, consents, covenants, etc. All the pertaining treaties tend to act in the manner which is similar to that of the contract, existing amongst all of the parties who are signing that specific treaty.

Being a contract, present in the written form, the States which are generally being considered as the party to the treaty are being able to recognize or identify to what all has been agreed to and also what all obligations are being owed by all of the members of the party and to whom.

Being the corollary to it, the treaties tend to have an application in the first place to all the pertaining States and also the to the policies being formed under the State. The State might tend to manipulate or modify these specific obligations within the treaty by making up of the reservation at the time of the signing up, rectification, acceptance, approval or the endorsement of the treaty.

Generally, all the states are being required to provide with the notification related to the secretary- general of many of the countries, at the time of the occurrence of such situations. And once the emergency gets over, all of the pertaining states are being expected to follow up with all of the treaty obligations, again, possessing an inclusion of any that might have been suspended.

The derogable treaties are being considered as all those treaties which are being non-derogable. There are only four rights are non-derogable: the right to life, the right to be free from torture, right to be free from slavery and right to be free from retroactive penal laws.

At the time, when the treaty or any of the section relating to that treaty are being non-derogable, then, all the obligations as well as the responsibilities present within that treaty, tends to continue for all the parties belonging to the respective States, even in case or at the time of the national urgency or at the time of the war.

Thus, the forbidding or the prohibition of the utilization of the torture is being an example of the obligation being non-derogative.

Even in case, when the State is being attacked by an army, it is prohibited to use torture, in any of the cases, against anybody, be it the citizens of their country, the military people, the members of the group who are attacking being in the opposition or anyone else.

1.2.5. Jus Cogens

The laws which are being made at an international level generally tend to contain the various rules and regulations that are referred to as the jus cogens or the norms being peremptory.

All these forms generally tend to provide the reflection of the law which is so fundamental that none of the States possess the caliber to ignore or avert it or try to contract out of it even with the help of the succeeding treaty.

The process of jus cogens is being acknowledged as the policy of the public belonging to the international law. The Convention of Vienna on the law of the treaties provides the definition regarding the norms being peremptory, similar to those norms which easily be agreed to and also being identified by the international community belonging to the state.

There is no derogation, or the process of derogation is not being permitted in here, and thus, it can only be manipulated or modified by the successive norm or the context related to the law which has been made at an international level and in accordance with the similar character.

The norms which are being accepted or agreed to as the jus cogens are basically genocide, slavery, torture, and piracy.

In accordance with the principles and standards, all the states have been forbidden from such actions; within the practice, this is basically the world which is being aspired to in consideration of the applicability of the various laws which has been made at an international level, in opposite to those domestic laws being made within the States.

All such obligations might continue to be persistent under the law which has been made under the laws being made at a global level, despite the domestic laws which have been owned by the state that might also contradict laws similar to these.

It has been said that the States might not be able to invoke the pertaining provisions within their respective constitutions or the laws it possesses, being the excuse for not having succeeded in performing up the duties, assigned to them.

1.3. INTERNATIONAL LAW: HISTORY

Four main or key periods of the growth and the development of international law have been identified by many researchers. All these existing four periods usually tend to correspond to both periods related to the evolution of the socio-politics as well as the technological one and are being segregated by the major wars (Figure 1.2).

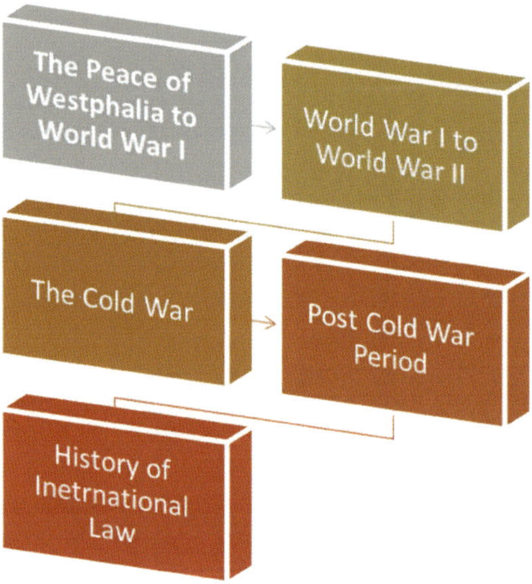

Figure 1.2: Four different phases of wars defining the history of International Law.

1.3.1. The Peace of Westphalia to World War I

The time from the peace of the Westphalia to the beginning of the First World War has been considered as one of the growths or the development of the today's state of the respective countries.

Prior to this, many of the countries did not possess any of the efficient or effective governments being centralized and also the various bureaucracies belonging to the government or any of the legit enforcement.

After this particular period, many of the people have seen much of the growth or development related to the current central government, along with the various bureaucrats and also the structure of the bureaucratic having an alternative to the dispersed fiefdoms and also the rule related to the nobility being formed locally.

Being the practical matter, there pertains none of the superpowers being dominant or the duopoly. All of the major powers tend to possess the sharing of the dominance along with their respective rivalries. The persistence of the wars amongst all these groups and also the states being related to them were considered to be common.

Various attempts have been made to handle or tackle with the pertaining relations or the connection amongst the powers as well as the process of resisting of the tendencies being revolutionary after the occurrence of the outcome from the upheavals in the process of development or growth, which is considered to be the series related to the treaty, which have been implemented in that particular time period.

Those major elements tend to include:

- Having a declaration of the various pertaining principles and the standards which tend to bind up the signatories to the existing standards related to the behavior which all are being based on the perception of the religion of the Christians.
- The alliance of the military, which are being based on the Treaty of Paris. The main reason for this was to provide them with the mutual assistance or help so that they could be able to suppress any of the components or the elements of the revolutionary and avert them from the process of renewal of all the movements, being revolutionary which has led to the great revolutions amongst the various countries.
- The occurrence of the meeting within the summit, periodically. This particular growth of the diplomacy being multilateral and also the meetings being occurring on a regular basis, wherein, all of the mutual concerns or the worries along with the interests might get discussed and then get settled ideally.

The efficacy or efficiency was somehow being restricted due to the emergence of many of the countries, being the world power, and also the proclamation which helped in providing with it.

Whereas the various other countries would not be intervening or interfering within the affairs of the colonials, and also that many countries would not be handling up with the interference of the colonials within the affairs of the states being independent, in those countries.

All the major powers of that particular time have provided the various parameters related to laws, which has been made at an international level and is usually being manipulated by the tenets on the various principles being based on Christians.

The growth or the development of the various laws near to the treatment of the various diplomats, the utilization of the force amongst the powers, the process of interference of the countries or the nations so that they could be able to protect their national interest in the ventures being commercial and also the existent laws belonging to the process of navigation and also the higher seas.

The process of codification as well as the growth or the development of the various process or the procedures for the resolution of the various disputes which started to move or shift the components of the power from other great powers to an approach which is being acknowledged as more balanced.

The process of adoption of the various conventions, amongst the various other treaties of the pertaining specified period, possessing a restricted capability of the powers so that they could make apt utilization of the various types or kinds of the weapons and thus, helps in dictating the existing treatment for the combatants.

More essentially, these specific treaties are being governed by the association or the connection amongst the signatories, but do not consider the colonial and also the nations which are not being secured or protected.

1.3.2. World War I to World War II

The events of World War 1 marked both the unsuccessfulness of diplomacy at an international level, but also the end of the period of the colonials.

The expansion of colonials has largely been ceased, and also the monarchies were being considered under the stress or the pressure, which was consistently increasing, along with many of the countries getting eliminated at the time of the revolution and demands of the treaty after the war ended.

This specific era or the period of time also have witnessed the elimination of various capitulation, which all were left, and thus, the considerate return of many of the laws being related to the local enforcement.

The occurrence of war with many of the deaths from both the military and the civilians, also provided them with the united requirement or the desire in order to have an efficient utilization of the diplomacy along with the rules and regulations which were being opposed to force the arms in order to have a dictation regarding the relation or the connection on an international level.

The increase of the technology in the weapons, as well as transportation, has made it easy to conduct both the warfare and trade, on a scale at an international level.

1.3.3. The Cold War

The time period after the end of the World War II, witnessed the law take up the center stage. The trials related to the war crimes as well as the incorporation of the various countries presented the pragmatic execution of various laws which were made at an international level on the global scale.

Instead of having a concentration or focus on the process of reparation against the powers of the Axis, individuals were identified and were tried for the respective crimes. The formal design of the process of resolution and the discussions pertaining to the major issues rose to the global level. Many of the countries were being incorporated into the discussions and the participation of the major and key powers of the world.

The superpowers, one being the United States, and the second one being the USSR, arose after the end of the world war. These two existing superpowers were being represented as having a competition with the military itself, the polarities, be it the legal one, the economic one or the political one, that will result in the segregation of the globe into the two respective camps who will be in opposition.

1.3.4. Post-Cold War Period

After the USSR fell from the position of being a superpower, the United States, then became the one and only superpower along with the assumption of the mantle of the policeman at an international level.

The interference or the intervention by this superpower, with or without the assistance of the UN, in many of the pertaining countries all across the globe, has left an opinion of the US being the hegemon of the world.

Thus, there continued to be the shift to the process of globalization which is resisted at the domestic level. The UK as of late has voted to quit the EU. It has been considered as the hint that it may happen and that the approach related to the enforced governance, at an international level, also has been highly structured, was being represented by the EU. That might not be acceptable by the various sovereign states.

1.4. INTERNATIONAL LAW: EVOLUTION

The phenomenon, 'Globalization,' which can be provided with the description as possession of the interconnection amongst the various interests depending on regions, people, social, ethnic, commercial as well as cultural one across the world that possess a great impact or influence on the distinct legit fields, having an inclusion of the international law as well.

- Reshaping or designing of the globalization with the help of various portent factors, the law which has been made at a global level has helped in changing or transforming itself from the set of the legitimate rules or regulations which have been set by the government so that they could be able to govern the relations within the state, to a critical or complex web of documents being transnational.

It generally helps in providing with the framework, which is normative in nature, for all types or sorts of distinct actors on the legit scene at an international level.

- The phenomena that have been utilized in order to connect with the realms within the nation are now being examined or assessed as well as are being monitored with the help of the legitimate lens at a global level.
- Our planet is "shrinking" because issues such as the environment, nuclear weapons, disease, and terrorism have become of global concern, and are thus measured by international law parameters.
- The laws being made within the nations, lost omnipotent, which is considered to be sovereign power and has now been supplemented, by the law, which has been made at an international level.
- Therefore, the law, which has been made at an international level, has been in the process, considered as being evolutionary, over the contemporary decades, changing itself from the instrument belonging to the resolution of the conflict within the state, to a global tool which is being acknowledged as quite powerful, existing regularly and is being quite impactful in many of the

policies as well as the decisions of the state actors and the entities which are not related to the states.

1.4.1. Transformation of International Law

The law which has been made at an international level, which has been studied by the various researchers with the help of traditional framework, and having an inclusion of two forms of systems being normative, is:

- One, which is being publicized by the states on their own for the relations within the nations; and
- The other one, which is generally being spread amongst the various states for the purpose of having good relations on an international level.

In addition, the organizations or the agencies which do not belong to the government or the NGOs do play a major role on the legal scene on a global level, similar to what the other regional agencies or organizations, institutions, as well as the judicial bodies, did.

The process of multiplication of the various actors in the international law possess the contribution in the multiplication of the legitimate norms or rules being made at an international level.

Therefore, in addition to this, even the veteran legitimate actors, via the courts, has played a vital role in changing of their role in the realm of the process of modernization of the laws being made in international law.

The phenomenon of globalization has been referred to as the process of stretching under which much of the associations or connections have been made amongst the distinct regions or the contexts of the society and thus, have become networked across the globe in totality.

1.4.2. The Role of International Law in Different Fields

The process of evolution, as well as globalization, has affected international law and the various distinct legitimate fields.

The three places where the impact of globalization is considered to be most striking are in the inclusion of the law made up for the rights of the human beings, the international law for the criminals, and the international law for the privacy.

The law which has been made at an international level has played a key role in the law for the human rights, being in its globalization or proliferation version, wherein the trend of evolution on the scene at an international level, possessed the major part.

- **Creation of International Norms:** The evolution of the law which has been made at an international level has made up or created many of the novel norms or standards for the rights of the human beings.

All through the twentieth century, much of the conventions regarding the rights possessed by the human beings have been started, and many of the norms or the standards related to the customary rights of the human beings, have emerged.

Thus, all of these pertaining novel rights for the human beings are considerate not just because of the number, which were expanded, but due to its evolutionary nature.

The actors belonging to state or non- state, therefore, started working together so that they could endorse, execute, and assess the myriad of the norms being set for the human rights, for developing the strong regime related to the regulation as well as protection or security of the rights of humans.

- **Limitations on State Sovereignty:** Due to powerful reach and the influence on the behavior of the state, various novel norms related to the rights of human beings do foster some of the severe as well as critical limitations on the sovereignty of the state. The states are being provided with the dictation that they might no longer be able to act according to its wish within its borders which is considered to be a contrary to the centuries related to the customary law being made at an international level.

Accurately, due to the version of the globalization belonging to the international law which generally tends to take into consideration the interests of the individuals, it provides more protection or security from the intrusion or the interference of the states into their own affairs by putting up a limit on the powers of the sovereign of the state.

1.4.3. The Impact of Globalized International Law

International law has been quite successful in changing or transforming itself over the few decades and thus, is currently presenting a complex body belonging to the global rules or regulations which generally apply to the great field of the actors belonging to the state as well as the non-state.

1.4.3.1. State Behavior

International law presents with the displaying of globalized shape: it covers up a vast variety of the legitimate fields; it generally surrounds a myriad of various distinct rules and regulations, and thus provides the governance for the behavior of the state as well as the non-state.

Thus, it provides the examination of two distinct phenomenons:

- If states do comply with the international law which has already been globalized, willingly as compared to what has been done years ago, when a more of traditional form got exhibited by the law, which has been made at an international level; and
- If the states are being considered as much more prone to the process of incorporation of the international law which has been globalized, into the law being made within the nation itself or the process of depending on the international laws being globalized in terms of the relations amongst different countries.

All such observations can be explained on a simple note, with the help of the facts which tends to line amongst the legitimate domains at national as well as international levels that has become much blurred that none of the states are being able to have a view of the international law, being the enemy.

1.5. INDIVIDUALS AS SUBJECTS OF INTERNATIONAL LAW

1.5.1. Individuals as Alleged Objects of International Law

The people who tend to publicize and think of individuals as the objects related to the international law specifically or in the principle are considered to be innumerable to get quoted. However, a person might speak regarding the individual being the object related to the international law only in the cases which are exceptional, in accordance with which the spirits of the current international law are being violated flagrantly.

1.5.2. States and Individuals as Subjects of International Law

The perception that the law which has been made at an international level not only rules the process of intercourse of the various states which are considered to be independent, but also the provisions it possesses which directly binds the individuals without the possession of any of the intermediary of that particular state.

This is being considered to be as old as the science of the international law. The legitimate capacity for the rights of the human beings as well as the legitimate capacity for the legitimate actions which generally is being related to the legit people and also to the physical people, to the individuals and the state as well.

1.5.3. Individuals as Exclusive Subjects of International Law

The doctrine which is being considered as dominant, belonging to the international law, is under attack by rising number of the people, who do the process of publicizing since the start of this specific century. The reformers tend to present their main objectives as:

- It is the decrement of the state sovereignty to the autonomy which is being acknowledged as similar to that of being enjoyed by the various members of the states belonging to the federation.
- Having an identification or the recognition of the entire primacy related to the international law over the law which has been made at a domestic level, unbothered of the question if concerned with the state or not, has been acceded or endorsed to the provided rules and regulations belonging to the international law.
- Identification of the complete unity of the law which is the legit monism and simultaneously similar to the 2nd objective regarding the principle that the law of the municipal generally tend to derive from the law which has been made at an international level.

In today's time the idea regarding the individual being the only subject related to the international law, possess just a small number of the supporters. It's been said that neither the state nor any of the collection can be considered to be the subject of the international law.

REFERENCES

1. Bloomsbury.com., (2018). [online] Available at: https://www.bloomsbury.com/au/transnational-organised-crime-in-international-law-9781841136905/ (Accessed on 12 April 2019).
2. Coursera, (2018). *Introduction - The History and General Principles of International Arbitration | Coursera.* [online] Available at: https://www.coursera.org/lecture/arbitration-international-disputes/introduction-9Qgsa (Accessed on 12 April 2019).
3. Donigan, G. C., (2000). *International Legal Mechanisms for Combating Transnational Organized Crime: The Need for a Multilateral Convention* (18th edn.). [eBook] p. 50. Available at: https://scholarship.law.berkeley.edu/bjil/vol18/iss1/2/ (Accessed on 12 April 2019).
4. En.wikipedia.org., (2018). *History of International Law.* [online] Available at: https://en.wikipedia.org/wiki/History_of_international_law (Accessed on 12 April 2019).
5. Encyclopedia Britannica, (2018). *International Law - Historical Development.* [online] Available at: https://www.britannica.com/topic/international-law/Historical-development (Accessed on 12 April 2019).
6. Hauck, P., & Peterke, S., (2018). *International Law and Transnational Organized Crime.* [online] Available at: https://global.oup.com/academic/product/international-law-and-transnational-organized-crime-9780198733737?cc=us&lang=en& (Accessed on 12 April 2019).
7. Legal bites - law and beyond, (2018). *Evolution of International Law.* [online] Available at: https://www.legalbites.in/evolution-international-law/ (Accessed on 12 April 2019).
8. Opil.ouplaw.com., (2018). *The History of International Law.* [online] Available at: http://opil.ouplaw.com/page/int-law-timeline (Accessed on 12 April 2019).
9. Oxfordbibliographies.com., (2018). *History of International Law, 1550–1700 - International Law - Oxford Bibliographies - obo.* [online] Available at: http://www.oxfordbibliographies.com/view/document/obo-9780199796953/obo-9780199796953–0036.xml (Accessed on 12 April 2019).
10. Peacepalacelibrary.nl., (2018). *History of International Law - Research*

Guide International Law | Peace Palace Library. [online] Available at: https://www.peacepalacelibrary.nl/research-guides/public-international-law/history-of-international-law/ (Accessed on 12 April 2019).

11. St. Korowicz, m., (2018). *Introduction to International Law*, p. 432.
12. Sterio, M., (2008). *The Evolution of International Law* (31st edn.). [eBook] p. 45. Available at: http://lawdigitalcommons.bc.edu/iclr/vol31/iss2/3 (Accessed on 12 April 2019).

2

The Concept of Transnational Organized Crime

CONTENTS

Transnational crime, often called as multinational systemic crime or international crime, is more than an extension of domestic crime. Hence, none of the countries can control and prevent different kinds of transnational crime. Furthermore, the control of transnational crime through international cooperation may be a supreme way. However, there are few major challenges for international cooperation, like the trend of westernization and different national interests. Consequently, international cooperation must have to worry about the national interests and social context of each country.

This chapter aims to study the concept of transnational organized crime (TOC), its different types, impacts, and whether the control of transnational crime through international cooperation is a better choice or not. The chapter will also discuss the relationship between globalization and crime to pursue comprehensive and in-depth understanding of transnational crime. It will regard transnational crime as a systematic issue and provide systematic analysis of multinational systemic crime.

2.1. INTRODUCTION

TOC has developed recently in many ways which place it at the topmost stage of international agenda. Modern communications and advanced technologies along with the global political economy have brought efficient changes in the way the TOC behaves and operates.

TOC is established around the globe, but their level of development in different countries varies. It is a diversified and fluid industry which is involved in hosting illegal activities such as human trafficking, piracy, drug trafficking, counterfeiting, etc.

It might affect powerful states, and it is above all weakened and conflict-affected states which are exposed to the predations of TOC and usually aid as base for international criminal enterprises. A major concern regarding the impact of TOC on the economic development is expressed by The World Bank's World Development Report 2011 (World Bank, 2011).

The stability of the strong states and the nation states are threatened by the global criminal markets. This is very much obvious in the case of conflict-affected and fragile states. Recent research shows that the major impact of TOC is that it badly affects the quality of governance of a state (van Dijk, 2007). As stated by some researchers, organized crime corrodes the long-term capacity of a state to enhance the profits for the public by compromising and affecting the integrity of the institutions and public officials.

The ability to bring public goods is the main element in a fragility level of a state. A state which is affected by prevalent corruption faces a reduction of validity which can compromise the capacity to be in power (Varese, 2000; West, 2006).

TOC can intrude the basic composition of various states, nourishing on weaknesses and ultimately improving fragility. Thus, organized crime has been established as the main reason for the failure of states, even if there is some discussion as to whether TOC is a cause or effect of fragility on states and eventually conflict.

This chapter analyses the effect of TOC on fragility and conflict. It concentrates on the changing aspects of TOC and its association to conflict-affected and fragile states, as well as on potential entry points and policy responses for novel initiatives which will help in tackling this problem.

The notion of TOC is not straightforward or clear-cut. Until now, there was no ordinary definition available for TOC in criminal or criminological law theories. Additionally, transnational criminal organizations diverge significantly from each other in various ways for example in organizational structure, types of activities, or size.

Various critical elements are evident in case of TOC even if there is a lack of consent on its definition. First, these kinds of organizations conduct criminal acts by violating licit outlines and booming out penalty outside the genuine procedures of law enforcement.

The people, who join the transnational organized groups intentionally, work under the influence of already established leaders to effectively execute their activities. They are not made up of strictly subordinated groups but they are very well-organized, and the structure is permanent.

In fact, TOC happens through a web of homogeneous groups which are associated to one another sometimes across borders by several forms of complicity, solidarity, and a hierarchical order. Moreover, transnational criminal organizations are dynamic in a diversity of fields.

The full spectrum of activities of TOC consists of cyber-crime, bank fraud and the illicit trafficking of people or goods. Additionally, these transnational criminal organizations are prepared to use bribery, violence, and various other activities in order to protect their comfort and attain their goals.

The major characteristic of these transnational organized groups is that the criminal activities of these groups are only limited to the national boundaries. As per the statement of the United Nations, an offense is transnational in nature. The statement was given in the Convention against Transnational Organized Crime (CATOC). The reasons behind this can be:

- It is dedicated in more than one State;
- It is dedicated in one State, but a considerable part of its planning, preparation, direction, or control occurs in another State;
- It is dedicated in one State but comprises an organized criminal group which is involved in criminal activities in more than one State; or
- It is dedicated in one State but has considerable effects in another State.

The United Nations listed various categories of TOC also. Those activities includes money laundering, theft of art and cultural objects, terrorist activities, intellectual property (IP) theft, aircraft hijacking, illicit arms trafficking, sea piracy, insurance fraud, land hijacking, cyber-crime, environmental crimes, trade of human body parts, trafficking of persons, illicit drug trafficking, infiltration of legal business, fraudulent bankruptcy, bribery, and corruption of public officials as described in national legislation, bribery, and corruption of party officials and elected representatives as described in national legislation, and other crimes devoted by organized criminal groups.

2.1.1. Types of Transnational Crimes

Usually, the classifications of 'TOC' highlight the background of transnational offenders, precisely their adherence to culturally described criminal groups. These criminal groups generally have the flexibility to search out the most worthwhile opportunities for the crime and once, the crime has committed to retreat the areas which provide major protection from law enforcement.

The TOC can be blend safely into travel, communication, migrant communities and international commerce (Shelley, 2005; Williams, 2001; Williams and Godson, 2002).

While considering the hurdles which can be faced by transnational offenders when they cross the borders and operate in a potential and an unfamiliar hostile environment, different light of transnational crimes appears. For example, provided the inclination to profile suspects, being familiar as outsiders discovers the transnational offenders more willingly than the domestic offenders to law enforcement scrutiny (van Duyne, 1998, pp. 278–279; Decker and Chapman, 2008, p. 71; Kenney, 2002, p. 106).

All forms of transnational crime are affected by the issues which are highlighted above. It seems that the differences can be captured practically by characterizing the activities of TOC as per the pattern of cross-border movement (Figure 2.1).

TOC can be defined by two major dimensions:

- The directionality of cross-border movement; and
- The nature of what crosses the border.

Figure 2.1: Two dimensions of transnational organized crime.

TOC includes the movement across the border of one or more of the goods, people, and information. It has been claimed that 'TOC,' and 'organized crime,' boils down to international smuggling activities (Kleemans and van de Bunt, 2002, p. 23).

For the furthermost part, this means the cross-border transportation of controlled, prohibited or highly taxed goods for example stolen motor vehicles, child pornography, pirated textiles, protected animals, drugs, illegally logged timber, embargoed technology, protected cultural goods, arms, human organs, hazardous waste, cigarettes or gasoline.

In the case of human smuggling and human trafficking, instead of objects, people are brought across the border. A question of the precise modus operandi is that whether the criminals accompany those goods which are smuggled. However, as an important element of the transnational crimes, called as cross-border predatory crimes, the criminal cross the borders.

For example, gangs which are involved in serial robbery and serial burglary in a country may function from bases in another country so that they can easily cross the borders whenever they move for robbery and burglary spree (Weenink, Huisman and van der Laan, 2004).

Different kind of transnational predatory crime engages simply movement of information across the borders, such as various cases of 419-frauds where the sufferers are bribed to transfer money to recipients present in abroad completely based on communication with criminals by phone, mail or fax (Ampratwum, 2009).

The type of crime varies with the directionality of the movement across the borders. As per the concept of TOC, directionality defines the patterns in which the borders are crossed for accomplishing the scheme of a crime. Smuggling can be defined as a unidirectional activity in which contraband is transported from a source to the destined country, possibly through one or more transit countries.

However, the payment for contraband goods will go in the opposite direction, possibly posing a different smuggling issue for transporting huge amount of cash (Reuter and Truman, 2004, p. 28). In the case of the illicit export of hazardous waste, the cross-border movement appears to be very unidirectional (Massari and Monzini, 2004).

Other schemes of transnational crime are bidirectional. For example, the case of serial burglars working from safe home bases. The endeavor of each criminal is completed only after crossing a border in each direction at least once.

Various schemes of cigarette-smuggling engage a hook-shaped movement pattern, specifically when cigarettes which are not taxed are procured officially for export to a third country to be trafficked back to the originated country for the distribution in black market (von Lampe, 2006).

'Carousel fraud' schemes which are directing towards the system of value-added tax reimbursement inside the EU may develop as a circular pattern connecting a number of fraudulent firms in different countries (Pashev, 2008).

To conclude, there are various crime phenomena which have complex transnational ramifications. For example, in the case of synthetic drugs, the illegal producers in the Netherlands may acquire precursor chemicals from suppliers in East Asia and Eastern Europe for the production of ecstasy to be trafficked through and into another set of countries (Blickman, Korf, Siegel and Zaitch, 2003).

2.2. DIFFERENT FORMS OF TRANSNATIONAL ORGANIZED CRIME

TOC is an industry which is ever-changing, creates new forms of crime and also adapts to the markets. It is not stagnant. In short, it is an illegal business which exceeds social, cultural, geographical, and linguistic boundaries and one which knows no rules and no borders.

For criminals, drug trafficking remains to be the most rewarding form of business with a projected annual value of $320 billion. UNODC in the year 2009 placed the projected annual worth of the total cocaine and opiate markets alone at $85 billion and $68 billion, respectively.

Human trafficking is a crime which takes place globally in which children, men, and women are used as products for labor-based and sexual exploitation. Although the figures vary, an approximate from the International Labor Organization (ILO) in 2005 specified the number of trafficking victims at any given time to be around 2.4 million, with annual profits of about $32 billion (Figure 2.2).

Figure 2.2: Human trafficking; a crime forcing people into slavery.

Source: https://cdn.pixabay.com/photo/2013/07/15/21/06/prison-162885_960_720.jpg

However, current research on the complete forced labor trends would recommend that the scope of the issue is very huge. In Europe, the trafficking of children and women for sexual exploitation brings in $3 billion annually, alone, and involves 140,000 victims at any one time, with an annual flow of 70,000 victims.

Migrant smuggling is a kind of well-organized business of transporting people around the globe by criminal groups, routes, and networks. Migrants are offered with a "smuggling package" by the groups of organized crime, and the handling they get along the route resembles to the price they pay to their smugglers.

In the course of being smuggled, the rights of migrants are generally broken, and they can be raped, robbed, beaten, held for ransom or sometimes even left to die, when the danger get too high for their smugglers. The smugglers do not care if migrants sink in the sea, suffocate in a container or die due to dehydration in a desert.

This trade is valued at billions of dollars, every year. In the year 2009, around $6.6 billion was produced by the illegal smuggling of 3 million migrants to North America from Latin America, while in the previous year 55,000 migrants were smuggled to Europe from Africa for a sum of $150 million.

Illegal trading in firearms brings in approximately $170 million to $320 million annually and sets pistols and assault rifles in the hands of gangs of criminals. It is hard to count the sufferers of these illegal weapons, but in some regions like the Americas, there is a robust association between percentage of homicides and the homicide rates by firearms.

Natural resource smuggling involves the trafficking of raw materials like diamonds and rare metals generally from the zones of conflict. The smuggling of timber in South-East Asia produces annual revenues of $3.5 billion.

In addition of criminal group funding, ultimately this element of criminal activity contributes to climate change, deforestation, and rural poverty. The illicit trade in wildlife another kind of profitable business for the organized criminal groups, along with robbers planning to export the body parts to foreign markets.

Smuggling of the parts of tiger, rhino horn and elephant ivory to Asia from South-East Asia and Africa generates $75 million criminal profits each year and also threatens the survival of few species. These organized crime groups also deal in live plants and animals intimidating their very presence to meet demand from collectors or unwitting consumers.

Smugglers illegally move around 100 million tons of fish, 440,000 tons of medicinal plants and 1.5 million live birds per year, as per the reports of the WWF. The sale of deceitful medicines is a disturbing business, because it represents a potentially dead trade for consumers.

Piggybacking on the rising legitimate trade in pharmaceuticals from Asia to other developing regions, criminals' traffic fraudulent medicines from Asia, in particular to South-East Asia and Africa to the value of $1.6 billion.

However, instead of preserving people, they can result in death or cause resistance to drugs used to treat deadly infectious diseases like tuberculosis and malaria. In addition to the methods of traditional trafficking, criminals continue to construct a profitable online trade in deceitful medicines by targeting developed and developing countries alike, due to which health implications for consumers can also be led.

Figure 2.3: Cybercrime - a digital form of crime.

Source: https://www.publicdomainpictures.net/pictures/270000/nahled/cybercrime.jpg

Cybercrime incorporates numerous areas, but one of the most lucrative for criminals is identity theft, which produces approx. $1 billion each year.

Criminals are progressively abusing the Internet to snip private data, access bank accounts and dishonestly accomplish payment card details (Figure 2.3).

2.3. THE PROFILE OF TRANSNATIONAL CRIME

The definition of TOC is the major issue. The concept of transnational crime which sometimes known as multinational systemic crime or international crime is much more than an extension of domestic crime (Martin and Romano, 1992).

Fijnaut indicates that "the adjective 'transnational' recommends that all of the kinds of crime described identify no national boundaries and, speaking geographically, take place in vacuum, as it were" (2000, p. 120).

An example in which many countries may be engaged in multinational crime systems is narcotics smuggling of Southeast Asian's Golden Triangle, where production of opium and refining of narcotics have majorly presented as a problem (Martin and Romano, 1992).

This area seems to be complex and sophisticated organization having close ties to a large number of countries on multinational level, including Burma, China, Hong Kong, India, Japan, Korea, Laos, Malaysia, Mexico, Pakistan, Singapore, Sri Lanka, Taiwan, Thailand, the Philippines, and United States (Royal Canadian Mounted Police, 1988).

Transnational crime is a kind of social phenomenon which involves people, places, and institutions, which is encouraged by a diversity of social, economic, and cultural determinants (Findlay, 2003). Therefore, different definitions of TOC are there in different countries depending upon the difference in philosophies.

According to Romano and Martin, "transnational crime may be defined as the behavior of ongoing organizations that involves two or more nations, with such behavior being defined as criminal by at least one of these nations" (1992, p. 15).

In fact, transnational crime is a concept of general-purpose, which covers various types of crime. The major categories of transnational crimes are espionage (Ranelagh, 1986; Rositzke, 1977; Corson and Crowley, 1985), terrorism (Adler, 1999), nuclear, and arms trafficking (Begley, 1996), drug-trafficking (Eck and Gersh, 2000), illegal wildlife trade (Warchol, 2004), money laundering (Gilmore, 1999), human smuggling for prostitution and low cost labor (Bensinger, 2000; Feve and Finzel, 2001; Zhang and Gaylord, 1996), and trafficking in art, antiquities, and bulk currency (US Department of Justice, 1994).

Transnational crime is a hybrid which is very complicated indeed. Hence, there are few doubts in drawing a line of division or separation of different types as transnational crime happens in diverse hybrid forms (Ruggiero, 1996).

2.3.1. Globalization and Crime

Globalization is a topic which has been discussed widely. In the literature of burgeoning globalization, there are various definitions of globalization present (AAS, 2007). There are basically five unique conception regarding globalization according to Scholte (2000). These includes "globalization as liberalization," "globalization as internationalization," "globalization as deterritorialization," "globalization as universalization" and "globalization as westernization or Americanization."

The process of globalization along with the changing role of the nation-state is not altered by these five conceptions. It is rather doubtful about the capacity and role of the state as a keystone of political community, government to oppose the juggernaut of globalization and social theory (Ohmae, 1990; Reich, 1991).

Globalization being a process of enhancing interaction and interconnectedness of the societies put forth constructive effects on the modern society for example, "the global economy makes different countries work as a unit in real time on a planetary scale" (Castells, 1996, p. 92), and "interconnectedness leads to 'information revolution' which has had a profound effect on all aspects of social life" (Aas, 2007, p. 9).

Additionally, the global village phenomenon makes it possible for the development of non-state actors, mainly economic forces or market forces, to avoid the state intervention and to get over the borders of a country.

The dark side of the process of globalization is emerging, however. According to Ass, "the great challenges to state sovereignty come, significantly, not only from the increasingly interconnected and autonomous global economy, but also from the global illicit economy" (2007, p. 11). Globalization helps in the transport of people, money, and goods through the global economy. It also facilitates the transport of 'dirty money,' counterfeit arms and goods, illicit aliens and nuclear material (Godson and Williams, 1998).

TOC groups in the context of globalization react to the incentives of the market and function with cooperative relationship in spite of their ethnic differences, mistrust, and different style of business. As a result, these TOC groups are made outside the structure of legitimate power and authority by multilateral cooperation (Mittelman and Johnston, 1999).

Therefore, it may not be concurrent that the increased ease of international travel, increased independence between various nations, the globalization of international networks of finance and the growth of multinational communications are the factors which basically contributed to the growth of, and to persist to make possible international criminal activities (Williams, 1994).

Additionally, globalization forms localized criminal groups equally from different regions and different countries which further works as a combined unit and finally become organizations of TOC. As a result of which, cooperation among the organizations of the criminal has enhanced the operational abilities and empowered the capacity of resisting governmental control (Godson and Williams, 1998).

In this situation, none of the countries has the ability contain and prevent different forms of transnational crime. In the 21st century, transnational crime has become a major challenge for the whole world.

2.4. ASSESSING THE POLITICAL IMPACT OF TRANSNATIONAL ORGANIZED CRIME

The modern nature of organize crime makes it easy to distinguish few facts which enforce significant challenges to the governance of democratic regimes. Thus, it must be noted that TOC is complex, diversified, and multidimensional phenomenon but not monolithic. In TOC, the collaboration between groups is much more recurrent as compared to confrontation (Williams, 1995).

In specific countries, TOC has different appearance and has been differently seemed throughout space and time. It never functions uniformly as it does not have a constant degree of influence on individuals, entities which are non-governmental and state agencies around the globe (Potter and Thomson, 1997).

The first impact of TOC in context of politics has to do with sovereignty. It is an old concept which is continuously dominating the sphere of relations between different states. Frontiers separate the states, due to which territories get divided and mark out levels of political culture and economic development also.

Criminal organizations are pitted against this because of their transnational and illegal nature. These organizations avoid sovereignty of the states and do not have any respect for boundaries when the concern is about their illegal business. Their expansion plans and strategies are not at all concerned with the concept of national authority. They are only concerned about the flow or movement of trustworthy people who can bring good earnings.

If these organizations think of state frontiers, then it is always in provisions of either precise criminal law systems along with different levels of risk and precise markets along with opportunities for illicit earnings, or the blurring of the trails of illegal activities through the international division of work. In spite of the process of economic globalization, the recent argument in the favor of free transportation of people, goods, and capital and the establishment of promising supranational structures have all intentionally corroded an important aspect of sovereignty, control of states on the movement of goods and services via its frontiers continues to sustain enough level of security for the general population.

Nevertheless, indiscriminate parallel routes have created by the organized crime so as to violate frontiers, and this defines a lack or deficit of control regarding the movement of goods and services into the country. This could grow in upcoming future and endanger crucial problems ranging to the democratic stability from public health.

These previously established illegal routes are well protected from the state irruption. The routes can be utilized for the of organized crime and subversive groups with sophisticated nuclear weapons or introduction of food without quality check and otter very dangerous products in the country.

Given that the ability of governments to decide of which individuals or merchandises cross national borders is a considerable and essential condition for assuring sovereignty and governability, the invariable far-reaching activity of organized crime which intrudes national frontiers with impunity supposes a serious challenge to the sovereignty of states.

As a result, the organized crime supervises to elude the principle of territorial control which is together always from the state and significantly erodes the concept of national sovereignty.

2.5. DOMESTIC VERSUS TRANSNATIONAL TERRORISM: DATA, DECOMPOSITION, AND DYNAMICS

This topic describes a method to divide the Global Terrorism Database (GTD) into domestic and transnational terrorist incidents. For the understanding of some terrorism phenomenon, this decomposition is very important when the two kinds of terrorism are hypothesized to have various impacts.

Transnational terrorism, for example, might have a major unfavorable effect as compared to domestic terrorism on the growth of economy. Additionally, the cause of these two kinds of terrorism may differ. After the separation of data, calibration method is applied to address few problems with GTD data namely, the missing data for 1993 and the different coding methods used before 1998.

Particularly, the GTD transnational terrorist incidents are calibrated to ITERATE the incidents of transnational terrorist to address GTD's undercounting of incidents in much of the 1970s, and it's overcounting of incidents in much of the 1990s.

The events of domestic errors in GTD are characterized, and thus the same calibrations are applied to adjust the incidents of domestic GTD. Lagged cross-correlations and contemporaneous for the two kinds of terrorist incidents are calculated for time series component including deaths, casualties, assassinations, armed attacks, and bombings. A huge cross-correlation between transnational and domestic terrorist incidents which persists over several periods.

A major finding is that shocks given to the domestic terrorism effect in constant consequences on transnational terrorism; but the reverse is false. This finding depicts that domestic terrorism can fall over to transnational terrorism, so that the countries who have prime targets cannot avoid domestic terrorism abroad and may require to help in reducing this terrorism which is homegrown.

In the subway of Moscow on 29. March 2010, two suicide bombers blew up themselves along with injuring around 60 people and killing around 40 people. The incident which took place was considered as a domestic terrorist event as the female perpetrators were Chechen rebels from a part of the Russian Federation.

Other domestic terrorist incidents which are remarkable involves Sarin attack of 20 March 1995 on the subway of Tokyo by Aum Shinrikyo, bombing on the Alfred P. Murrah Federal Building of Oklahoma City by Timothy McVeigh and many more suicide attacks by the Tamil Tigers in Sri Lanka.

However, maximum of the empirical literature on the concept of terrorism has concentrated on TOC; domestic crime also reflects a considerable threat. Domestic events, in fact, are counted to be much more than the transnational incidents of terrorism many times (Jongman, 1992).

The analysis of the impact of terrorism on the growth of economy mandates a distinction between transnational and domestic terrorist events as the transnational terrorism may have a major influence by demanding border defenses which are highly expensive and by scaring away growth-enhancing foreign direct investment.

The discrimination of economy which is directed at the domestic minority groups is the main cause of domestic terrorism but not transnational terrorism. Because of the availability of data related to the terrorist event, transnational terrorism has past fixation.

The International Terrorism Attributes of Terrorist Events (ITERATE) data set since 1970s used to code various variables for example target entity, date, casualties, country location and perpetrators for the incidents of transnational terrorism. Nowadays, ITERATE is covering 1968–2009, and it used to get updated very frequent (Mickolus et al., 2010).

Until now, in data sets of other events, the coverage of domestic incidents of terrorism is very limited. For example, RAND data set and the National Memorial Institute for the Prevention of Terrorism (MIPT) started recording the events of domestic terrorism in 1998.

Only transnational attacks by the terrorists for 1968–1977 are coded by MIPT. Engene's (2007) data set that is Terrorism in Western Europe: Event Data (TWEED) records 'internal attacks' for only 18 European countries for 1950–2004. When the terrorists attack within their own country of citizenship, then the terrorist act is known as internal.

The internal attacks of TWEED sometimes can be transnational for example, when a Spanish official in France is murdered by a French terrorist. The first global dataset which constitutes transnational and domestic incidents of terrorism for an extended period of time is the GTD, which is managed by the National Consortium for the Study of Terrorism and Responses to Terrorism (START). At present, START's (2009a) GTD data cover 1970–2007. Although, domestic incidents of terrorism are not distinguished per se from the transnational ones. After the four hijackings of 11 September 2011, the interest in research regarding terrorism has enhanced greatly. Most of the research is empirical and relies on the data of ITERATE. A scholar of Google on 14 November 2010, searched for "ITERATE and terrorism" and found out around 3,500 references. Many researchers are using the data of GTD after its release.

Until this date, the active interaction between transnational and domestic terrorism is unknown totally. For example, if the domestic terrorists ultimately move to transnational terrorism to acquire more exposure, then domestic terrorism can be regarded as a driver of transnational terrorism.

Domestic and transnational terrorism can be interconnected if novelty adopted by the authorities or the terrorists for any one kind of the terrorism influence the entities of another kind of terrorism. For the investigations of dynamic interrelationships, Vector Auto Regression (VAR) techniques are applied to study shock induced responses of impulse, Granger causality tests and variance decomposition.

2.6. IMPACTS OF TRANSNATIONAL ORGANIZED CRIME ON CONFLICT AND FRAGILITY

On one hand, TOC is associated with fragile and conflict-affected states; there is some debate over whether it is primarily a cause or an effect of fragility and internal conflict. West (2006, p. 11) commented that a lot could happen when there is organized crime at an international level, and its presence can be "a symptom of state weakness it has created its own dynamics that intensify the causes of state failure and is itself best conceptualized as a proximate cause" (Figure 2.4).

Talking about the impact of TOC, the main victim is Afghanistan. Poppy growing and the subsequent heroin trade are some of the symptomatic weaknesses of the Afghan state. They have also been found to be key elements in defeating the state's efforts to establish a strong rule of law throughout the country.

West further argues that, "The drug trade there provides funds …for non-state actors [local warlords in this case] to challenge the state and maintain an enduring violence…." Van Dijk in the year 2007 stated that "one of the most important impacts of TOC on a state is the harm it does to the quality of its governance."

Figure 2.4: Impact of transnational organized crime on conflict and fragility.

It is due to these TOCs, that there are many countries that are compromising the integrity of public officials and institutions through corruption and intimidation. The impact is so adverse that it has undermined the state in the two key areas of capacity and legitimacy. Those two key areas are:

- The state's capacity to deliver basic public goods and citizenship rights; and
- Its legitimacy as the political entity in charge of government (Varese, 2000; West, 2006).

Such adverse impact or after-effects have different sort of implications for peace processes, where it somewhere subtracts from the legitimacy of the actors involved, as well as that of the process itself. There are several international organizations which have understood and realized the risk that is involved when there is any kind of TOC in any of the state which is weak or not ready to fight against it.

The United Nations High-Level Panel on Threats, Challenges, and Change in the year 2004 stated that "TOC is a menace to States and societies, eroding human security and the fundamental obligation of States to provide for law and order" (United Nations, General Assembly, 2004, p. 52).

It is the same document which also talks about that how important it has now become to handle such issues which should be in regards to post-conflict situations where former combatants may seek to "exploit criminal connections…undermining peacebuilding efforts" (United Nations, General Assembly, 2004, p. 53).

The risk from criminalized elements in post-conflict scenarios is such that it may act as a peace spoiler, undermining the possibility of successful peacekeeping operations (Cockayne and Pfister, 2008). These three main impacts of TOC on fragile states are explored in more detail below:

2.6.1. Eroding the State's Capacity to Deliver Public Goods

Generally, TOC is prevalent in those areas where there is non-existent formal state control. This implies the characteristic of low contract enforceability, states that lacks border controls, and no much provision provided to the public goods. But, this does not necessarily mean that the state is in its absent stage. This clearly shows that the state is behaving in such a way as to favor the emergence and arrival of TOC.

According to Arias, 2006, "The traditional view that sees TOC and the state as competing entities fails to take into account the complex relationships between these two actors and the civil society in which they are nested." In fragile and conflict-afflicted states, there is a huge possibility that TOC would have the capability to harm the state's capacity to deliver much-needed public goods such as safety, health, and sustenance.

In this particular context, pre-existing fragility can be referred to something which begins with the state and a situation where the state is not that liable enough to provide such public goods to its citizens or common people. In such situations, TOC would find an opportunity to establish itself in a market and set up its informal networks there. It also tends to infiltrate formal institutions as well as the legitimate economy through corruption of its agents (van Dijk, 2007).

This infiltration can be referred to as a form of cronyism (Kaufman, 2003; Kaufman and Kraay, 2002) that certainly have an adverse impact over the economic development of that State. This is because the climate of uncertainty that TOC creates makes investment and even aid very difficult (van Dijk, 2007). By further weakening already debilitated states TOC impairs public goods provision and ultimately undermines development and good governance.

2.6.2. Harming the State's Legitimacy

The social and economic development of any State is directly or indirectly connected with its legitimacy. For example, if one fails the others also start diminishing simultaneously. It is believed that TOC is regarded as a prime catalyst in this process. Also, somewhere or the other it is now quite visible that TOC is generally prevalent in those states that are weak and it becomes easy to establish criminal markets and enterprises there.

This process is usually characterized by systematic and pervasive corruption and cronyism. By appearing to be captured or favoring criminal networks, a state can fall irretrievably into a legitimacy crisis (Varese, 2000) by which the general population loses trust in the state's capacity or willingness to provide for their wellbeing.

Loss of legitimacy results in a weak and unsupported state structure that may fall further into conflict and fragility, further degrading the capacity of the state to provide basic public goods. TOC may also provoke other issues of legitimacy that can impair a successful peace and state-building process; if a state's control of the use of violence and force over a territory is undermined by TOC, the role of the state as the sole protector of the population is undermined (Tilly, 1985).

2.6.3. Affecting Peace Processes

It is believed that TOC in weak and conflict-afflicted states came into existence due to various conflicts already prevalent in those states, for example, gun trafficking networks. This is one reason which further gives rise to various other illegal activities in such states. Alternatively, TOC may have been there before the conflict and survived through it.

In any case, the biggest challenge to peace processes and disarmament, demobilization, and reintegration (DDR) are those criminal groups that are responsible for various criminal activities like, corruption, and terrorism and through their links to the political establishment they have managed to establish threat in such states (Ashdown, 2006). Apart from this, there are other forms of crime that are prevalent in post-conflict scenarios. According to various researches, in some African countries, there has been a tremendous increase in the crime rate in the aftermath of conflict, including armed robbery, child prostitution and drug dealing (Baker, 2009).

Not just African countries, an increase in urban crime in Central America has been witnessed which has a similar dynamic and that represents an important policy challenge. Criminalized elements in post-conflict scenarios undermine the possibility of successful peace-keeping operations (Cockayne and Pfister, 2008). Therefore, it is highly essential to manage organized crime in an effective manner by involving equal participation of all the countries, which demands for various peace-keeping interventions. It is no secret that in many cases peace missions have had to engage directly with TOC in order to be able to operate (Cockayne and Pfister, 2008; Cockayne and Lupel, 2011).

2.7. THE CONSTRUCTION OF THE TOC THREAT

The HDR analyses the usual suspects, such as, the Japanese Yakuza and Chinese Triads, the Sicilian Mafia, Mexican, and Colombian cartels and evolving Russian organized crime groups. The question here arises is that do they exist as transnational, organized criminal corporations and what is the exact scope of their financial resources and power to corrupt societies?

2.7.1. Rapid Succession of Acts and Actors Challenging the Fashion Industry

These days, various researchers agree that the TOC is understood better as a very dynamic and flexible, loose, fragmented configuration sometimes competing and sometimes collaborating networks. "Network structures have now become predominantly established in contemporary organized crime, characteristics that help make them enormously difficult to combat."

The illicit organized crime consortium is not the same as huge transnational legal business corporations. Here the question arises that, what it means for the evaluation of their economic power, and the assumed threat to the process of globalization?

However, the conventional model of hierarchy of the Mafia is substituted by more confused and diverse notion of small entrepreneurial groups which associate in business alliances, although the criminal networks and organizations are gradually more observed as a worldwide threat.

The US National Intelligence Council noted in an analysis of global trends that the criminal networks and organization will develop the scope and scale of their activities. Economic power will be used by them to disrupt societies and states. Loose alliances will be formed by them with small criminal entrepreneurs, with one-another and for specific operations with insurgent movements. They will corrupt leaders of economically fragile, failing or unstable states, cooperate with insurgent political movements to control substantial geographic areas and insinuate themselves into troubled banks and businesses.

Since the attacks of 9/11, the 'criminal underworld' is progressively combined with that of political terrorism and created into one underground 'axis of evil' which is a major national security threat. According to the Department of US State: "As we move through the first decade of the 21st century, the United States faces grave threats from international terrorist networks and their allies in the illicit drug trade and international criminal enterprises to its security. TOC, terrorism, and international drug trafficking concurrently target Americans and American interests both at home and abroad."

According to Nordstrom, there is an extension of new political and economic formations which ignore national borders. In the form of shadow or surrogate states, these power blocks follow their own logic of territorial development which are difficult to achieve access to. They offer some of the world's most political marginal and unstable economic regions with mercenaries, arms, food, medicine, and luxury commodities.

These power blocks provide better opportunities for association with rising political strongmen or warlords who want unlimited profits and power. Political control and economic power go hand in hand. Entire regions such as Liberia and Sierra Leone or the Congo come to mind, but the condition in the slums of Rio de Janeiro which are conquered by drug gangs does not differ that much – while these are just zones of an otherwise more or less functioning state or even a city.

According to Margaret Beare, the Convention disregards the 'fringe, the professionals without whom organized crime would often not be possible. The missing piece is the heading of the fringe professionals that enable transnational crimes and still tend to be slapped rather than manacled.

The requirement to grasp the corporations and companies which are liable for involving in or benefiting from serious crimes engaging organized crime groups as well as activities of money laundering is addressed by the Convention. There is still very little admiration that the corporation may be the organized crime group.

2.8. TRANSNATIONAL ORGANIZED CRIME GROUPS IN A CHANGING SOCIO-POLITICAL AND SOCIO-TECHNICAL ENVIRONMENT

Modern social network media are the main reason behind changes in the environment of socio-technical. These changes are producing modern lateral forms of social communication through globalized networks. Culturally driven hierarchies or traditional social class are being bypassed by these lateral forms of communication. These forms are actively changing opinions and expectations by either polarizing them or collecting them together.

Socio-technical changes catalyze the changes in the socio-political environment. The socio-technical changes cause the rejection of neo-liberal hegemony and the decline of progressive neoliberalism which together mixes lethal forms of capitalism and the truncated ideals of emancipation (Fraser, 2017).

The main driver here is a lust for change and public anger which is evolving within the heavily populated, out of the inconsistency emerging from the illusion of neo-liberal ideals against the hard edge reality of modern capitalism of exclusion from achievement of wealth by high housing costs, zero hour contracts, minimal pension, increased education costs with less certainty of benefits, predatory debt, minimal pension and protection measures for example those once provided by Unions and hesitant attitudes towards the diversity of religion.

The modern post-progressive-neo-liberal socio-political environment demotivates individuals by making them feel that they must matter, but in reality, is avoided and, as such, will never attain their personal potential.

It has the cause of substituting accessible political norms with a 'new political normal.' In this case, the explanations which are based upon the conventional values do not apply anymore, they are declined, which lift ups questions about what is acceptable as well as modern in the advanced world of globalization.

Therefore, the rise and success of disruptive politics in the USA; the surprise at the anti-Renzi reforms vote in Italy; Brexit, 2016 and the 2015 failure of poll predictors in the UK; through to the various 'Arab spring' movements in Tunisia, Egypt, and elsewhere; the rise of the National Front in France, Germany, and elsewhere; and finally. This modern 'disrupted' socio-political environment is perhaps making new behavioral norms which new transnational terror networks and TNOCs are now exploiting, for example, the transfer of huge populations to Europe from Africa and also religious attitudes and extreme politics.

2.9. CONCLUSION

The containment of TOC by international cooperation can be a model method of systematic solution, due to the systematic understanding of the internal workings of transnational criminal systems as how they correlate to their criminal and noncriminal external environments both, how these systems cooperate with each other, and how these criminal organizations thrive and under which circumstances they refuse depending on information-sharing system among United Nations (Martin and Romano, 1992).

Additionally, when there is consistency in the interest of the United States, these can be attained easily by international cooperation, sharing of essential information and empowering multilateral cooperation will not be a major hurdle (Godson and Williams, 1998).

When these interests are compared with the national interests, however, involving national political and economic interests along with the essential national information, the containment of TOC by multinational cooperation may be a thing which cannot be attained.

Ultimately, it might be debated that the control and prevention of the transnational crime by multinational cooperation would have to be reliable with the appropriate social context, for example, social interests, political orientation, cultural characteristics and economic interests of the implementing regions or nations.

2.10. CASE STUDY: DEUTSCHE BANK MONEY LAUNDERING SCHEME

2.10.1. The Deutsche Bank Money Laundering Scandal

After Russia's incursion into Crimea, sanctions by the European Union and the U.S. against Russia forced President Putin to declare "offshorization" illegal in an attempt to keep Russian businesses at home and prevent the declining exchange rate of the ruble from damaging the Russian economy.

As a result, Russian billionaires resorted to a more discreet way of funneling money offshore via mirror trading whereby a relatively small amount is traded in each transaction. Thus, creating the Deutsche Bank money laundering scandal. This scandal raises questions about the effectiveness of systems and controls implemented to prevent the occurrence of these types of unethical violations.

2.10.2. Key Players

The central players in the Deutsche Bank money laundering scandal, which gained media attention in late 2016 include:

Deutsche Bank AG: Deutsche Bank is a global German banking and financial services company with more than 100,000 employees in over 70 countries and a large presence in Europe, the Americas, and Asia-Pacific. The company is headquartered in the Deutsche Bank Twin Towers in Frankfurt and was the largest foreign exchange dealer in the world with a market share of 21 percent in 2009.

The company offers financial products and services for corporate, institutional, private, and business clients. Deutsche Bank provides services that include sales, trading, research, origination of debt and equity, mergers and acquisitions (M&A), risk management products, such as derivatives, corporate finance, wealth management, and transaction banking.

U.S. Department of Justice (DOJ): The United States DOJ is a federal executive department of the U.S. government, responsible for the enforcement of the law and administration of justice in the United States, equivalent to the justice or interior ministries of other countries.

The Department is headed by the United States Attorney General, who is nominated by the President and confirmed by the Senate and is a member of the Cabinet. The current Attorney General is Jeff Sessions.

New York State Department of Financial Services (DFS): The New York State DFS is the department of the New York state government responsible for regulating financial services and products, including those subjects to the New York insurance, banking, and financial services laws.

The department's mission is to foster the growth of the financial industry in New York and spur economic development through judicious regulation and vigilant supervision.

Organized Crime and Corruption Reporting Project (OCCRP): The OCCRP is an impartial and non-partisan consortium of investigative centers, media, and journalists that operates internationally in Eastern Europe, the Caucasus, Central Asia, and Central America. It is the only existing full-time investigative reporting organization that specializes in organized crime and corruption in the world.

Transactions: In a press release published on the 30th of January 2017, the New York State DFS states it found Deutsche Bank and several of its senior managers responsible of neglecting opportunities to detect, intercept, and investigate a long-running mirror-trading scheme facilitated by Deutsche Bank's Moscow headquarters and involving its New York and London branches. Deutsche Bank employees used a mirror-trading scheme to help wealthy Russians move $10 billion out of that country from 2011 through 2014.

Specific companies that were clients of the Moscow equities desk operated through the equities desk at Deutsche Bank's Moscow branch. They issued orders to purchase Russian blue-chip stocks. These companies would always pay for the stocks in rubbles. Through Deutsche Bank's London branch, a related counterparty would then sell the identical Russian blue-chip stock sometime thereafter in similar quantities and at the same price in US dollars.

Money laundering practices take place through mirror trading as mirror trades bypass currency controls, anti-money-laundering laws, and, possibly, tax controls when moving money overseas. The investigation carried out by the New York State DFS exposed Deutsche Bank for violations that include the following:

- The bank conducted its banking business in an unsafe and unsound manner, failing to maintain an effective and compliant anti-money laundering (AML) program.
- The bank failed to maintain and make available true and accurate books, accounts, and records reflecting all transactions and actions.
- The Deutsche Bank Trust Company of the Americas (DBTCA) unit was unresponsive to efforts made by outside sources to stop the mirror trading scheme. In addition, the senior compliance employee did not take any steps to investigate the basis for the European Bank's inquiry.
- The bank's Know Your Customer (KYC) processes were weak, functioning merely as a checklist with employees mechanically focused on ensuring documentation was collected. Virtually all

the KYC files for the companies involved in the scheme were insufficient.

- The bank failed to accurately rate it's country and client risks for money laundering throughout the relevant time and lacked a global policy benchmarking its risk appetite.
- The bank's anti-financial crime, AML and compliance units were ineffective and understaffed.

The DFS worked closely with the Financial Conduct Authority of the UK on the investigation to uncover Deutsche Bank's failure to detect, investigate, and stop the mirror trading scheme due to extensive compliance failures. This negligence allowed the scheme to continue for years.

2.10.3. Outcomes

So far, three Deutsche Bank employees have been suspended, two Co-CEOs of the bank have announced their resignation and new Co-CEO, John Cryan, has announced the forthcoming closure of all investment-banking activity in Russia. Currently, the bank is under investigation by the U.S. DOJ, the New York State DFS and financial regulators in the U.K and in Germany for allegations of money laundering in Deutsche Bank's Moscow office.

Furthermore, within 30 days of the selection of the independent monitor, Deutsche Bank, DBTCA, and the New York branch must submit to DFS an engagement letter, for DFS's approval, that provides for the independent monitor to review and report on, among other things:

- The elements of the bank's corporate governance that contributed to or facilitated the improper conduct and allowed it to go on for such a long time.
- Relevant amendments or reforms to corporate governance that the bank has made since the time of the improper conduct and whether those changes or reforms are likely to significantly enhance the bank's AML compliance programs going forward.
- The thoroughness and comprehensiveness of the bank's current global AML compliance programs.

In addition, Deutsche Bank must submit a written action plan to enhance its current global AML compliance programs that pertain to or affect activities conducted by or through DBTCA and the New York Branch.

2.10.4. Policy Recommendations

As stressed in the DFS's 30th January 2016 press release, the DFS's new risk-based anti-terrorism and AML regulation, which became effective on January 1, 2017, is significant in regulating financial institutions and preventing similar scandals involving financial institutions from reoccurring.

DFS's regulation requires regulated institutions to maintain programs to monitor and filter transactions for potential AML violations and prevent transactions with sanctioned entities. It also requires regulated institutions to submit an annual board resolution or senior officer compliance finding confirming the steps taken to ascertain compliance with the regulation.

In addition, DFS has proposed a first-in-the-nation cybersecurity regulation, effective March 1, 2017, requiring DFS regulated institutions to establish and maintain a cybersecurity program designed to protect consumers and ensure the safety and soundness of New York's financial services industry. To ensure safe and honest transactions, Deutsche Bank officials should consider applying the regulations as proposed by the DFS.

2.10.5. Conclusion

Bottom line, based on the information in this case study of the Deutsche Bank money laundering scandal, Deutsche Bank acted unethically because:

- The institution failed to act impartially and transparently when faced with institutional compliance and legal governance conflict of interest issues arising from mirror trading schemes. These schemes aided corruption and criminal activity because they normalized the act of money laundering in financial institutions.
- The institution failed in its fiduciary duty to act on the various opportunities to detect, investigate, and stop the mirror trading schemes taking place throughout the years by its employees.

REFERENCES

1. Gachúz, J., (2016). *Globalization and Organized Crime: Challenges for International Cooperation*. [eBook] p. 4. Available at: https://www.bakerinstitute.org/media/files/files/37efaacf/BI-Brief-070616-MEX_Globalization.pdf (Accessed on 12 April 2019).
2. May, C., (2017). *Transnational Crime and the Developing World*. [eBook] p. 166. Available at: https://www.gfintegrity.org/wp-content/uploads/2017/03/Transnational_Crime-final.pdf (Accessed on 12 April 2019).
3. Miraglia, P., Ochoa, R., & Briscoe, I., (2012). *Transnational Organized Crime and Fragile States*. [eBook] p. 36. Available at: https://www.oecd.org/dac/accountable-effective-institutions/WP3%20Transnational%20organised%20crime.pdf (Accessed on 12 April 2019).
4. Reinares, F., & Resa, C., (2018). *Transnational Organized Crime as an Increasing Threat to the National Security of Democratic Regimes: Assessing Political Impacts and Evaluating State Responses*. [eBook] p.85. Available at: https://www.nato.int/acad/fellow/97–99/reinares.pdf (Accessed on 12 April 2019).
5. *Transnational Organized Crime – The Globalized Illegal Economy*, (n.d.). [eBook] p. 4. Available at: https://www.unodc.org/documents/toc/factsheets/TOC12_fs_general_EN_HIRES.pdf (Accessed on 12 April 2019).
6. *United Nations, General Assembly*, (2004). p. 52.
7. Van Der Laan, F., (2017). *Transnational Organized Crime*. [eBook] Netherlands Institute of International Relations 'Clingendael, p. 25. Available at: https://www.clingendael.org/sites/default/files/pdfs/clingendael_strategic_monitor_2017_transnational_organised_crime.pdf (Accessed on 12 April 2019).
8. Von Lampe, K., (2012). *The Practice of Transnational Organized Crime*. [eBook] Routledge, p. 14. Available at: https://www.researchgate.net/profile/Klaus_Von_Lampe/publication/299461494_The_Practice_of_Transnational_Organized_Crime/links/56f9a3ee08ae38d710a3033f/The-Practice-of-Transnational-Organized-Crime.pdf?origin=publication_detail (Accessed on 12 April 2019).
9. Wall, D., (n.d.). *Understanding Transnational Organized Crime*. [eBook] p. 24. Available at: http://www.paccsresearch.org.uk/wp-

content/uploads/2018/01/TNOC-Research-Integration-Report-FINAL-Dec-17.pdf (Accessed on 12 April 2019).

10. Wang, P., & Wang, J., (2009). *Transnational Crime: Its Containment Through International Cooperation.* [eBook] Canadian Center of Science and Education, p. 8. Available at: https://pdfs.semanticscholar.org/f046/90614bdfc8a0b0ad477fbf9d1fbad75693af.pdf (Accessed on 12 April 2019).

3

Impact of Transnational Organized Crime on States and Societies

CONTENTS

The international collaboration in the fight averse to the organized crime has been considered as an indivisible part of the growth or the development of the cooperation of the criminal police at an international level, as such. The theoretical part of it generally tends to emerge from the unclear definition or the description related to the subject matter, the crime which has already been organized, whilst the factual complexity has been linked with the complicatedness, which has been inherent in the enforcement of the law and also the collaboration of the judicial on the global level.

This particular subject has been placed within the intersection of the two provided disciplines, i.e., the criminology and the relations amongst the various countries. This chapter basically talks about the adverse effect the transnational organized crime (TOC) might possess on the states as well as the society.

3.1. INTRODUCTION

The influence or the effect of transnational crime, which has already been organized, on the pertaining communities, is being considered as much of critical or complex and are not that simple to provide with description. No easy or simple description exists which will cover the entire essence of the effect or the influence the organized crime possesses, also the repercussions, it has, for societies, states, and rules or norms related to the law.

An approximation to the various distinct issues and also the challenges the societies or the communities have to suffer due to the arising transnational crime which has already been organized (Figure 3.1).

It has been considered as a universal fact that the TOC, in accordance with the definition, is being known as the phenomenon of the cross- border which is firmly in relation with the darker part of the process of Globalization, which tends to make it much more critical as well as difficult to provide with even the brief regarding the account which is based on the problem.

Not even one or a single set of the effects or the influences that the transnational crime which has already been organized possesses on the communities or the existing societies surrounding the globe.

These effects might be similar to those in the different nations or the countries, but, nonetheless, the repercussions of TOC, for the various societies tend to be distinct considering the different countries and even ranging from region to region.

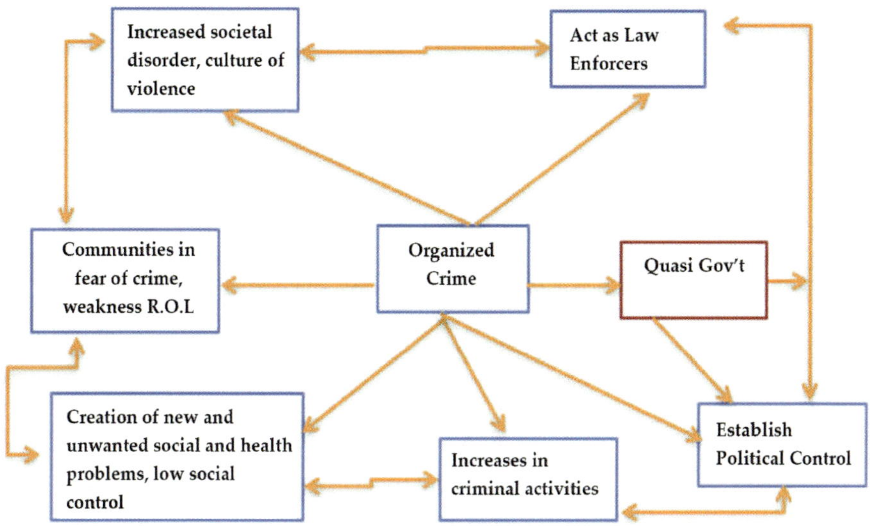

Figure 3.1: Social impacts of organized crime.

Source: https://www.researchgate.net/figure/Social-Impacts-of-Organized-Crime-in-the-Caribbean_fig1_321808834

For instance, the recent fight against drugs in various countries puts in the repercussions on the several states of those countries and the societies as well, which are considered to be destructive and distinct from the various other wars related to drugs in the remaining countries.

The crimes related to environment, which has already been organized in the various south regions and are being grasped and dealt with by the states and the societies or the communities of those southern regions, in a manner which is being acknowledged as distinct from the usual ones.

The other complexity, which the research of the criminology is witnessing, is the process of dealing with the crime that has already been organized, has been considered as the major question related to the definition being provided, which could not get simplified by the process of adding up the terminology of transnational to it.

Many of the people who do the research in criminology have also worked on the provided definition, but the context belongs to the crime, which has been organized, tends to stay firm on being one of the terms that has been contested the most, in the research of the process of criminology.

This is all because of the fact that the pertaining variations, be it the structural one or the organizational one, relating to that of the phenomenon, have been considered as quite vast.

The issue with having a debate regarding the provided definitions is that it generally tends to provide a threat related to the killing of the considerable debate belonging to the cause itself.

Some questions might arise related to the concern for the differentiation between the organized crime and the TOC.

The crime which has already been organized tend to operate or function, at an increasing rate, on an international level even more so that they could be able have a difference regarding the virtual borders as well as the geographical borders. This tends to become more of outdated, and thus, similar to this is the difference amongst the crime which has already been organized and the transitional organized crime.

However, the main facet of the research in the transitional crime which is already been organized is generally to do the process of recognition or identification of these particular crimes, already being organized at a domestic level, which tend to become international. And to what extent in these particular cases are these crimes international.

The transitional organized crime is being acknowledged as one of the most critical as well as complex phenomenon. Socially in the world which has been globalized and is even more complex, and thus, is consistently trying to adapt itself to the challenges that has been add by current conditions.

Nonetheless, the world belonging to international crime, which has already been organized, and the world belonging to the civil society, is being considered as the two sides of the same coin.

The organizations which possess the criminals exist only when the society or the community starts to demand various goods and services, and wherein the whole of marketplace is being available to the general public, within which the various goods and services are being provided.

Having a sound understanding regarding the harm or destruction the international crime which has been organized can cause, means there must be various developing models for the purpose of analysis that helps in tracing of the harms being caused.

This will certainly prove to be of great assistance to the makers of the policies in the execution of the various policies related to the enforcement of the law, placing of the financial resources, and thus, assessing the required measures which are being taken. Being specific, the process of measuring the costs incurred related to the organized crime, can play a vital role in the process of evaluation or assessment of the effect on the crime belonging to the spending of the money as well as the efficacy of the policies being made for the process of the reduction of the crime.

It can provide assistance in order to make it a priority and to possess a focus on the policies related to the resources which are scarce and which possess the capability of actually reducing the destruction or the harm caused by the organized crime, instead of having a decrement in the number of the crimes.

3.2. IMPACT OF ORGANIZED CRIME ON THE LEGAL ECONOMY: IDENTIFYING STRATEGIES TO DISRUPT CRIMINAL INVESTMENT IN KEY SECTORS

Many of the conferences have been organized by the ministry of the development or growth within the economy, so that they could have much focus on the three major topics (Figure 3.2), which are:

- The process of forging and the crimes related to the environment, being the source of providing funds for the crimes which have already been organized;
- The opinions or the perspectives on the process of reinvesting of the capital, known to be the illicit one, into the legit economy; and
- Various creative as well as innovative methods of managing the seizing of the assets possessed by the criminals.

The crime, which has already been organized, has showed rising capability of the process of adaptation with the fast changes taking place in the arenas belonging to politics as well as economy, specifically in the current years.

Since many of the years passed be much of the organizations' possessing the criminals have been successful in having an increment within their sphere of the action, maintaining a vicious cycle which is inseparable as well, amongst the process of managing the activities, being illegal, and the process of reinvesting the capital within the legit economy.

Having the reinvestment of the revenues collected from the activities, being illegal, and the markets which are known to be illicit, into the assets as well as the legitimate economy.

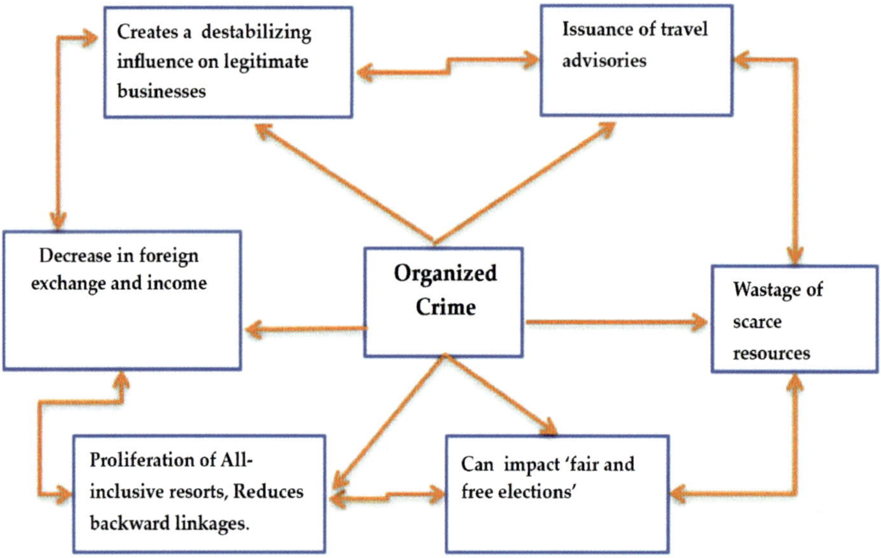

Figure 3.2: The economic impact of organized crime.

Source: https://www.researchgate.net/figure/The-Economic-Impact-of-Organized-Crime-in-the-Caribbean_fig5_321808834

The various negative repercussions related to this process are specifically for the government as well as the society.

The illicit economy is not being properly filtered by the groups involving in the criminal activities, the competition is considered to be twisted, and the pertaining resources have been diverted from the services rendered by the general public.

In addition to it, this process is basically being facilitated by the complex mechanisms related to the process of laundering of the money, which generally makes it quite difficult for the government to segregate the legal economy from the illegal economy.

Making the way for the rising corresponding approaches as well as the strategies, being the representatives from the academia, the various civil societies, the enterprises or the organizations being present in abroad and the government, who all will be providing with their respective aims or objectives, their personal experiences and the outcomes generated. Amongst the various participants, there pertain the representatives from the various departments across different countries.

Moreover, the people participating in it from the private sector will be providing with the illustration regarding how the war against the power of the economy belonging to the crime, which has already been organized, would be providing with their assistance regarding the creation of the environment within the business, wherein the economy would be able to thrive.

3.3. IMPACTS OF ORGANIZED CRIME

The prevalent nature of the crime which has already been organized in the various legitimate commercial markets, be it the global one or the domestic one, possess a great effect on all the provided arenas of the various societies.

Domains including the healthcare sector, the various systems for safety as well as the financial security or safety, are all being present at the front of all those areas which are being severely affected by the crime, already being organized, and is far from the reach (Figure 3.3).

Figure 3.3: The impact of organized crime.

Source: http://umich.edu/~eng217/student_projects/nkazmers/index1.html

The crimes related to the economy, are being committed by the various groups belonging to the crime which has already been organized that generally costs quite a higher value to many of the countries each year.

Thus, the effect of the organized crime generally tends to go way ahead of the impacts related to monetary terms. Corruption, menacing, and violence are all considered to be the mainstays belonging to the groups related to the crime which has already been organized.

They tend to possess an impact on the confidence of the general public in many of their respective fundamental sources being related to the solace as well as the security of the houses, the neighbors as well as the communities or the societies.

The various agencies are being committed to provide people with assistance so that they could be able to provide with an assurance regarding the safety of the homes and the communities as well.

The crime which has already been organized possesses an impact on the various rights of human beings related to the peace, order, and having good governance.

The various acts related to the violence or the process of menacing within the respective societies or communities; the corruption pertaining in the systems related to the politics and the government; depreciating quality of the life; sacrificing the personal security; and the disturbance within the life of the family, are all being considered as the major effects or the impacts which have been felt from the functions or the operations related to the groups of the people committing organized crimes.

3.4. THE DIRECT AND INDIRECT IMPACTS OF ORGANIZED CRIME ON YOUTH, AS OFFENDERS AND VICTIMS

Although the crime, which has already been organized, possesses an effect on the young generation which is both of bold as well as straightforward, often it might be having more of the considerate affect being a consequence to the various impact, being indirect, which are all being taken into consideration specifically at the level of the community or the society.

This particular research helps in the process of exploration of the effect, both the traditional criminal activities as well as the non- traditional criminal activities, which has already been organized, might possess on the youth or the young generation (Figure 3.4).

Figure 3.4: Effects of organized crime on society.

Source: https://classroom.synonym.com/effects-of-crime-on-society-12081764.html

It provides with the discussion regarding the impact of the crime which has already been organized, on the perception or the opinion of the public, wherein the population of the young generation are often being addressed as vulnerable, and also the process of policing the allocation of the various resource possessing the inclusion of the measures for the process of reducing both the supply as well as the demand.

The research which is based on crime, already being organized, in respect to this particular context, is considered to be restricted in terms of the number of the pertaining areas.

The further research depending on the effect of the crime, which has already been organized, on the younger generation, for instance, might be having an inclusion of the various issues which belongs to the perceptions or the opinions of the general public and the process of collection of the data being apt.

An approach being ethnographic might also provide with the assistance in having an expansion of the understanding regarding much of the effects or the impacts.

The policies belonging to the communication, be it the external one or the internal one, of the local effect of the crime, which has already been organized, has to get assessed properly, and also which all are being related or associated with the entry of the data, guarding the allocation of the pertaining resources, and the issue regarding the reduction of the demand as well as the supply.

Many of the researchers did complete their latest examination or the assessment of the pertaining impacts or the effects of the activities performed by the people involving in the organized crime in various countries.

These researches, however, did not put in much of the concentration or the focus on the particular segments or the parts related to the population which might the one getting affected the most. The effects of the activities belonging to the crime, on the young generation, particularly were not being examined or assessed in many of the countries.

Currently, much of the verbal links of the groups having an involvement in the activities related to the organized crime to the young generation, being the offenders, and not mandatorily being the victims.

The sole purpose of conducting such a research was to show up an analysis based on both the quantitative as well as the qualitative domains regarding the effect or the impact of the crime, which has already been organized, on the young generation, both being the victims as well as the offenders.

However, this particular task is not being considered as possible, being provided with the restricted studies or the researches accessible belonging to this specific topic.

Rather, the major part of this particular research would be focusing on the pertaining literature which helps in assessing the indirect as well as the direct effects such crime possess on the young generation, both at the domestic level as well as the international level.

It also possesses the discussion regarding the complexity or the difficulty in the process of assessing the crime which has already, having an inclusion of the dearth of the consensus being present on the provided definition or the description.

Many of the traditional activities related to the domestic organized crime have been highlighted, as all of them are being quite unique and generally possess an impact which has already been shared, on the younger generation. Whereas all of the people within the young generation belonging to the population, much of the parts related to the population belonging to the young generation, might be more of vulnerable to the crime which has already been organized, in comparison to the others.

Thus, this particular research tends to put in the main focus on the children belonging to the young generation, the youth being the aboriginal, the youth belonging to the explicit minority, and all the distinction in accordance with the respective gender.

This will be providing the review of not just the process of assessing the pertaining circumstances. The provided organization or the enterprise possesses the various listed crimes which have already been organized. Terrorism, as well as the young generation amongst the priorities it has, shows the link or the connection which is actually being required amongst those priorities.

This report regarding the research being conducted will be assessing the varied, as well as secured, perceptions of domestic organized crime.

Therefore, having a sound understanding regarding the pressures on the various agencies of the police, their respective designs and the several patterns or the trends in the process of enforcement will provide the assistance in getting a deeper understanding regarding wherein the police tend to put in much of focus their respective energies as well as allocation of the resources.

3.4.1. The Direct and Indirect Impacts of Organized Crime on Youth- Drugs

Generally, drug activities are directly associated with the organized crime. Various other criminal activities must be analyzed for their effect on youth. Related to the illegal trade of drugs, organized crime has direct impact on the youth.

Youth are and can be directly involved in the process of production, exportation, smuggling, and purchase of drugs. The involvement of organized crime in drugs offers simple and easy availability of illegal substances and the enhanced use of drugs by youth (Adlaf et al., 1995).

Youth aged under 12 are brought into the world of drug by older or adult youth offenders. Neighborhood youth are recognized as potential resources which can produce extra income for low wages and partial or full immunity from the law (Haberfeld, 1992). By this, the use of youth or children as mules for the exportation of drugs can be directly promoted. It also encourages the idea of using drugs to subdue youth into prostitution (Dimmock, 2002; Estes et al., 2001). The behavior of drug traffickers is then modeled by the youth of community and can be quickly learned.

Drug use may have various consequences on youth and society. Groups which are involved in organized crime supply drugs to fulfill the existing requirements. Unsuspecting and native youth can rapidly become addicted to the drugs. Theft and property crimes are also committed by people who are under the influence of drugs to get more drugs (Pernanen et al., 2002).

There are various impacts of using drugs such as social, physical, and emotional as well. These also involve grave life-threatening diseases attained by the chronic health effects of drugs like MDMA/MDA or by sharing needles (Mathias et al., 2001).

Additionally, when drugs are promoted at raves by organized crime groups, it can lead to unintended accidents and sexual assaults, such as teenage pregnancy and car accidents (Addictive Drug Information Council, 2001).

The participation of organized crime in the production of marijuana also has the impact on communities. For instance, for growth preparations of marijuana, the use of rental properties may prevent poor families from getting suitable rental accommodation in the community where rental housing is either restricted or the prices are exaggerated by huge payments organized criminals pay to property owners.

Safety becomes a major issue if the growth operations are planned to be performed near community parks by the organized crime groups for tactical reasons, basically to capable to observe and defend against burglars (Tyakoff, 1998).

The children of those parents who are involved in the production of marijuana may be exposed to dangerous electrical wiring and 'booby traps. If their parents are arrested, the children might be turned over to child welfare ("28 Children caught up in Homegrown Seizure Raids," 2002).

If young traffickers who are at the lower end of the supply are used to smuggle drugs to other youth, they may also be exposed to weapons or turf issues (Gordon, 2000). Youth are facing troubling problems around socialization, value, and trust by being familiarized with the network of drug trafficking by older drug dealers.

Therefore, they may grasp their criminality views for a long period of time than those who perform crimes which are not associated with drugs.

Though, only a minority of youth who trade drugs become regular dealers (Haberfeld, 1992).

Evidence documentation indicates that more enforcement of police is directed towards the involvement of organized crime in supply, in contrast to efforts to decrease the demand. Some illegal drugs get more priority as compared to others. Economic models suggest that a drug can influence the future consumption of other drugs.

When prices increase for one drug, it could lead youth to some other substances. For example, as a result of police seizures, a lower supply of marijuana could result in enhanced ecstasy use. Additional use of tobacco or marijuana is resulted by contraband alcohol seizures. With the decrease in demand, a focus on other gateway commodities like alcohol and tobacco could donate to decreased demand and supply for all the three substances as tobacco, alcohol, and illegal drugs (Kenkel et al., 2001). At this point, the three issues which are related to drugs warrant attention.

First is the US government has started educating and advertising on the role of American youth to subsidize the terrorism by consumption of drugs. Information connecting Canadian consumption to the groups of terrorists is speculated from the facts available in the report. However, it is not validated through proof (Criminal Intelligence Directorate, Drug Analysis Section, RCMP, 2002).

No documented evidence is available about the associates, or members of terrorist groups are resorting to drug smuggling to finance the activities of various terrorists. Another problem is the perception of police related to organized crime drug trafficking.

Research in various countries has shown that medium to high-level drug smugglers are most likely to be not career criminals, but once law-abiding business people that is small business pinched to high margins of profit (Woodiwiss, 2001; Desroches, 2002; Williams, 1999).

It could be dangerous as well as difficult for the police to invade and this size of criminal group. This may demonstrate why it gets less credit by the agencies of law enforcement. Ultimately, about the recent CCSA-sponsored research on drugs and crime (2002), there is an attained fear from crimes associated to the consumption of drug.

This observation may be more admirable for crimes including alcohol. These kinds of research findings may cause police and different service providers to go back to their policies (Pernanen et al., 2002).

3.4.2. Human Smuggling and Child Sexual Exploitation (Prostitution and Pornography)

Organized criminal groups are engaged in human smuggling and child sexual exploitation activities to varying degrees. Pornography, human smuggling, and child prostitution are generally committed in tandem. After men, women, and youth are trafficked into a country, the women and children are enforced to tolerate various forms of sexual exploitation and abuse (Figure 3.5).

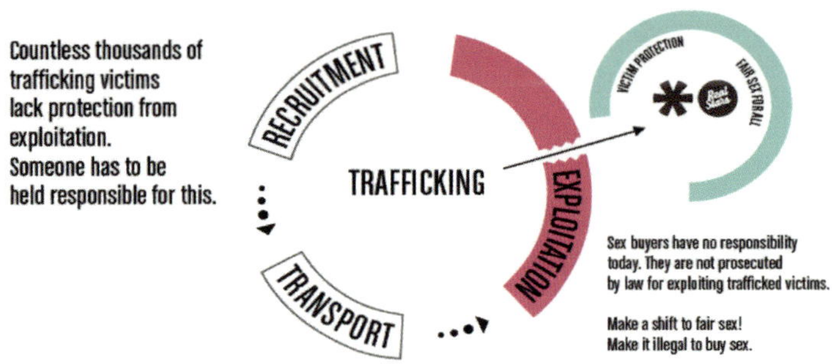

Figure 3.5: Sex trafficking.

Source: https://en.wikipedia.org/wiki/Sex_trafficking

Child sexual exploitation is a profitable business which is preferred by the organized crime. This is another kind of service in their 'portfolio' of crime. The use or abuse of youth and children has left apparent impressions on the lives of those who are directly engaged in sexual exploitation and human smuggling.

As per the Criminal Intelligence Service Canada, 2001, the average age of youth prostitutes in Canada is 14. To keep and employ youth or children, ploys are used by the organized crime groups. They also provide drug and financial incentives to get same-sex peers to employ other youth. Drugs are given to sexually exploited youth to sustain their activities and to feed their addiction (Estes et al., 2001).

For the basic requirement of money, cloth, food, and shelter, organized crime groups sustain street children by having them engage in different forms of exploitation (Estes et al., 2001; Rodriguez, 1999). Trafficked children and adults work off sustained debts as prostitutes and indentured servants.

Many times, they are forced to engage in different types of criminal activity like being mules for drugs (Estes et al., 2001). Human trafficking is very risky as people may die during their transport, or face various consequences if trapped and returned to their homeland. Adults are caught up in the mandate for goods and services.

The continued supply of youth or child pornographic material is facilitated to the adults directly by organized crime groups. This generally provokes the commitment of crimes against the youth or children. Organized crime is engaged in the supply of goods and services linked to child sexual exploitation. But other players are also mandatory, comprising members of the tourism industry who provide sex tours, villagers who sell their children, domestic, and international police/peacekeepers and foreign aid workers (Williams, 1999; Limonowska, 2002).

Runaway or homeless children around the age of 12 and above are the key targets of organized crime groups for sexual exploitation. There is evidence to suggest that the infants of youth prostitutes are also taken by the organized crime groups. This makes the crime rings able to apply superior control over these youth (Estes et al., 2001).

The social, physical, and social toll of being sexually exploited as a child and the consequent adolescent is an adult or delinquent whom exhibits maladjusted behaviors including committing suicide, drug use and domestic violence should be considered also (Zickler, 2002).

The distribution of goods like pornography material to vulnerable and unsuspecting youth through the internet is another indirect impact. Generally, trafficked humans find that their probabilities of earning income through welfare assistance and employment in their new country are reduced.

As a result, they are preyed upon by the trafficking group and various other criminal organizations. In Europe, more of the illegal immigrants, especially children and women may be forced into labor to survive, as compared to North America. Migrant trafficking can lead to xenophobic sentiments from the bigger community and fuel racial prejudices, closer to home.

This could contribute to the feelings of 'second class citizenry' and diminished funds for immigrant integration. Recent immigrants lack the understanding of the norms of society, which results in deviant behavior (Adamoli et al., 1998; Estes et al., 2001; Wolln et al., 2001).

As compared to the native population, the real or publicly alleged growth in crime committed by illegal immigrants creates terror and misconceptions regarding the good character and intentions of the smuggled people. Ultimately, the transport of smuggled people can serve to grow the demands for child prostitutes and foreign prostitutes by the western world. These individuals are deemed safer when it comes to sexually transmitted diseases (Adamoli et al., 1998).

3.4.3. Terrorism/Narco-Terrorism

The western world was awakened on September 11 to organized criminal activity in the context of terrorism. Since the actions of that day, only a small period of time has passed so there is little information available regarding the involvement of youth in this area (Figure 3.6).

Figure 3.6: Narco-terrorism.

Source: https://nccounterdrug.com/events/narcoterrorism/

Since 1977, the maximum recorded terrorism casualties were 2,652 wounded and 311 dead (Williams, 1999) and in the year 2001, the number increased to 3000 dead people.

There is an argument regarding the use of terrorist groups who behave as drug smugglers to transfer funds for criminal activities within the countries like Canada (Vaillant, 2002). This is further known as narcoterrorism. However, the US government and RCMP both claim that American and Canadian youth drug consumption is probably connected to the financial support of terrorism abroad.

The reason is that terrorist organizations are directly as well as indirectly engaged in the production of drugs in various areas like the Middle East,

Asia, and South America (Office of National Drug Control Policy, 2002; Criminal Intelligence Directorate, Drug Analysis Section, RCMP, 2002).

Terrorism or narco-terrorism impacts the youth directly by socially, emotionally, and physically destroying communities here and abroad. There is evidence present which shows that terrorist organizations use drugs as weapon to intentionally target the children of their enemies and consumer countries (Lyman et al., 1998).

In proximity to host countries or terrorist organizations youth are modeling different behavior. For example, militaristic training for joining terrorist cells, suicide bombings, and other dangerous activities.

There are more extensive and wider indirect impacts of terrorism or narco-terrorism on youth. One of which is the retribution of post-September 11 against countries like Afghanistan. This has negative impacts greatly on nutrition, emotional well-being and physical safety of Afghani children.

The 'follow the money' policy post-September 11 by Western governments may strictly limit the capability of genuine Western charities from obtaining funding to provide help to susceptible children and women in the Middle East. This allows countries like Afghanistan to be a more prolific incubator of criminal activities in the coming future (Naylor, 2001).

September 11 is the stimulus, for the push of U.N., for long-term change with respect to the decrease of social and economic despair, and corruption. For breeding groups of terrorists, they are supposed to be the main ingredients. However, the children of developing countries will suffer from decreased social and economic aid, for a short period of time (Blustein, 2002).

Also, there are emotional effects for witnessing events like September 11, and they are of long-consequences. These may consist of anxiety, fear, the subsequent use of alcohol or drugs to comfort the stress and absence of trust among children and parent who is documented already (National Institute on Drug Abuse, 2002).

After major criminal activities, the new amplified state of alert aids the safety of children, but civil rights may be dishonored as countries may not bear actions like protesting basically regarded as a 'right of passage' for youth (Ellard et al., 2002). After September 11, a new violence standard was set. Consequent attacks may engage susceptible populations like children more easily (Brynen, 2002). After the incident of September 11, few decisions are rationalized easily by the nations.

3.4.4. Gambling

Gambling has been considered as the traditional activity which heretofore has been the major crime which is associated with organized crime. It generally tends to provide the contribution of rising accessibility of gambling, which will certainly be affecting the frequency as well as the rates of gambling-related problems, specifically among the young generation (Figure 3.7).

Figure 3.7: Gambling.

Source: https://stockhead.com.au/tech/casino-cash-machine-increases-gambling-spend-by-up-to-18pc/

The problems related to the process of addiction to gambling which, in case, has been attained at an earlier age, increases the chances of being more inclined to continue the addiction in their adulthood. The process of problem gambling is generally being connected with the activities of the criminals and the absentees at work or the school.

A risk of violence has been associated within the gambling, also known as the illicit gambling when the time for the collection of the respective debts comes. This illicit gambling might also cause the gambler to seek funding with a loan shark or other undesirable persons or groups to cover up their gambling. As a result, instead of seeking help for the addiction, they dig a bigger hole by being in debt and contending with the gambling illness.

Finally, much of freedom provided by the parents or the attitudes which provides them with the encouragement in the gambling generally tends to provide the younger generation with the view that it is fine to illegal gambling and to cut school.

3.4.5. Money Laundering

The process of laundering of the money is considered as the peculiar activity which is related to the crime which has already been organized so that they could be able to address them in terms of the effects, be it the direct one or the indirect one.

The activities are in themselves is an indirect effect or the impact of the various other forms of the activities being in relation with the domestic organized crime.

The process of movement or the transferring of the assets belonging too many of the criminals are to get accomplished so that they could be able to have a realization of the gains as well as the power.

The overview regarding the effect of the laundering of the money which can never be acknowledged without having addressed much of the current provincial various policies at the domestic level as well as international level are being enacted so as to provide a cure to those pertaining activities.

There pertain much of the direct effects relating to the process of laundering of the money and all the policies which tend to accompany based on the young generation or the youth.

There pertains the enlarged presence, for example, of the various groups being involved within the organized criminal activities within the countries, wherein the policies related to the laundering of the money is more slacked.

Thus, it helps in bringing much security and protection implications to the pertaining societies or the communities.

The groups involving within these organized crimes tend to make the apt utilization of the legitimate companies or the organizations so that they could be able to transfer the money, specifically all those which tend to serve for the typical requirement of the young generation to the old generation.

Therefore, it tends to possess the involvement of the various arcades of the videos, entertainment, clubs, etc. the renewed policies of the enforcement regarding the following the money, within many countries, might be having specific groups involving in the activities related to the organized crime for the financial incentives as well as the scope of their respective functioning.

It is also motivated in some underprivileged crime areas like Russia, to utilize laundered money from organized crime to finance the legitimate businesses to service the growing requirements of Russian families (Solomon et al., 2000).

There is a policy named 'follow the money' to address the financial activities by criminals which contributes the resources to crimes performed after the fact, as in contrast to inhibition and education of youth, parents, and communities. Because of the estimated cost of operation, this policy is not helpful in inhibiting large scale criminal acts against the civilians like that which happened on September 11.

Accounts of many terrorist accounts were frozen by US investigators since 1988, but this never halt consequent attacks (Brynen, 2002; Naylor, 2001). As stated previously, due to current stringent money laundering policies, there is an enhancing requirement for organized crime to become engaged in tobacco trafficking networks in Europe and Columbia in order to launder other crime money (Center for Public Integrity, 2002)

3.4.6. Corporate Organized Crime

Describing corporate organized crime as organized crime takes its illustration into a distinct sphere of understanding. In various aspects, organized crime causes much harm to youth and society as different other crimes like human and drug trafficking.

According to Michael Woodiwiss (2000), during the discussion of the scope of organized crime, the criminal behavior of three elements such as professionals, corporations, and governments has to be included. Banks and corporations have been caught laundering money for crime groups (Figure 3.8).

By considering corporate crime as organized crime, it could produce some reflection on the present political importance of 'corporate social responsibility.' In the 1960s, corporation introspection was very popular but has yet to be rejuvenated in context of research interest.

To meet the expected requirements of this kind of crime, police resourcing is very low. It could be very difficult to get evidence of corruption or collusion from corporations as it is from biker gangs. It is not only the corporations which are involved in this kind of corporate organized crime. Every level of government is vulnerable too.

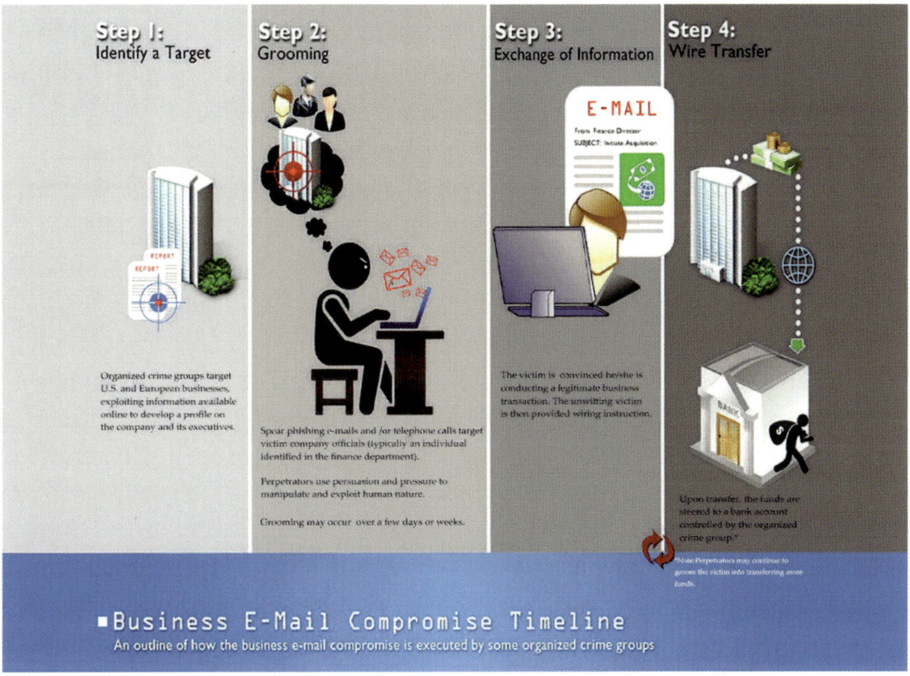

Figure 3.8: Organized crime groups.

Source: https://www.fbi.gov/news/stories/business-e-mail-compromise-on-the-rise

The RCMP was recently alerted to alleged corruption within government by the Auditor General of Canada. Since a criminal investigation has launched into various contracts of federal government.

Porteus (1998) contended that organized criminal groups, within Canada, are engaged in transferring and illicitly discarding toxic wastes. In the long-term adulteration of environments, corporations have also participated. There are various impacts on youth and children to such acts as significantly polluting waterways.

Waterway pollution has definite effects on societies which exist in nature. The Reed Co. Pulp and Paper Mill in Dryden, Ontario, dumped mercury into the river way which caused Minamata disease through the Aboriginal community of White dog and Grassy Narrows. The Aboriginal people by 1970, declined to believe that the water was polluted. All this had a severe impact on the livelihood and future expectations of the people of this reserve (Elmy, 2000; "Mercury and Lake Superior: The White Dog First Nation and Mercury Poisoning on Northwestern Ontario," 2002). The Sydney Tar Ponds in Nova Scotia accumulated 700,000 tons of polluted sentiment of kerosene, benzene, and various other chemicals. This was the consequence of dumping for 100 years by the Sydney Steel Company. In 1967, the provincial government bought the company to diminish the impact of job cuttings in Sydney. When the huge pollution became known, the company was forced to close. People living around the company complain of nosebleeds, headaches, and serious breathing problems.

After 30 years of company closings, the amount of environmental harm on children through birth defects, miscarriage, and cancer was maximum (Selinger, 2001). There are various other examples of the impacts of corporate organized crime on youth. For instance, RJR, and Northern Brands International were effectively sued in 1999 by the Canadian government for racketeering fraud, and helping to bring trafficked cigarettes into the marketplace.

These products, in turn, are bought by the more economically deprived and price-sensitive customers, such as youth (Center for Public Integrity, 2002). Recently, it got confirmed that eight corporate vitamin producers were price fixing vitamins, like folic acid, beta carotene and B6 which are required during the pregnancy and by children and youth ("Vitamins Price Fixing Lawsuits," 2002).

There are accusations also, that top corporations manufacturing baby formula have involved in immoral and violent marketing practices. These go against current standards are signed by governments of the Western world. It is been resolved that baby formula is a dangerous and an unwise choice for infants in developing nations due to unmet standards on use and storage (World Health Organization, 2001).

There are convinced unintended impacts of corporate organized crime on youth. Vitamins, for instance, are found in many food products, for example, cereals, and drinks. Therefore, corporations which purchase vitamins at exaggerated prices may choose not to comprise those required for healthy human development in their products.

Those maximum affected are young children and parental, particularly from economically underprivileged areas (European Union in the US: Eurocom, 2001). Even though standards do exist keeping out the assertive marketing of baby formula, this kind of marketing possibly will generate a perception that it is the only choice for women. Formula-fed infants can be less capable of resisting disease, and severe complications or deaths can happen in minor developing areas where the formula cannot be made properly, stored properly or sustained properly (International Baby Food Network, 2002).

3.5. THE IMPACT OF ORGANIZED CRIME ON LOCAL COMMUNITIES

Modern research on the impact of organized crime on local communities is done by the Perpetuity Research and the Police Foundation. The research found that around 17% of crime happening in the neighborhoods could be accredited to organized crime.

As identified by the police, majority of the crimes occurring in the neighborhood are related to fraud, drugs, and violence. Researchers, who are connected to organized crime offenders, assessed that only 4% of crimes are organized.

In a different city-wide study, 27% of police recorded shoplifting and theft Offenses was estimated which are associated with organized crime group. It is suggested from qualitative analysis that the substantial impact of organized crime groups on neighborhoods is linked with the high grade of social control which they applied.

The recent police snap-shot of organized crime is incomplete and also fails to reflect the diversity and scale of organized crime happening in these communities, and certainly the knowledge of local level practitioners in police and different agencies.

3.6. IMPACT OF ORGANIZED CRIME ON SHADOW ECONOMY: SOCIAL IMPACT ASSESSMENT

National security determines the development of a country as an independent state and economic sovereignty. It is provided with safety and abolition of the evolving threats. To the national security, the threats are the shadow economic relations having an undermining effect on the economy of a nation. Their extension leads to destruction and distortions of the link between an individual and the state. It also contributes to the declining the ethical and moral foundations of society, wears away the measures for the choice of means to attain the aims and the boundaries between prohibited and permitted activities.

In the meantime, the shadow economy is not something which is introduced from outside and goes together with the life of any state, irrespective of the existing socio-economic system. Therefore, the roots of this modern phenomenon lie in the current Soviet past.

Analyzing the features of the socialist economy, it was highlighted that the shadow economy remains an integral part, but it is not an island of capitalism (Sampson, 1988).

Various western economists have noted that the key characteristics of the Soviet shadow economy production and distribution of goods and services for acquisitive ends in destruction of legal norms. This phenomenon was called as "unofficial economy" (Grossman, 1977), "counter-economy," "second economy" (Karol, 1971) or "parallel market" (Simes, 1975).

For example, in the shortage condition, the enterprises have generally formed unrecorded excess goods so as to exchange them for other goods projected for executives or employees (Berliner, 1952).

In that way, the chief identification characteristic of the shadow economy is "unaccounted value creation" (unearned value creation), it refers to any economic activity which contributes to formation of the economic values of the country but is not involved in its gross domestic product.

Specifically, any activity of creating goods and services, related to tax-exempt or tax evasion but not counting the financial transactions or property transfers, numerous illicit or criminal activity without making valuables (Cassel, 1986).

The shadow economy consists of all legal and illegal elements of economic activity in the state and cooperative organizations also, which adds all the unrecorded activities and all forms of legal, semi-legal, and illegal economic activity (Marrese, 1981).

While developing the above approaches, Feige (1990) analyzed four different types of underground economic activities as:

- **Illegal economy:** When illegal goods and services, for example, speculative currency exchange, drugs, etc. are produced and circulated;
- **Unregistered economy:** It is not covered by the statistical

authorities and reproduces the unreported income;

- **Unreported economy:** It consists of violations of tax rules and producing the difference between the actual and estimated collected tax revenues; and
- **Informal economy:** It comprises private expenses and revenues attained by informally operating economic structures (Feige, 1990).

3.7. CASE STUDY: TRANSNATIONAL CRIME IN THE DEVELOPING WORLD: THE ILLICIT TRADE OF HUMAN ORGANS

In August 2010, the bodies of 72 immigrants were discovered in Tamaulipas, a state in northeastern Mexico. While nobody knows the sequence of events that led to this massacre, it is well known that Tamaulipas is at the center of a turf war between two powerful drug cartels, the Zetas and the Gulf Cartel. It is also well known that lately, these cartels have expanded their criminal operations to include fuel bunkering, prostitution, kidnapping, and even software piracy.

Across the Atlantic, in October 2010, 11 people were arrested for alleged organ trafficking between Syria and Egypt. The criminal group is believed to have transported poor donors from Syria to Cairo, where their kidneys were sold "to wealthy patients from Saudi Arabia and the United Arab Emirates." A human kidney can sell for as much as $15,000 on Cairo's black market, with most of the profits going to hospitals, laboratories, and middlemen.

Donors rarely receive more than $2,500. One need not look too hard to find stories like these in newspapers the world over. The simple fact is that TOC is big business in an increasingly globalized economy. From China to Nigeria to Mexico, entrepreneurial criminals will navigate around laws and across borders, supplying illegal or illegally acquired goods and services to meet the demands of the highest bidders. Whether it is drugs, human kidneys, human beings, illegally harvested timber, weapons, or rhinoceros' horns, as long as someone is willing to buy it, someone will be willing to sell it.

3.7.1. Overview

Decried as "neo-cannibalism" by leading experts in the field, the illicit trade in human organs reveals the dark complexities of humanity, medical ethics, and law in the global economy. The practice of human organ trafficking is fueled by increasing demand and supplied by donors coerced through force, the threat of force, or the promise of payment. Though it is primarily centered on kidneys, the human organ trade also includes the sale of livers, hearts, pancreases, lungs, corneas, and human tissue.

Unfortunately, voluntary organ donation remains insufficient and most countries fall dramatically short of meeting demand. A 2008 Economist article stated that, while 30,000 transplants are performed yearly in the United States, 100,000 people remain on waiting lists, "with 4,400 names being added each month." As a result of this shortage, and in spite of laws which exist in almost all countries prohibiting the sale of one's organs, a thriving illicit organ trade has risen to supply demand.

3.7.2. Estimated Value of the Illicit Organ Trade

The kidney is the most commonly transplanted organ, with a global estimate of 68,500 transplants performed per year. This is followed by the liver (20,100), heart (5,200), lung (3,250), and pancreas (2,800). While there is a distinct shortage of data on the price and frequency of illegal organ transplants, experts have estimated that globally, 5 to 10 percent of kidney transplants are a result of trafficking. This means that illegal trafficking accounts for some 3,400 to 6,800 kidney transplants per year.

The $50,000 broker's fee plus medical and transportation expenses bring the price of each transplant to approximately $150,000, meaning the retail value of the global illicit kidney market would range from $514 million to $1 billion per year. With 20,100 transplants per year, the partial liver transplant is the second most common procedure. There are no estimates as to how many of these include illegally acquired partial livers, however, according to a 2009 Reuters report, "the World Health Organization estimates about 10 percent of all organ transplants worldwide involve unacceptable or illegal transplants." Therefore, using a conservative range of 5 to 10 percent, it can be estimated that a yearly range of 1,000 to 2,000 partial liver transplants involve illegally acquired livers. According to a 2007 article in the Pittsburgh Tribune-Review, a liver transplant could be purchased, "within 90 days at a South American hospital for about $100,000." At this rate, the global illicit liver market would range from around $100 to $200 million. Combining these two markets, this report estimates the global retail value of the illicit organ trade at between $600 million and $1.2 billion per year. This estimate does not include estimates for heart, lung, or pancreas transplantation, for which data are insufficient.

3.7.3. Analyzing the Flow of Illicit Organs

As with other forms of trafficking, the illegal kidney trade generally "flows from poor, underdeveloped countries to rich, developed ones." Common countries of origin for donors include China, India, the Philippines, Turkey, Egypt, Moldova, Romania, Brazil, Bolivia, and Peru. Buyers are known to come from developed countries including the United States, Canada, Japan, Italy, and Australia, as well as the wealthy classes from developing countries such as Saudi Arabia, Israel, and Oman.

Recently China, Pakistan, and the Philippines have taken steps to prohibit 'transplant tourism,' which the United Network for Organ Sharing defines as "the purchase of a transplant organ abroad that includes access to an organ while bypassing laws, rules, or processes of any or all countries involved." These efforts have dramatically slowed the practice of open transplant tourism, but experts believe that the practice continues as "an underground criminal activity."

3.7.4. Profit Distribution

In many ways, the illicit organ trade is the perfect criminal enterprise. When viewed from the perspective of the desperate buyer, there is a strong case to be made in favor of organ trafficking. The gap between global demand and the supply of licit organs is so vast that illicit donors will be viewed by many as heroes. Unfortunately, these heroes, citizens of the world's most impoverished communities, are more often than not motivated by their own desperation.

This context, where both buyers and sellers are driven by their most basic need for survival, is primed for criminal exploitation. A middleman usually offers a donor around $5,000 for a kidney or partial liver and often ends up paying less than that. In China, for example, a 19-year-old was offered a little more than $5,000 for part of his liver. After the surgery, when he approached the middleman for payment, he was beaten and paid a mere $3,660. The middleman then arranges the transplant, charging the buyer approximately $150,000. This fee will usually cover travel and other expenses, after which the middleman nets around $50,000.

3.7.5. Illicit Organ Trafficking and the Developing World

Organ traffickers operate in the vast chasm that exists between the world's wealthy and the world's poor. In developing countries, economic stagnation and deficiencies in law enforcement combine with increasing globalization and improved communications technology to create the perfect space for this criminal enterprise. The lack of economic opportunity forces people to consider options they might otherwise find dangerous or reprehensible, while inadequate law enforcement enables the traffickers to operate with little fear of being arrested or fined.

At the same time, thanks to technological advancements in travel, trade, and communications, traffickers now have access to the major markets in developed countries all over the world. In essence, this allows them to buy an organ at the lowest price from the poorest donor, and sell it to the highest bidder in the richest country. Though the global shortage has fueled a debate as to whether or not organ sales should be legalized, the practice is currently banned in every country except Iran.

This pushes the practice underground which can have serious economic and health-related repercussions. Economically, there is the obvious loss of government revenue due to tax evasion. Everyone from the donor to the middleman to the person performing the transplant has a strong incentive to keep the transaction undercover. Not only would taxes reduce profits, but transparency would also open the door to prosecution. In this way, as with most transnational crime, even what appears to be financial inflow to a developing country has very little impact on the official economy, and does little to spur development.

The illicit organ trade can also involve serious health risks for donors and recipients alike. According to Nancy Scheper-Hughes, a leading expert on organ trafficking, "recovery from surgery is much more difficult when you don't have clean water or decent food." This is quite often the case for donors in developing countries, even if the transplant is performed in a certified hospital.

For the recipients, complications can involve fungal infections, compromised grafts, or tuberculosis, although these risks are probably weighed against the possibility of not getting a transplant at all. In short, for the developing world, there are very few redemptive aspects to the illicit organ trade.

Donors are paid next-to-nothing relative to the overall trade, while the huge profits of the middlemen disappear into the shadow economy, further promoting the self-interest of criminals and others who would profit from poverty and state weakness. Also, the shortage of legitimate donor organs is not only a problem for developed nations. By making human organs available to the highest bidder, traffickers prevent the poor from having access to the organs that they too so desperately need. In these ways human organ trafficking profits from and perpetuates the inequities that exist in the global economic system.

REFERENCES

1. Classroom.synonym.com., (n.d.). *Effects of Crime on Society | Synonym*. [online] Available at: https://classroom.synonym.com/effects-of-crime-on-society-12081764.html (Accessed on 12 April 2019).
2. Emeraldinsight.com., (2018). *Emerald Insight*. [online] Available at: https://www.emeraldinsight.com/doi/abs/10.1108/13590790610660926 (Accessed on 12 April 2019).
3. Haken, J., (2011). *Transnational Crime in the Developing World*. [eBook] Available at: https://www.gfintegrity.org/storage/gfip/documents/reports/transcrime/gfi_transnational_crime_web.pdf (Accessed on 12 April 2019).
4. Hofmann, K., (2018). *The Impact of Organized Crime on Democratic Governance*. [eBook] p. 9. Available at: http://library.fes.de/pdf-files/iez/global/06697.pdf (Accessed on 12 April 2019).
5. Midgley, T., Briscoe, I., & Bertoli, D., (2014). *Identifying Approaches and Measuring Impacts of Programmes Focused on Transnational Organized Crime*. [eBook] p. 58. Available at: http://file:///C:/Users/acer/Downloads/identifing-and-measuring-programmes-focused-on-transnational-organised-crime.pdf (Accessed on 12 April 2019).
6. Rcmp-grc.gc.ca., (2018). *Impacts of Organized Crime - Royal Canadian Mounted Police*. [online] Available at: http://www.rcmp-grc.gc.ca/soc-cgco/impact-eng.htm (Accessed on 12 April 2019).
7. Richter-White, H., (2002). The direct and indirect impacts of organized crime on youth, as offenders and victims. *Trends in Organized Crime, 7*(4), pp. 79–111.
8. Richter-White, H., (2003). *The Direct and Indirect Impacts of Organized Crime on Youth, as Offenders and Victims*. [eBook] p. 52. Available at: http://www.turtleisland.org/news/orgcrime.pdf (Accessed on 12 April 2019).
9. Scialert.net., (n.d.). *Impact of Organized Crime on Shadow Economy: Social Impact Assessment - SciAlert Responsive Version*. [online] Available at: https://scialert.net/fulltextmobile/?doi=ajaps.2014.644.651 (Accessed on 12 April 2019).
10. Stockley, L., (n.d.). *The Impact of Organized Crime on Local Communities - Perpetuity Research*. [online] Perpetuity Research.

Available at: https://perpetuityresearch.com/2604/the-impact-of-organised-crime-on-local-communities/ (Accessed on 12 April 2019).

11. *The Economic, Financial & Social Impacts of Organized Crime*, (2013). [eBook] p. 86. Available at: http://www.europarl.europa.eu/RegData/etudes/etudes/join/2013/493018/IPOL-JOIN_ET(2013)493018_EN.pdf (Accessed on 12 April 2019).
12. *Transnational Organized Crime and the Impact on the Private Sector*, (2017). [eBook] p. 78. Available at: https://www.unodc.org/res/cld/bibliography/transnational-organized-crime-and-the-impact-on-the-private-sector_-the-hidden-battalions_html/gitoc_tocprivatesector_web-3.pdf (Accessed on 12 April 2019).
13. Unicri.it., (n.d.). *The Impact of Organized Crime on the Legal Economy: Identifying Strategies to Disrupt Criminal Investment in Key Sectors*. [online] Available at: http://www.unicri.it/news/article/organized_crime_ (Accessed on 12 April 2019).

4

Terrorism and Transnational Organized Crime

CONTENTS

Organized crime has become a transnational phenomenon for the past two decades, and its impression is still far from being known completely and understood by the common people. The forms of manifestation of this phenomenon are eternally adapting or evolving whether explicit or subtle. As a result, its intrusion from the areas which are legal, along with the activities makes it problematic to recognize and act accordingly. After a huge time-gap, it has become a peripheral phenomenon and tends to be a major risk for the social, economic, and political stability of the states.

Through its goals and nature, as well as through the intricacy of its forms of manifestation, transnational organized crime (TOC) signifies a key challenge for the state and non-state organizations who deal with national and international security. This chapter mainly focuses on the phenomenon beginning from the most influent theories in international relations, offers the present features of transnational organized criminal groups and examines the sources and the supporting elements of the phenomenon, as well as the impression of the phenomenon upon national and international security at the social, economic, and political level. The method is an interdisciplinary one which covers the nexus between TOC and international terrorism.

4.1. INTRODUCTION

During the last few years, swift developments and turbulences have led to redefinition of the concept of TOC. Hence, presently, regarding the transnational organized crime there are no universally accepted definitions to define it properly.

There are basically two major variables which influence the conceptual framework that is built around the idea of TOC. First is, the space within which the process takes place and the second is, the time needed for its analysis.

These two defined variables acquire sense if and only if they are regarded as a collection of situations and historical, economic, technological, and socio-political developments in case of first variable that is space or as a collection of specific ideas in case of second variable that is time.

Hence, it is valuable noticing that definitions evolve unceasingly, but the main content of the definition is affected by the theoretical approaches to the process they define. Additionally, the discipline itself, the methodology for research and the level of analysis are the factors which renders the variability of the definitions describing this process. The meticulousness of various geographical spaces, the economic and political interests of states, as well as the variances in method definite to different theories related to the international relations additionally hamper acquiring consent about what TOC signifies for a defined period of time.

Sometimes, there is a lack of consent about what TOC signifies. But this does not prevent researchers from getting an agreement about some features of the process, considered intrinsic to its transnational character (Figure 4.1):

- Perpetrators: They are persons or organized groups who cross national borders by utilizing modern technologies in communication and informatics physically or virtually during the development of their activities.
- The object of the organized crime is represented by: "illegal goods which are manufactured from the services field; legal goods stealth or those which make the object of smuggling outside the country; the legal goods bought from a country by violating the rules regarding their export; the legal goods imported from a country by violating the rules regarding import or international embargo"
- The subject of the organized crime mainly comprises of foreigners involving in illegal acts on the territory of other state.
- The aim of organized crime comprises of attaining profit from illegal activities. The contribution in illegal activities assumes acquaintance to risks sustained by national legislation constraints. It does not necessarily mean that TOC organizations evade high-risk states.

If the last one provides lucrative and attractive markets, then they will turn out to be targets for transnational organized groups that will involve in illegal activities, trying to bound or to decrease their risks, but continuing to operate from states where the authority presents reduced risks for them.

- The digital signals which denote to the transferring of the electronic messages pointing at destroying or attacking the informatics systems or stealing from the financial institutions.

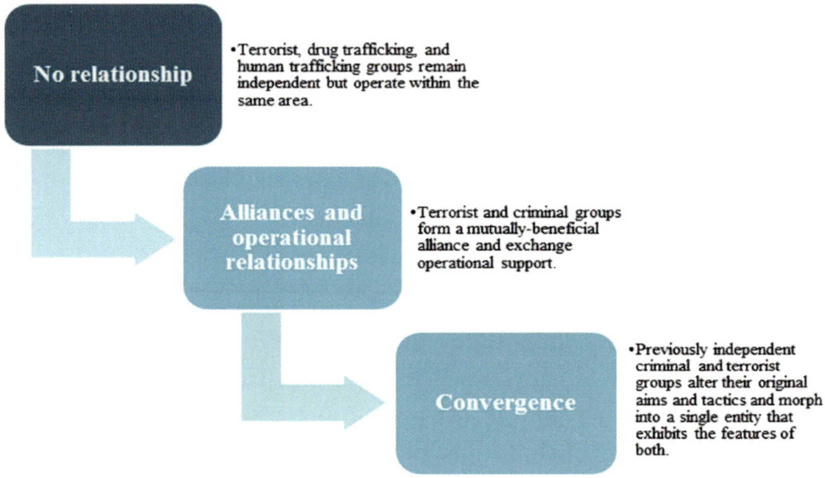

Figure 4.1: Module of organized crime.

Source: https://www.unodc.org/e4j/en/organized-crime/module-1/key-issues/similarities-and-differences.html

An operational definition evolves from all the above features which define that TOC has three different features which separate it from its initial national manifestations:

- It works at regional or global level;
- It has formed extended trans-border connections; and
- It has the ability to challenge national and international authorities.

4.2. CONCEPTUAL PERSPECTIVES OF TERRORISM AND TRANSNATIONAL ORGANIZED CRIME (TOC)

As stated earlier, the method to the process of TOC agonizes from the influence of various trends in leading international relations theory, namely Liberalism, Realism, Social Constructivism, and Marxism.

It is an obligation for every member of the human society to obey the essential values of the community, as per the perspective of Political Realism. To make social order under control, the state has legal authorization to interfere.

To offer benefit to the complete society, the dominant legal system needs to be preserved. Generally, state institutions function to preserve these dominant legal systems. As per the Clausewitzian perspective, in the core, the organized crime represents a persistence of economic activities utilizing illegal means that is legal working approaches are combined with illegal ones such as the use of corruption, violence, blackmail, and intimidation by the TOC groups.

This theory of Clausewitzian proposes the major solution to eliminate the phenomenon, robust measures against those who are involved in such kind of antisocial deeds. In fact, that must represent exact signals to the individuals who are part of a social organization is given. The signal involves the information that the state is very strong and determined to take those measures which are essential to discourage those which has the intentions to challenge the authority of state.

Liberalism highlights the human freedom and considers society as a unitary and harmonious mechanism. In this mechanism, the citizens share a mutual set of values that are significant to their community. According to this framework, the criminals are described as the persons who have a deviant behavior.

In general, the theoreticians of Liberalism identified that globalization and trade liberalization have donated to extending TOC. Though, they claim that sometimes this represents a secondary effect which cannot be shadowed by the aids of globalization and free trade.

There are basically two solutions to the issue according to this theory. First is that they give up of the criminals on their own will or due to the pressure of the society in which they are living, their nature and become alike other members of the society. Second is that they eliminate themselves from the society and will tolerate the significances of their behavior.

As per the experts of Liberalism, the phenomenon can be clashed by forming huge international institutions having attributions in this field and through cooperation among different states. The Marxist theory describes the phenomenon of TOC as the constant determination on behalf of capital owners to increase their own benefits and, indirectly, as a consequence of their greediness or lack of interest, to bound the access to well-being for other social classes.

Once disregarded, the latter do not have any substitute to survive. The researchers who belongs to this kind of thinking regarding international relations has the solution in adjusting the ratio between capital and work as far as goods and services are concerned on the world market, in service of work.

Social Constructivism finds crime as a collection of elements whose basis is at the crossroad between the concrete reality and social process sphere. Reality is a social construct as per the constructivist researchers, and the way in which people behave in a society has a substantial impact upon the behavior of people.

The researchers who belong to this school of thought contend that the phenomenon is a result of the existing social organization, of the way in which members of the society observe themselves in relation to the institutions defining the state and of some individual psychological features (Figure 4.2).

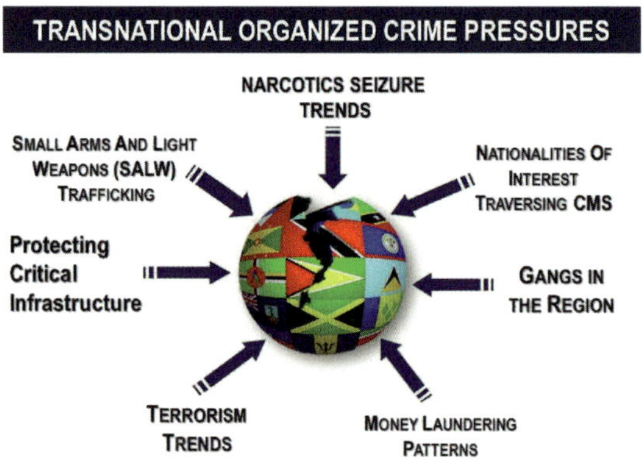

Figure 4.2: Pressures in transnational organized crime.

Source: https://slideplayer.com/slide/10788943/

Concerning the things from the viewpoint of Alexander Wendt, the organized crime is powerfully shaped by the thoughts and ideas which are prevailing in the society. From the perspective of this school of thought, the solution must be required in the course of redefining and rethinking the social processes that which regulate the behavior of the people present in the society.

Each of the theories mentioned above has their own limits in describing the phenomenon. Social misfits which are there in every society are generally ignored by the Realist theory. Special kind of treatment is required for these misfits. However, due to huge effort, huge cost and ineffective nature, just about all contemporary societies are not prepared to invest in this direction.

Liberalism acknowledges the hypothesis which is mentioned above. It also reflects that this is a natural fact and the citizens themselves are the only responsible for their acts, taking into consideration that state institutions must have only a limited involvement in regulating a given activities of the society.

The Marxist theory is not able to explain why only few individuals from the demoralized social categories are involved in criminal acts, and others do not. Beyond the merits of Social Constructivism, in recognizing the limits of the other schools of thought, it is not that articulate to form the solutions of those problems which are under discussion.

The research programs which are proposed by Social Constructivism is indicative and yet not as much of conclusive in analyzing concrete solutions. TOC suffers from an implicitly and partial analysis from an inadequate understanding.

That is also highlighted by various concerns which are linked to human, drug, and arms trafficking activities, illegal immigration or other activities, as well as by the exclusion from the definition of the phenomenon of other illegal activities done out by the legal actors or in which these actors are essentially involved.

Therefore, the crimes which are carried out by the transnational corporations mainly those which operate in the field of oil, tobacco, international finance or chemical products or those which are carried out by some state institutions such as intelligence services.

The politico-diplomatic relations which are accepted by the states and the existential symbiosis between state and non-state groups of criminals are the major causes of this approach. Hence, the subjective and imitative character of the recent research in the field can be explained better, despite the fact that the objective character claimed by scientific research must rise above these practices that, most of the times, have a brief character and are not necessarily anchored in the social requirements of the citizens which they are supposed to serve.

Basically, the illegal activity which is oriented towards the profit which crosses national borders defines the TOC. There are varieties of activities in this sphere which are carried out on translational bases but not all organized crime forms are transnational. There are premises at the same time for extending the criminal activities outside the national borders, firstly, due to the differences in the supply of the illegal goods and services and character of the demand.

An exclusive list of the criminal activities comprises of drugs trafficking, persons' smuggling, persons' trafficking, arms,' ammunition and forbidden substances trafficking, maritime piracy, cyberspace crime, and fake goods trafficking (Figure 4.3).

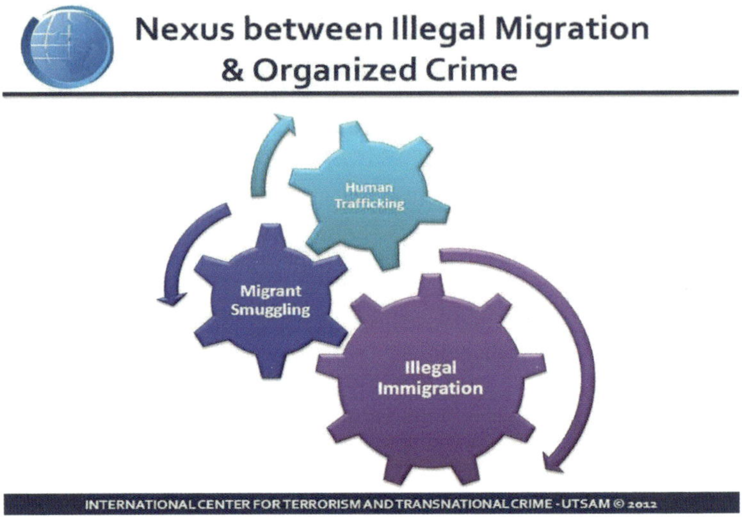

Figure 4.3: Nexus between illegal migration and organized crime.

Source: https://slideplayer.com/slide/2529257/

4.3. MEASUREMENT OF TRANSNATIONAL ORGANIZED CRIME (TOC)

An increase has been observed in extent and scale of the transnational criminal activity. It is becoming a worldwide threat which is very complex. The transnational criminals cross the borders and move huge money via international financial system which is so big. They minimize the combined economy of various nations.

Generally, they are involved in multi-crime businesses and have capitalized on development in international transportation and communication to increase criminal operations and make potent alliances. The destructive activities of transnational criminal groups do not threaten specific regions or countries anymore as was the case before cold war era. They usually threaten all the nations. Transnational organized crime is a kind of law enforcement issue. It is challenging, and the threat to national and international security is increased by it. TOC is not a modern concept, but still, there is no standard and universally accepted definition of this criminality in the law theories of criminology.

During an international symposium in 1988, in Saint Claude, France where the headquarters of Interpol is located, few definitions related to the TOC came into existence. The symposium was completely based on the organized crime. Before this international symposium, a total of 84 participants from 46 member-countries of Interpol decided to settle with the working formula as a base of additional discussion.

TOC is a criminological term having no claim to provide a juridical concept. The transnational factor of the organized crime across the boundaries of the globe was very important and literally helped it for the treaties and programs of the international organization.

TOC has a commanding potential, and it is dynamic also. Hence, it possesses a major risk to the existence of single state as well as the community of world as a whole. These criminal groups are very equipped and well-organized.

It is not an easy task for the organs of the law enforcement to find out their path in the organizational structures of these groups as they perform in the spheres of authority of various states and most of them are based upon the ethnicity.

The authority of legal power is challenged, and the democratic institutions get weaker by their activities. They destruct economies and financial markets of various states. The governmental resources which are structured to resolve various social and economic issues are not that much sufficient balance the criminal organizations at all.

Many of them combine their associations with ethnic, religious, and militant movements. A set of elements encourages the potential of rings of transnational crime. For example, they behave as parasites in some cases where governments are weak and do not have political power as well as the resources to defeat them.

Basically, they thrive on the bizarre amount of money which they get by doing various illegal activities mainly the process of production and selling of drugs. They are capable of acquiring benefit from the increased migration of people by continents and countries.

The groups have suitable technologies and advanced weapons at their disposal. These are significant means for the protection and realization of interests of the transnational criminal groups. Many states and international organizations are not able to coordinate and design efficient anti-criminal programs. This results into a suitable environment for the criminal community to operate in their battle to law enforcement organs.

Hence, it is very essential to develop the suitable countermeasures to the activities of TOC. The main type of activity under TOC consist of various illegal businesses such as women and children trafficking, illicit migration, theft, corruption, illicit transport of cultural property, body parts trafficking, flora, and fauna trafficking, software piracy, computer crimes, money laundering, drugs trafficking, etc.

There are other activities related to organized crime which has transnational implications and transnational character. If in any situation, it is not certain to categorize particular organized criminal activities in the defined range, their distinctive and most common feature is that it incorporates the crossing of national borders and jurisdictions.

Thus, control measures are specifically important on the international level and also within pretentious countries if these measures have international implications.

4.4. THE TERROR-CRIME INTERACTION SPECTRUM

As compared to military units, the crime and terrorist groups are miscellaneous in nature. They may be hierarchies or networks, they have a range of cultures instead of a disciplined code of behavior, and their aims are far less clear.

According to Hoffman, terrorist groups on the basis of their organization can be categorized further. Various researchers have created important evidence of interaction between organized crime and terrorism generally to support the general observation which might converge, the basic motives of crime and terror groups would assist to keep them at arm's length and hence the term "methods, not motives."

Certainly, the differences between the two are abundant: terrorists follow religious or political objectives through explicit violence against military targets and civilians. They turn to crime for the money they require to operate and survive.

On the other hand, criminal groups are aimed at making money. Any use of violence tends to be buried, and is usually engrossed on tactical goals, for example, eliminating competitors, intimidating witnesses or obstructing investigators.

So far, the similarities are equally clear as both functions universally, use flexible network structures to replace or balance formal hierarchies, and prosper in messy environments with weak rule of law or shaky regulation.

These common traits are mainly striking in disordered states where efficient rules and regulations of law have broken down. These two groups find a shared cause in the corrupt environment. Generally, terrorists find it necessary and convenient to deal with unknowns to attain logistical support and funding for their operations.

When these interactions are repeated, again and again, various concerns arise which terrorist and criminal organizations will assimilate and form new kind of organizations. The seminal work of Sutherland can provide support to this point. The work of Sutherland has argued that the duration and intensity of an association with criminals makes an individual more expected to adopt criminal behavior.

There are intensive interactions in the region of conflicts between terrorists and criminals; there is more common behavior and an approach of mutual learning which goes on. The same process can also be observed in urban areas of developed countries and in the prisons of Western Europe, Canada, and the US—both locations where professional criminals interact with terrorists.

Similar patterns were seen in conflict zones, where these kinds of interactions generally include more large-scale criminal elements. The vital relationship between transnational crime and international terror has essential strategic implications for the United States.

Williams, Naylor, Dishman, and Makarenko are the crime-terror interactions which are linked to its empirical results by the TraCCC (Terrorism, Transnational Crime and Corruption Center) team. The terror-crime interaction spectrum forms which shows the relationship between criminal and terror groups.

Each kind of interaction represents specific and different threats along with the opportunities for the process of detection by intelligence agencies and enforcement of laws. As an example, the principle of activity appropriation is outlined below which means that drug dealing, small to medium fraud and smuggling can be observed in the complete significance of it as possible evidence of cell activity of terrorists.

Small scale criminal activity can provide a distinctive clue such as common knowledge which further involves individuals as well as outlines of behavior that gets fit into the watchpoints. For instance, the major importance of cash business is specified by Naylor's and various other money laundering studies as the laundering phenomenon for gains which are illegal.

The unit of crime investigation conducted an interview with a retired member of Chicago. The interview revealed that taxi owners and taxi companies are investigated as money launderers who are totally cash based. According to the logic, it is assumed that terrorists might also be acquiring benefits from this scheme.

In the case of 9/11 investigations, this kind of investigations was not followed, even when two of the hijackers were drivers of the taxi. Different processes such as activity appropriation, symbiotic relationship, nexus, hybrid, and transformation of this spectrum demonstrates various kinds of interaction between an organized crime group and a terrorist group along with the nature of a single group who are involved in organized crime and terrorism both.

These kinds of conditions may have dynamic movements as demonstrated further, as a few of the groups may skip a level or may move backward while others may never move forward a specific kind of interaction. Having these kinds of interactions, this scheme can be portrayed as a continuum. When the organized crime groups and terror groups work by adopting other methods without even working together, then the activity appropriation takes place.

Usually, to increase the funds, terrorists turn to drug dealing, card fraud, smuggling, and money laundering. For example, John Horgan has mainly recognized how the cells of Provisional Irish Republican Army are involved in a variety of organized crime activities without having any association with the organized crime groups.

Similarly, the Al Qaeda cells present in Italy and Spain utilized SIM card fraud and credit card fraud to finance those strike cells which are based in France and Germany. On the other hand, Hezbollah utilized smuggling of cigarettes in the U.S. and abroad. Whereas both Al Qaeda and Hezbollah have smuggled diamond-like commodities in Africa.

When the authorities threatened the existence of organized criminals, they appropriated the terror tactics less commonly. All through the initial attempt by the authorities to stop these activities in 1993, the Lateran Church in Rome and the Uffizi museum in Florence were bombed by the Sicilian Mafia bombed.

Activity appropriation captures the merger of methods, but it does not signify the organizational associations between the terror and crime groups. Activity appropriation is a method by which the terrorists are exposed to the organized crime activities. As noted by Chris Dishman, this can lead to terror cells transformation into organized crime groups. A terror group which is using the approaches of organized crime does not always continue to a nexus arrangement.

The reason behind it is that none of the crime groups wants to do business with it, or the terrorists find no use of doing business with the outsiders as there is no benefit of doing that. Alternatively, there is a process called transformation where a terrorist group gets very much involved in criminal activities and make profits out of it that walk out on terrorism altogether.

Another indication given by officials of British security was related to the Belfast bank robberies happened in December 2004. This followed relative inactivity by Republican terrorists in Northern Ireland for really a long period. Officials of British security told a process to the process team by which IRA, itself was transformed into an organized crime group. Abu Sayyaf in Philippines began as an affiliate of Al Qaeda. He is now involved more in kidnapping which is motivated economically for huge ransoms and in piracy than in case of terrorism.

In the same way, criminal groups can be transformed into terrorist groups. However, there is no clear example of this phenomenon. There are various cases where the organized crime has transformed into terrorism. This transformation is found to be temporary and hence can be defined as the process of activity appropriation.

There are very rare occasions where such relationship results into a nexus. For example, when Colombian drug lord Pablo Escobar appointed ELN terrorists to pay a campaign of bombing on his behalf, against the government. When this kind of convergence between terrorism and organized crime is not captured as an activity, there is a loss of explanation of why terrorist groups and organized crime might converge.

As per the Sutherland principle of differential association, these kinds of activities might bring terror groups into consistent contact with the organized crime. When they try to get the launder money, forged documents or pay bribes, then it is quite obvious step to draw on the expertise and support of the criminal group, which is expected to have much more experience in these kinds of activities. It is referred as a nexus here.

Remarkably, this progression is a kind of the contraposition of Makarenko. He observed that alliances of organization occur previous two groups who are appropriating the activity of others. On the other hand, Williams assured this progression by noting that the terrorists first get involved in 'do it yourself' kind of organized crime and then get involve into organized crime groups specific services such as money laundering or document forgery.

In several cases, the criminals who provide goods and services to the terrorists for payment which can work in both the directions are involved in Nexus. A nexus does not infer a short-term relationship in which the criminals share the conceptual understandings of the terrorists simply that the transactions provide.

Ultimately, they have various common requirements such as safe havens, evasive tactics, false documentation and other strategies to decrease the risk of being detected. Transnational criminal gangs have hired different terrorist groups to protect their drug processing plants, in Latin America.

Protection has been provided to terrorists in Northern Ireland, for the operations of human smuggling by the Chinese Triads. Such low-cut contact may look unimportant and spontaneous to an investigator and hence might be overlooked.

The relation will get much stronger if the nexus remains to provide benefits both sides for a long period of time. If members of both the groups cooperate more, then the groups will form procedures and structures for the transaction of their business, share transfer skills and best practices.

It can be closely referred like more constant cooperation as a symbiotic relationship. It is defined as a relationship of common dependence and benefits. Well, it is practical to observe few related examples that exist. Distinctions of the close connections of the Albanian crime gangs and Kosovo Liberation along with the liaison between the trafficking groups in Colombia and the FARC can also be observed by the existing examples.

These two groups cooperate in the next stage for a long period of time, and the members of the organized crime group starts sharing conceptual aims of the terrorists. They grow gradually and ultimately, and they merge together.

The outcome of the process is a dark and hybrid network which has remarkably been defined as terrorist by day and criminal by night. Such kind of organization has a political agenda and involves criminal acts. Both political and criminal ends are forwarded by using corruption and violence.

These developments are resulted from a set of opportunities which can lead to the next level of cooperation, but are not inevitable. However, it is essential to analyze that when these two groups reach the point of hybrid, there will not be any reason per se to be uncertain about the follow up of transformation.

Similarly, a group may continue with the methods which are borrowed methods for the near future without constantly continuing to cooperation. Crime groups in Italy who are involved in terrorism never get a terrorist partner and hence continued at the activity appropriation stage.

In the end, they finished their activities of the terrorists and get back to the comprehensive pursuit of organized crime. The project team did not get any evidence of existing hybrid organization from the case of Aum Shinrikyo cult in Japan, certainly. It is a proof to various hurdles which hinders their formation.

Investigators generally use the interaction spectrum of terror crime to recognize the nature and behavior of terrorists and criminals both, and also to assume the future strategies of them. Above statement is argued with regards to the Sutherland that the group of terrorists are tracked down most probably and if the connection with other criminal groups, they are infiltrated.

In other words, the investigators are harmonized to the connection of crime-terror. The investigators may find it very easy to introduce counter terrorist operations which mainly concentrates on the criminal group and hence giving support to the terrorist group.

Remarkably, none of the examples were found by the TraCCC team in which a group of terrorists are involved in organized crime, either through an organizational linkage or through activity appropriation, arose into conflict with a group of criminals.

Neither the interviews nor the archival sources exposed such a battle about "turf," however as per the logic, organized crime groups would definitely react to these kinds of competitions. Certainly, not a part of the spectrum has provided its concentration on 'interaction' between terrorism and organized crime, in terms of operations and organizations both. Non-interaction and conflicts should remain as the classes of the relationship between terrorism and organized crime.

Precise models of the criminal-terrorist cooperation evolution are not formed by the spectrum. The proofs given here and various other studies suggest that there is no single path available for crime-terror interactions.

Factors of the environment which are outside the control of any of the organization and the different needs of specific terrorist or organized crime groups are the two main reasons that interactions happen more idiosyncratic than generalizable.

Therefore, to form a method for analysts and investigators to recognize the occurrence of the cooperation, to observe such a relationship and answer suitably when a trend become apparent either at local stage or at international stage, needs a methodological approach which considers a broad variety of potential modes of interaction.

Analysts and investigators can acquire the understanding about the terror crime intersection by using the PIE method, by identifying the evidence obtained from financial transactions, communications, behavior, and organizational charts.

Different methodologies can also be applied by the analysts and the investigators to identify the watchpoints where the two entities interact. Ultimately, by using electronic, physical, and data surveillance, they can easily develop indicators which shows the point where the watchpoints get translated into the practice.

The outcome is a method for mapping where and how terror or crime interactions may take place, adding proofs to that particular hypothetical map, and then analyzing the emerged patterns. There are some semi-automated software tools which allow the analyst to observe the emerging interactions between terror and crime without even delegating the method completely to a computer system.

4.5. THE SIGNIFICANCE OF TERROR-CRIME INTERACTIONS

The interactions of terror-crime can take place in various settings and the research done pointed towards two major categories of specific interest. The first is that the cities which are present in developed countries where terrorists are generally supporting themselves by a variety of apparently insignificant but organized crime activity. Examples can be seen from the case of Madrid bombers of 2004 who were engaged in fraud practices of mobile phones and also Chechen groups of United States were engaged in pornography in Los Angeles.

Generally, such kind of interactions can be easily classified as an activity appropriation along with the terror groups by assuming the crime groups' activities. There is no merger of terrorism-crime as observed in the zone of conflicts.

However, various related examples exist where this terror group's formation has taken place. Mostly, they have formed in prisons or urban areas, where these criminals are forced to move. Close associations are formed there, between the terrorists and the organized criminals.

The main terrorists used to hire different individuals to promote their criminal and terrorist activities. Jamal Ahmidan, the central member of the Madrid terror cell and a former dealer of drugs at an international level get converted to Islam when he was in prison and commissioned his past as a criminal after getting released from the prison to supply the requirements of logistical cells which consist of exchanging of drugs used as explosives during the attacks.

The case of Ahmed Ressam is very well documented and can be considered as a significant example of various interaction of terror-crime in the urban areas of developed countries. He got arrested prior to his attempt of bombing an International Airport in Los Angeles during the celebration of millennium.

This case of Ahmed Ressam depicts the process that how the interaction of terror-crime functions in Diaspora urban communities of Europe and North America. The enforcement of laws in these neighborhoods never appreciated the importance of organized crime which is at low-level and supporting the activity of terrorists.

Ressam was very much active in crime and also a major part of terror groups of Algerian Islam which were co-located in Canada, France, Roubaix, and Montreal. A few common characteristics are evolved by analyzing this case.

First, similar compositions of Diaspora and a deficiency of interested or significant policing were shared by both the neighborhoods. Second, both of the terror groups had very strong associations to the shadow economy. The list of activities which are staple for the men of the Montreal cell includes theft, shoplifting, credit card fraud, document fraud, etc.

The Roubaix cells fits exactly in the class of activity appropriation. This cell was always involved in armed robberies so that the terrorist activities can be financed easily. Mainly three factors are shared by these cells as demonstrated by this case, such as a tradition of organized crime, a sense of traditional separation among the cells which is usually supported by the nature of neighborhoods of Diaspora and poor governance.

These factors are not just limited to urban neighborhoods of developed countries. Enforcement of law and U.S. Intelligence are inclined naturally to concentrate on indicators of terrorism and organized crime in their country. They would definitely be benefited by analyzing the patterns and studying the behavior of crime in different countries and areas which are potentially relevant to the terrorism.

A person can easily differentiate between the ancient crime groups and their presently formed counterparts while turning to the situation over the globe. Colombia is an exceptional case, who established large associations of crime organizations with the terrorists.

These groups hold long-standing interests of finance which would suffer the structure and design of the state and the financial community at international level comes to be destabilized. These groups reduced the danger of prosecution by moving into the lawful economy and corruption and hence, they do not have any fear of the power of institutions of the states.

Generally, new groups of transnational crime are succeeding in a state of political chaos or the conflict which is ongoing. The urgent requirement of financing the military actions defines that they have very less concern for the current financial institutions.

Every type of criminals usually tries to avoid the enforcement of laws and the regulation. The TraCCC team found these new groups to be encouraged by a need to contempt or undermine the already established order. This is the main reason of their association to the terrorism.

In a comprehensive sense, all types of criminal activity are likely to succeed in a huge shadow of economy, where illegal, undeclared, unregulated, and illicit transaction occurs and where there is slight legitimate economy.

The scope and size of the phenomenon varies broadly. For instance, it accounts around 70 percent of the total national economy in Georgia as compared to approximately 5–10 percent in the U.S. Hence, it is desirable to concentrate on various geographical areas as the interaction of nexus of crime-terror.

A critical difference is there between the illegal activities in the shadow economy in the United States and in the not so regulated states of the former USSR, as mentioned in the PIE analysis of the Georgia banking sector. A research done by Naylor established that money laundering takes place in an environment where there is a combination of legal and illegal funds.

According to the enforcement of law, there truly exists an illegal banking in an illegal economy and large shadow which is examining international criminals same as exist in Georgia and Moldova. Current investigations of FBI in these countries shows the difference in nature of the illicit activities within these minute economies.

Economic and ideological foundations are provided for both terrorism and organized crime within their borders by developing countries having weak economies, by history of government which is not stable, hungry, and desperate people, etc. They relatively have more ability to contest any of them.

Huge opportunities for corruption and smuggling has provided traditionally by the conflict zones. The conflict zones diminish the overnight ability because enforcement and regulatory almost become wholly directed towards the target of military. Hence, they are specifically vulnerable to both violent activity and grave organized crime. For the goals related to politics, these two are directed at the civilian people as well as the collaboration between those who are involving in violence which is motivated politically and those who are involving in complete criminal activities.

Such cooperation is likely to spawn post-conflict zones. As such fields generally hold weak enforcement ability for small period of time following an end to recognized conflicts. There are certain kinds of locations in total, where both the terrorism and organized crime have boomed.

Based upon the features which make them more generous to terrorism and organized crime, they can be grouped. In turn, this will make it possible to recognize the terrain that enables both terrorists and criminals to succeed. They exhibit various regions on the map of the world, and the major list comprises:

- The regions such as Georgia, Colombia, portions of Myanmar and Sri Lanka, the Sumatra peninsula of Indonesia, Chechnya, the Trans-Dniester region of Moldova and the breakaway states of Georgia such as South Ossetia and Abkhazia, where the central state has lost control over some of its territory.

- The regions such as the Tri-Border Area of Paraguay, Brazil, and Argentina, Pakistan's North West Frontier and the Pamir Mountains in Tajikistan which is spanning various jurisdictions or national borders.
- Conflict zones such as Tamil areas of Sri Lanka and almost complete Nepal, where separatists are battling the forces of government. Areas of countries having robust rule of law but fragile control over few slums and neighborhoods like Diaspora neighborhoods of cities, for example, the northern sections of Naples, the outskirts of Marseilles, the favelas in Brazil, etc.
- Penal institutions where the correctional authorities are further concerned with sustaining order instead of penetrating the crime-terrorism interactions within their institutions. This is all relevant to enforcement of law and intelligence in the U.S. as these patterns of organization and behavior of criminal can evolve from areas as assorted as the conflict zones present at overseas to the neighborhoods in the U.S. cities.

The challenging combinations of traditional separation from bigger society, poor governance and a tradition of criminal activity which is commonly international are the major concerns behind this wide taxonomy of geographic locales for the interaction of crime-terror.

4.6. CONCLUSION

Organized crime has attained various dimensions and become a threat and translational phenomenon to global security. The latent challenge raised by the organized crime leans towards a major danger for the social, economic, and political stability of the states.

The present stage of organized crime has emerged out in corresponding with new frameworks and has been simplified by new frameworks in which international trade has been carried out, as well as by the uprisings in transportation and communications.

The prolonged admittance of modern technologies, the lessening hurdles in human mobility and financial resources permit the group of criminals to challenge the stability of the states and demoralize the democracy in various areas of the globe, mainly in the weak states and where the pluralist administrations are not merged up.

The significance of countering measures essentially rests on two aspects. First one is the understanding of the phenomenon and the second one is the incorporation of responses at national level within a significant international strategy. Presently, there are two distinct patterns of analysis of transnational organized crime, one which concentrates on the criminal groups who are operating in different areas of human activity. Other concentrates on the illegal market.

None of these pattern analyses reflect the issue in its difficulty as they do not hold all the relations between the appropriate elements.

Till now, the first approach profited from an enlarged consideration on behalf of researchers. Though, this approach is not that significant because it is rather reactive when it needs to be pro-active. The eradication of the present organized crime groups does not reduce the risk for other groups to substitute the current ones, as long as there is a call for illegal goods and services.

As showed by a UN report on the issue, majority of the illegal goods and services drifts are the consequence of market forces and the activities of criminal groups. A comprehensive abolition of this flagellum is barely expectable, but the fading of its present extension - by more efficient and more active participation, both of states and international organizations – is a viable goal.

4.7. CASE STUDY: THE TRI-BORDER AREA OF PARAGUAY, BRAZIL, AND ARGENTINA

Hezbollah is mostly thought of as a terrorist group operating in the Middle East and is strongly associated with attacks on Israeli targets in Lebanon and Israel. In fact, Hezbollah has struck far away from its home base of operations—in South America.

On March 17, 1992, a van bomb outside the Israeli embassy in Buenos Aires killed 29 people and injured 250. Two years later, another car bomb attack in Buenos Aires practically destroyed the Jewish-Argentine community center, killing 87. In both cases, the evidence pointed to Hezbollah as the perpetrator, the staging area for the attacks was the Paraguayan city of Ciudad del Este in the so-called Tri-Border Area, a nexus for terrorist and criminal activity of all kinds. CDE has become notorious as a remote place where the spotlights of law enforcement are dim and where everything may be purchased at the right price from the right people. Originally a village, this rapidly-expanding city of some 250,000 people was developed by Julius Stroessner, who turned Paraguay into a haven for fugitives from the law—including the Nazi war criminal Josef Mengele.

Stroessner himself is suspected of having run a drug-trafficking organization. CDE is also an international crossroads where the borders of Argentina, Paraguay, and Brazil meet. For many years these three countries have been blaming each other for tolerating widespread crime activities in the Tri-Border Area, yet achieved very little.

Argentina has recently suffered a catastrophic economic crisis. Huge disparities in incomes and prices, combined with prohibitive import tariffs in all three countries, have created a smuggler's paradise. Paraguayan tax laws and other regulations are lax and poorly enforced.

The shadow economy in Paraguay is estimated at between 40 percent and 50 percent of gross domestic product. All kinds of goods including sophisticated military hardware and all kinds of weapons are available for purchase in the shops.

The resulting business opportunities have attracted Diaspora communities from all over the world, including tens of thousands of people from the Middle East, Africa, and Southeast Asia. The Tri-Border Area includes a significant Muslim population, which is susceptible to extortion and a suitable hiding place for extremist elements.

Organized crime groups of all types thrive in the tri-border area. Paraguay's return to democracy and the free market in 1993 brought in a sharp relaxation of regulation characterized by ineffective law, rising corruption, and weak state institutions.

As the legitimate economy slumped, international criminal groups moved in. The Tri-Border Area is now a meeting place for the Yakuza as well as Colombian and other Latin American gangs, who pass illegal drugs through CDE on their way to the ports of Brazil, Argentina, and Uruguay, and thence to the U.S. and Europe.

Chinese Triads such as the Fuk Ching, Big Circle Boys, and Flying Dragons are well established and believed to be the main force behind organized crime in CDE. CDE is also a center of operations for several terrorist groups, including Al Qaeda, Hezbollah, Islamic Jihad, GamaaIslamiya, and

FARC. The 1992 bombing of the Israeli Embassy in Buenos Aires provided the first evidence of this. While Islamic Jihad claimed responsibility, the U.S. State Department and others believe that the claim was a smokescreen for Hezbollah.

- **Watchpoints:** Crime and terrorism in the Tri-Border Area interact seamlessly, making it difficult to draw a clean line between the types of persons and groups involved in each of these two activities. There is no doubt, however, that the social and economic conditions allow groups that are originally criminal in nature and groups whose primary purpose is terrorism to function and interact freely.
- **Organizational structure:** Evidence from CDE suggests that some of the local structures used by both groups are highly likely to overlap. There is no indication, however, of any significant organizational overlap between the criminal and terrorist groups.

These groups are traditional hierarchies, each commanded by a single leader. Terrorist groups in the area, including Hezbollah, Al Qaeda, and al Gamma al Islamiya, have a loose hierarchical structure in which some groups work as financial wings (raising money and remitting it to the Middle East), while others are responsible for secure communications with the rest of the world.

- **Organizational goals:** In this region, the short-term goals of criminals and terrorists converge. Both benefit from easy border crossings and the networks necessary to raise funds. Some terrorists operating in the Tri-Border Area raise money through drugs and arms smuggling.

In May 2002 Ali Assi, who ran a coffee shop in the Islamic Welfare Center in CDE, was arrested at the Beirut airport with 10 kilograms of cocaine. Assi is the father-in-law of Ali Hassan Abdallah, who is one of the key operatives of the Hezbollah financial network in the CDE area and also a business partner of Sobhi Mahmoud Fayad, a convicted Hezbollah lieutenant.

- **Culture:** Cultural affinities between criminal and terrorist groups in the Tri-Border Area include shared ethnicities, languages, and religions. Both Arab and Chinese criminal groups maintain local cells that specialize in imposing their rules on the local Diaspora communities.
- **Illicit activities and subterfuge:** The evidence in CDE suggests

that terrorists see it as logical and cost-effective to use the skills, contacts, communications, and smuggling routes of established criminal networks rather than trying to gain the requisite experience and knowledge themselves.

Likewise, terrorists appear to recognize that to strike out on their own risks potential turf conflicts with criminal groups. Trafficking in stolen automobiles is big business in the region, and Paraguayan authorities estimate that out of 450,000 vehicles registered annually in that country, more than half are obtained illegally.

- **Open activities in the legitimate economy:** The knowledge and skills potential of CDE is tremendous; one of the recent cases investigated by the Central Bank of Paraguay involved counterfeit Iraqi currency. Business intelligence is so good that a few years ago, faked versions of famous French perfumes were available for purchase in CDE even before they were officially inaugurated in Paris.
- **Support or sustaining activities:** The Tri-Border Area has a usually large and efficient transport infrastructure, which naturally assists organized crime. In turn, the many criminals and terrorists using cover require a sophisticated and reliable document forgery industry.

In February 2002, the entire Tri-Border Area was searched by local law enforcement and international intelligence agencies in pursuit of five Afghanis believed to be linked with Taliban and Al Qaeda. Each of them was believed to use three or four sets of identity documents.

Khalid Sheikh Mohammad, the former number three in Al Qaeda who was captured by U.S. forces in 2003, spent about twenty days in Foz do Iguaçu, the Brazilian sister city of CDE. And Brazilian intelligence services have evidence that Osama bin Laden visited CDE in 1995 and met with the members of the Arab community in the city's mosque to talk about his experience as a mujahedeen fighter in the Afghan war against the Soviet Union.

Criminal groups and terrorists in the area have also cooperated on the purchase and shipment of arms. At least two Chinese criminal families based in the Tri-Border Area had been reported engaging in illegal business ventures with the operatives of Egyptian GamaaIslamiya.

- **Use of violence:** Contract murder in CDE costs as little as one thousand dollars, and the frequent violence in CDE are directed at business people who refuse to bend to extortion by terror groups. Ussein Mohamed Taiyen, president of the CDE Chamber of Commerce, was one such victim—murdered because he refused to pay the tax.

Another motive is retribution against officials who attempt to crack down on crime. In October 2002, Uruguayan Customs Director Victor Lissidini was shot at by four shooters on two motorcycles. Lissidini had received threats of revenge for his confiscation of counterfeit materials headed for CDE—calls that were later linked to organized crime groups suspected of working on behalf of Islamist terrorists.

- **Financial transactions and money laundering:** In 2000, money laundering in the Tri-Border Area was estimated at 12 billion U.S. dollars annually. In 2003, an estimated 50 percent of all banking transactions in CDE were suspected to be of an illicit character.

It is not just criminal elements who take advantage of the many international banks and illicit money exchanges. Between 1999 and 2001, at least 50 million U.S. dollars, and some officials say that the amount is probably much higher, was sent from Foz do Iguaçu to extremist Islamic groups through the CDE banks and exchange houses.

- **Use of corruption:** Most of the illegal activities in the Tri-Border Area bear the hallmark of corruption. In combination with the generally low effectiveness of state institutions, especially in Paraguay, and high level of corruption in that country, CDE appears to be a perfect environment for the logistical operations of both terrorists and organized criminals. Paraguay's government itself is highly corrupt – Transparency International declared Paraguay 129th out of 133 countries in its 2003 Corruption Perceptions Index.

The Consul General of Taiwan in CDE, Jorge Ho, stated that the Chinese groups were successful in bribing Paraguayan judges, effectively neutralizing law enforcement moves against the criminals.

In sum, for the investigator or analyst seeking examples of perfect conditions for such cooperation, the Tri-Border Area is an obvious choice.

REFERENCES

1. Albrecht, H., (n.d.). *Concepts of Terrorism and Organized Crime*. [eBook] p. 51. Available at: http://www.etc-graz.at/cms/fileadmin/user_upload/humsec/SAc_08_PPP/PPP_Hans_J_rg_Albrecht.pdf (Accessed on 12 April 2019).
2. Cartwright, R., & Bones, F., (2017). *Transnational Organized Crime and the Impact on the Private Sector: The Hidden Battalions*. [eBook] p. 78. Available at: http://globalinitiative.net/wp-content/uploads/2017/12/GITOC_TOCPrivateSector_web.pdf (Accessed on 12 April 2019).
3. *Convergence of Terrorism & Transnational Organized Crime,* (2017). [eBook] p. 13. Available at: https://www.chds.us/coursefiles/hsx/modules/convergence_of_terrorism_and_transnational_organized_crime/story_content/external_files/Convergence%20of%20Terrorism%20&%20Transnational%20Crime.pdf (Accessed on 12 April 2019).
4. Makarenko, T., (2004). *The Crime-Terror Continuum: Tracing the Interplay between Transnational Organized Crime and Terrorism*. [eBook] Global crime, p. 17. Available at: https://www.iracm.com/wp-content/uploads/2013/01/makarenko-global-crime-5399.pdf (Accessed on 12 April 2019).
5. Martin, G., (2018). *Terrorism and Transnational Organized Crime*. [eBook] Research gate. Available at: https://www.researchgate.net/profile/Gus_Martin2/publication/292833533_Terrorism_and_transnational_organized_crime/links/5989fda6aca2724358516a29/Terrorism-and-transnational-organized-crime.pdf?origin=publication_detail (Accessed on 12 April 2019).
6. Shelley, L., Picarelli, J., Irby, A., Hart, D., Craig-Hart, P., Williams, P., Simon, S., Abdullaev, N., Stanislawski, B., & Covill, L., (2005). *Methods and Motives: Exploring Links between Transnational Organized Crime & International Terrorism*. [eBook] NCJRS, p. 115. Available at: https://www.ncjrs.gov/pdffiles1/nij/grants/211207.pdf (Accessed on 12 April 2019).
7. Stoica, I., (2016). Transnational organized crime: An (inter) national security perspective. [eBook] *Journal of Defense Resources Management*, p. 18. Available at: http://journal.dresmara.ro/issues/

volume7_issue2/02_stoica_vol7_issue2.pdf (Accessed on 12 April 2019).

8. Voronin, Y., (n.d.). *Measures to Control Transnational Organized Crime, Summary*. [eBook] U.S. Department of Justice, p. 22. Available at: https://www.ncjrs.gov/pdffiles1/nij/grants/184773.pdf (Accessed on 12 April 2019).

5

Conventions for Transnational Organized Crime

CONTENTS

Transnational organized crime (TOC) is rapidly increasing day by day, but there is no standard definition of it present till now. The spectrum of activities under TOC comprises cybercrime, money laundering, trafficking of goods and people, etc. to combat and prohibit these crimes conventions were made as "The United Nations Convention against Transnational Organized Crime (UNTOC)."

The main objective of the Convention is to encourage cooperation to battle and stop TOC more efficiently. The Convention characterizes a key step forward in the struggle against TOC and implies the acknowledgment by Member States of the significance of the issues posed by it, as well as the requirement to foster and improve close international cooperation to challenge those issues. The chapter describes the objectives of these conventions along with the articles which are made to eliminate the terrorism globally.

5.1. INTRODUCTION

To fight against the TOC, the major instrument which plays a role is "The Convention." On 12–15 December 2000, the conventions opened for signature by the Member States in Palermo, Italy, and on 29 September 2003, it got entered into force. The convention signifies a key step in the struggle against various TOC comprising drugs trafficking, money laundering, human trafficking, etc. It implies the requirement to improve and foster the international cooperation to challenge these kinds of issues.

Various numbers of measures are taken by the states against TOC, who has approved these conventions, to battle the increasing number of crimes in the society. These consists of the formation of domestic criminal Offenses, the acceptance of new inclusive framework models for expulsion, joint legal assistance and enforcement of law cooperation, and the advancement of technical assistance and training for upgrading or building the important ability of national authorities.

The United Nations UNTOC is a 2000 United Nations-sponsored multidimensional treaty which is formed against TOC. On 15 November 2000, a resolution of the United Nations General Assembly adopted these conventions. Further, it is also known as the Palermo Convention. There are three supplementary protocols of the Palermo Protocols. It includes:

- Protocol to Prevent, Conquer, and Penalize Trafficking in Persons, especially Children and Women;

- Protocol against the Smuggling of Migrants by Air, Land, and Water; and
- Protocol against the Illegal Manufacturing and Trafficking in Firearms.

All these instruments comprise elements of the present international law on arms trafficking, human trafficking, and money laundering. Every element has some of the protocol related to the terrorism. The United Nations Office on Drugs and Crime (UNODC) turns as custodian of the UNTOC and its protocols (Figure 5.1).

Figure 5.1: Human trafficking affecting lives of many.

Source: https://famvin.org/en/2018/07/28/july-30-international-day-against-human-trafficking/

On 29 September 2003, these Conventions which are related to the TOC came into existence. The United Nations UNTOC, as of 19 September 2017 has 189 parties which further consists of 184-member states of United Nations, the Holy See, the Cook Islands, Niue, the State of Palestine and the EU (Figures 5.2 and 5.3).

Figure 5.2: Smuggling through waterways.

Source: https://famvin.org/en/2018/07/05/unodc-issues-first-global-study-on-migrant-smuggling/

Figure 5.3: Trafficking of arms and ammunition for harming people at a global level.

Source: http://theconversation.com/how-illegal-firearms-find-their-way-onto-british-streets-despite-tough-laws-61239

5.2. THE PROVISIONS FOR INTERNATIONAL COOPERATION

The UNTOC comprises very less procedural framework model to be utilized to make able the cooperation with regards to the Offenses in the Convention and Protocols. It offers various obligations to improve the needs of significant police cooperation and exchange of information and to approve effective policing measures also. An informative platform is settled by the framework of conventions for better formal legal assistance and for extradition.

Ultimately, provisions are formed for cooperation in appropriation and reclamation of assets. OCG involvement and transnationality functions as for the application of this procedural administration. The container Offenses set up by the UNTOC, which are eventually derived from unidentified and serious domestic Offenses.

It makes possible the cooperation in a container-to-container fashion, as it were, providing any expressive condition of double criminality for such cooperation. This also gives out with an understood criterion of proportionality between the level of cooperation presented by a requested state party and the significance of the basic Offense (Figure 5.4).

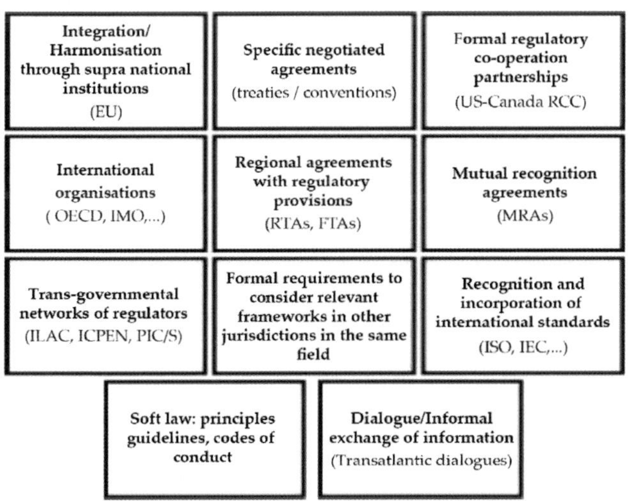

Figure 5.4: International regulatory co-operation.

Source: http://www.oecd.org/gov/regulatory-policy/irc.htm

Despite engendering the common trust required for cooperation, it produces distrust among different states parties. Some accountability for this must be with the negotiators who followed the development of a 'toolbox' on approaches of international cooperation and did not deal effectively or with any interest with the conceptual problem of defining organized crime.

The conceptual problem became secondary to the search of a global legal assistance convention. As per the National Interest Analysis (NIA), The United Nations UNTOC provides a universal approach to prevent and combat TOC.

The key purpose of the convention is "to outlaw crimes committed by organized criminal groups, to battle money laundering, and to simplify international cooperation in the fight against TOC."

5.3. CONVENTIONS AND ARTICLES TO ERADICATE CRIME AT A GLOBAL LEVEL

The Convention on TOC can be further categorized into the following: definitions and scope (Articles 1–4); criminalization of specific Offenses and establishment of penalties (Article 5–12 and Article 23); investigative measures and international cooperation (Articles 13–22 and 26–27); protection and assistance to victims (Articles 24 and 25); information sharing, training, technical assistance, economic development and prevention of organized crime (Articles 28–31) implementation and other technical issues (Article 32–41).

The main aim of the Convention was to enable international cooperation against TOC. Certainly, the very priority was the implementation of a toolbox of measures to implement organized crime and to support international cooperation (Figure 5.5).

Therefore, the majority of the 41 Articles of the TOC Convention deal with international cooperation and investigative measures. The explanation of organized crime and its illegalization demonstrated from the start to be among the most difficult complications. Few of the negotiators even debated that the explanation of TOC was not ultimate and that there was no rigorous requirement for it. This depicts the major issues in attaining a harmony among different legal and political traditions.

However, the final text of the Convention covers a definition of organized criminal groups and the necessity to criminalize the involvement in an organized criminal group. The impact of the European Union has been significant in attaining an agreement on these subjects.

Figure 5.5: UN global counter-terrorism strategy.

Source: https://www.un.org/counterterrorism/ctitf/en/un-global-counter-terrorism-strategy

Certainly, the final definition of organized criminal group is constant with the Joint Action on framing it a criminal fault to involve in a criminal organization (98/733/JHA), accepted by the European Union in 1998, which has a similar definition of criminal organization.

Specified the complications in accomplishing an agreement on the description of organized crime and the minor priority of this problem equated with the improvement of international cooperation, the definition caused in the most controversial provision. Truly, definitions unavoidably influence the whole building of the Convention and its protocols.

Article 1: Statement of Purpose

This statement states that the main idea of this Convention is to help the states by providing agreement on matters and promote cooperation to avoid and fight TOC more successfully.

Article 2: Use of Terms

For the purposes of this Convention:

- The convention defines an organized criminal group and is

required because the convention aims at directing policy, law, and practice which help in preventing and combating organized crime and committing one or more serious crimes or offenses. It also helps in other material benefits.

- The convention also focuses on serious crime issues by giving punishment and providing no liberty for these kinds of crimes of at least four years.
- Structured group does not have any developed structure and defined roles for the members.
- The property is the assets of every kind, whether tangible or intangible, movable or immovable, corporeal or incorporeal and legal documents or instruments showing interest in these assets.
- Proceeds of crime are defined as any property which found directly or indirectly through the commission of an offense.
- The freezing or seizure is the similar terms which are used for the movement of property or control of property based on an order issued by a court or other competent authority.
- Confiscation is a lack of property to provide punishment by the court or other competent authority.
- Predicate offense is any crime where large number of profits is generated.
- Controlled delivery is a technique of allowing illegal packages to pass into the region of one or more States. It helps with the knowledge and under the supervision of their competent authorities, with a view to identify the persons or search for a crime involved in the commission of the offense.
- Regional economic integration organization is an organization founded by free states of a given region by which the member of the states has transferred competence in respect of matters governed by this convention and which has been properly approved. State Parties must follow the conventions, and it can be applied to all organizations with the internal procedures, to sign, ratify, accept, approve or accede to it.

Article 3: Scope of Application

1. This Convention is applied to the prevention, investigation, and prosecution of:

- The crimes established in accordance with articles 5, 6, 8 and 23 of this Convention; and
- Serious crime as defined in article 2 of this Convention; where the Offense is international in nature and involves an organized criminal group.

2. For paragraph 1 of this article, an Offense is international in nature if:

- It is committed in more than one State;
- It is committed in one State but a substantial part of its planning, controlling, preparation or direction takes place in another State;
- It is committed in one State that includes organized criminal group which involves in criminal activities in more than one State; or
- It is committed in one State but has large effects in another State.

Article 4: Protection of Sovereignty

1. Under this convention, states parties will carry out their responsibilities in a manner constant with the principles of sovereign equality and territorial integrity of States and that of non-interference in the domestic affairs of other States.
2. State Party are not allowed to take the area of another state because of this convention and is states that the exercise of authority and performance of functions that are kept exclusively for the authorities of that other State by its domestic law.

Article 5: Criminalization of Participation in an Organized Criminal Group

1. It is necessary for each state party to adopt legislative and other measures to find the criminal faults when committed intentionally:

(A) Either or both of the following as criminal offenses distinct from those involving the attempt completion of the criminal activity:

- Domestic law is required when one or more persons commit a serious crime for a purpose relating directly or indirectly to the obtaining of a financial or other material benefit, involving an act accepted by one of the participants in maintenance of the agreement or involving an organized criminal group;
- The Organization examine the behavior of the person who has the knowledge of the general criminal activity of an organized criminal group or its intention to commit the crimes in question,

takes an active part in the crime.

- Criminal activities of the organized criminal group which includes blackmailing, bombings, bookmaking, and illegal gambling;
- The participation of the people in activities of the organized criminal group will contribute to the achievement of the above-described criminal aim;

(B) Organizing, directing, aiding, abetting, facilitating or counseling the contract of serious crime involving an organized criminal group.

2. The purpose, aim, knowledge or agreement referred to in paragraph 1 of this article may be inferred from objective factual circumstances.
3. States Parties who follow domestic law are involved in the organized criminal group for the resolutions of the crimes established in accordance with paragraph 1 (a) (i) This article shall ensure that their domestic law covers all serious crimes which are involved in organized criminal groups. These state parties whose domestic law requires an act in furtherance of the agreement for purposes of the crimes established in accordance with paragraph 1 (a) (i) This article helps to inform the Secretary-General of the United Nations to deposit their instrument for acceptance, confirmation, or approval to this Convention.

Article 6: Criminalization of the Laundering of Proceeds of Crime

1. Each State Party adopt the fundamental principles of its domestic law, such legislative and other measures as may be necessary to establish as criminal Offenses when committed intentionally:

- The property can be shifted by knowing that the property is the proceeds of crime, for concealing or hiding the illegal origin of the property or of helping any person who is involved in the commission of the predicate Offense to avoid the legal consequences of his or her action;
- The disguise or concealment of the true location, movement, nature, source or ownership of rights with respect to property by knowing that such property is the proceeds of crime.

2. There are some basic concepts of the legal system:

- The control, achievement or use of property at the time of receipt, that such property is the proceeds of crime;

- Participation in, association with or conspiracy to commit, attempts to commit and aiding, counseling, supporting, and facilitating of any of the Offenses established in accordance with this article.

3. For purposes of implementing or applying paragraph 1 of this article:

- Each State Party shall seek to apply paragraph 1 of this article to the widest range of predicate Offenses;
- Each State Party shall include as predicate Offenses all serious crime as defined in article 2 of this Convention and the Offenses established in accordance with articles 5, 8 and 23 of this Convention. Each State Party shall provide the Conference of the Parties with information on its programs, plans, and practices, as well as legislative and administrative measures to implement this Convention, as required by the conference of the parties.
- For the purposes of above paragraph, its predicate Offenses shall include Offenses committed both within and outside the jurisdiction of the State Party 9 in question. However, Offenses committed outside the jurisdiction of a State Party shall constitute predicate Offenses only when the relevant conduct is a criminal Offense under the domestic law of the State where it is committed and would be a criminal Offense under the domestic law of the State Party implementing or applying this article had it been committed there;
- For subsequent changes, each state party shall supply copies of its laws that give effect to this article;
- If required by fundamental principles of the domestic law of a State Party, it may be provided that the Offenses set forth in paragraph 1 of this article do not apply to the persons who committed the predicate Offense;
- The Purpose, Knowledge or intent is essential as an element of an Offense and this article may be inferred from objective factual circumstances.

Article 7: Measures to Combat Money-Laundering

1. Each State Party:

- The Drug traffickers and other criminals throughout the world use the banking system to channel the proceeds of illegal transactions into the economy in a manner that makes them appear to have been honestly acquired. Money laundering is the activity whereby an individual or legal entity acquires or receives for itself or others' gains from a criminal Offense and it shall institute a comprehensive domestic regulatory and supervisory regime for banks and non-bank financial institutions and other bodies particularly liable to money-laundering, in order to deter and detect all forms of money-laundering, which regime shall emphasize requirements for customer identification, record-keeping, and the reporting of suspicious transactions;

- This implies that, without prejudice to articles 18 and 27 of this Convention, there should be the assurance implying over administrative, regulatory, law enforcement and other authorities which are generally dedicated to combating money-laundering (including, where appropriate under domestic law, judicial authorities).

Such activities can cooperate and exchange information at the national and international levels within the conditions prescribed by its domestic law and, to that end, shall consider the establishment of a financial intelligence unit to serve as a national center for the collection, analysis, and dissemination of information regarding potential money laundering.

2. States Parties are considered to implement possible measures to perceive and monitor the movement of cash and appropriate negotiable instruments across their borders which subject to safety measure to make sure that the proper information are used without delaying. It may include a requirement that individuals and businesses report the cross-border transfer of suitable instruments and substantial quantities of cash.
3. The domestic regulatory and supervisory rule is established under the terms of this article, and without bias to any other article of this Convention, States Parties are called to use and follow the guidelines to take care of regional, interregional, and multilateral organizations against money-laundering.
4. States Parties attempt to promote and develop regional, global, subregional and bilateral cooperation among judicial, law enforcement and financial regulatory authorities are the measures to fight money-laundering.

Article 8: Criminalization of Corruption

1. Each State Party shall adopt such legislative and other measures

as may be necessary to establish as criminal Offenses, when committed intentionally:

- The unnecessary promises are made to the public, directly or indirectly that the official act or refrain from acting in the exercise of his or her official duties;
- The solicitation or acceptance by a public official, directly or indirectly, of an undue advantage, for the official himself or herself or another person or entity, in order that the official act or refrain from acting in the exercise of his or her official duties.

2. Each State Party follow the same law to stop corruption and should adopt such legislative and other measures as it becomes necessary to establish as criminal Offenses conduct referred to in paragraph 1 of this article involving a foreign public official or international civil servant.
3. For the purposes of paragraph 1 of this article and article 9 of this Convention, the public official is defined in the domestic law and public official is a person who provides a public service and applied in the criminal law of the state party in which the person in question to perform that function.

Article 9: Measures against Corruption

In addition to the measures set forth in article 8 of this Convention, each state party should adopt:

1. Administrative, legislative or other effective measures to promote honesty and to prevent detect and punish the corruption of public officials.
2. Each State Party should take measures to ensure effective action taken by the authorities in the detection, punishment, and prevention of the corruption of public officials in the future.

Article 10: Liability of Legal Persons

1. Each State Party is consistent with its legal principles and adopts such measures which is necessary to establish the liability of legal persons for participation in serious crimes involving an organized criminal group and for the Offenses established in accordance with articles 5, 6, 8 and 23 of this Convention.
2. The liability of legal persons that are civil, criminal or administrative are subjected to the legal principles of the state party.

3. Such liability shall be without prejudice to the criminal liability of the natural persons who have committed the Offenses.
4. Each State Party are subjected to proportionate, effective, and dissuasive criminal or non-criminal sanctions including monetary sanctions to ensure that legal persons held liable in accordance with this article.

Article 11: Prosecution, Adjudication, and Sanctions

1. Each State Party should charge for these crimes which established in accordance with articles 5, 6, 8 and 23 of this Convention.
2. Each State Party under the act of domestic law should have open legal powers to the prosecution of persons for offenses. This convention is exercised to maximize the effectiveness of law execution measures in respect of those Offenses and with due regard to the need to prevent the commission of such offenses.
3. In the case of Offenses established in accordance with articles 5, 6, 8 and 23 of this Convention, each State Party under the domestic law should respond appropriately to the rights of the defense, to ensure that conditions imposed in connection with decisions on release pending trial or appeal to take into consideration for the need.
4. Each State Party shall ensure that the courts or other experienced authorities bear in mind the serious nature of the offenses covered by this Convention when considering the prospect of early release or liberation of persons convicted of such offenses.
5. Each State Party is established under its domestic law a long statute of limitations period in which to commence reports for any crimes covered by this Convention and a longer period where the so-called criminal has avoided the direction of justice.
6. The applicable legal defenses or other legal principles controlling the lawfulness of conduct is reserved to the domestic law of a State Party and nothing controlled in this Convention shall affect the principle and that such Offenses shall be prosecuted and punished in accordance with that law.

Article 12: Confiscation and Seizure

1. States Parties must adapt their domestic legal systems if it is possible and such measures as may be necessary to enable confiscation of:
   - Proceeds of crime provide the confiscation derived from offenses covered by this Convention or property the value of which links to that of such proceeds;
   - Equipment, property or other instrumentalities are designed to use in crimes covered by this convention.
2. Profits, income or other benefits resulting from proceeds of crime and the property which also resulting from proceeds of crime have been change or converted and that property is also responsible to the measures referred to in this article to the same extent and in the same manner as proceeds of crime.
3. If proceeds of crime have been combined with property acquired from valid sources, such property shall, without prejudice to any powers relating freezing or seizure is liable to confiscation up to the assessed value of the combined proceeds.
4. If proceeds of crime have been changed, transformed or converted into other property, so that property should be responsible to the measures referred to in this article instead of the proceeds.
5. States Parties should implement such measures as may be necessary to enable the tracing, freezing, identification or seizure of any item referred to in paragraph 1 of this article for eventual confiscation.
6. State parties should not fail on the ground of bank privacy and the purpose of this article and article 13 of this Convention is that each state party should allow the authorities or courts to order that financial, bank or commercial records be made available or be seized.
7. States Parties may consider the possibility of requiring that an offender demonstrate the lawful origin of alleged proceeds of crime or other property liable to confiscation, to the extent that such a requirement is consistent with the principles of their domestic law and with the nature of the judicial and other proceedings.

Article 13: International Cooperation for Purposes of Confiscation

1. A state party that has received a request from another state party to have authority over an offense covered by this convention for confiscation of equipment, property, crime or other instrumentalities referred to in article 12, paragraph, of this Convention situated in its area and the greatest extent possible within its

domestic legal system:

- If an order is approved for the better results than the state party submit the request to its competent authorities.
- State Party in accordance with article 12, of this Convention which relates to equipment, property, proceeds of crime or other instrumentalities are situated around the requested state party.

2. The demand is made by another state party to provide authority over an offense covered by this Convention and the invited state party shall take measures to trace, identify, trace or recognize the property, equipment, proceeds of crime or other instrumentalities referred to in article 12, of this Convention for the purpose of final confiscation to be ordered either by the requesting State Party or pursuant to a request under paragraph 1 of this article.
3. The conclusions, activities, decisions or actions are provided in paragraphs 1 and 2 of these articles which is be taken by the requested state party in agreement with and subject to the provisions of its domestic law and its technical rules or any agreement or arrangement to which it may be certain in relation to the requesting state party.
4. Each state party can provide the copies of the laws and regulations that give effect to this article and of any following changes to these laws and regulations or a description thereof to the Secretary-General of the United Nations.
5. In this article, the teamwork can be rejected by a state party if the offense to which the request relates is not an offense covered by this Convention.
6. States Parties may finish their agreements or arrangements to increase the effectiveness of international cooperation undertaken pursuant to this article.

Article 14: Disposal of Confiscated Proceeds of Crime or Property

1. Property or Proceeds of crime removed by a state party pursuant to articles 12 or 13, paragraph 1, of this Convention because the State Party is with the agreement of its domestic law and administrative procedures.
2. State parties give payments to the victims of the crime or property to their legitimate owners and they give importance to those state parties who are suffering from crimes.
3. State party gives more attention to conclude agreements or ar-

rangements when the request is made by another State Party in accordance with articles 12 and 13 of this Convention.

Article 15: Jurisdiction

1. Each State Party should adopt such measures that are necessary to have control over the crimes in accordance with articles 5, 6, 8 and 23 of this Convention when:

- To investigate the matter that the crime is committed in that State Party; or
- The Offense is committed on board a vessel that is flying the flag of that state party or an aircraft that is registered under the laws of that State Party at the time that the Offense is committed.

2. For the purposes of article 4, of this Convention is that each state party should adopt such measures which is necessary to control the crime covered by this Convention. When the alleged offender is present in the area and it does not transfer such person by just claiming he or she is one of its nationals.
3. This convention does not eliminate the exercise of any criminal jurisdiction by a state party in accordance with its domestic law.
4. If a State Party has noticed that other state parties are doing the same thing as investigating or examining the crimes than the experienced authorities of other states should consult one another with a view to coordinate their actions.
5. Without prejudice to norms of general international law, this Convention does not exclude the exercise of any criminal jurisdiction established by a State Party in accordance with its domestic law.

Article 16: Extradition

1. If the request for extradition includes several separate serious crimes like political nature of the alleged crime, failure to fulfill dual criminality which is not covered by this article and the requested state party may apply this article also in respect of the latter offenses.
2. This article applies that each of the Offenses is considered to include an extraditable offense in any extradition treaty existing between states parties. States Parties undertake to include such offenses as extraditable offenses in every extradition treaty to be concluded between them.

3. This article applies that this convention is a legal basis for extradition in respect of any Offense as if a State Party that makes extradition conditional on the existence of a contract receives a request for extradition from another state party with has no extradition treaty.
4. This article applies that states parties do not make extradition conditional on the presence of an agreement to recognize offenses between themselves.
5. Extradition is not available at the request of members of the public. State Party or by applicable extradition treaties, including, inter alia, conditions in relation to the minimum penalty requirement for extradition and the grounds upon which the requested state party may refuse extradition.
6. This article applies that states parties are focused to their domestic law and try to rush extradition procedures to simplify evidentiary requirements.
7. This article applies that by requesting the state party to take a person whose extradition is required and who is present in its region into custody and to take some measures to ensure that the presence of that person at extradition proceedings.
8. Every time a state party is allowed under its domestic law to transfer or surrender one of its citizens only upon the condition that the person will be returned to that state party to serve the sentence imposed because of the proceedings or trial for which the extradition or surrender of the person was required.
9. This article applies that each person is guaranteed to get fair treatment at all stages of the proceedings including enjoyment of all the rights and guarantees provided by the domestic law of the state party in the area.
10. State party has enough grounds for believing that the requests have been made for punishing or accusing a person based on the person's sex, nationality, political opinions, race, religion or ethnic origin that would cause harm to that person's position for any of these reasons.
11. Before refusing extradition, the state party should also consult with another state party or request them to provide information and opportunity to present its opinions relevant to its allegation.
12. To improve the efficiency of extradition, the state parties shall

seek to conclude bilateral and multilateral agreements or arrangements.

Article 17: Transfer of Sentenced Persons

The Convention on the Transfer of Sentenced Persons is an international agreement regulating the extradition and social rehabilitation of imprisoned persons. This convention covers the states parties which may consider entering into bilateral or multilateral agreements or arrangements on the transfer to their territory of persons sentenced to custody or other forms of lack of liberty for Offenses in order that they may complete their sentences there.

Article 18: Mutual Legal Assistance

1. Generally, Mutual legal assistance is governed by treaty and can also be authorized by domestic law and shall fully be afforded possible under relevant laws, arrangements, agreements, and treaties of the requested state party with respect to prosecutions, investigations, and judicial proceedings in relation to the Offenses for which a legal person may be held liable in accordance with article 10 of this Convention in the requesting State Party.
2. Mutual legal assistance may be requested for:

- The authorities are responsible to have relevant evidence or statements from the person who is involved or who is the witness to any of the crime or illegal activity;
- Effecting service of judicial documents;
- Executing searches and seizures, and freezing;
- Examining objects and competent sites;
- Providing information, evidentiary items and expert evaluations;

3. The authorities who are experienced can transmit information related to criminal matters in another state party and they believe that this information will help the authority for taking responsibilities or could result in a request formulated by the latter state party.
4. The provisions of this article are that the contracting parties shall, in accordance with this treaty, provide each other with the widest measure of mutual legal assistance in criminal matters.
5. States Parties shall not decline to render mutual legal assistance pursuant to this article on the ground of bank secrecy.
6. A person who is being detained or is serving a sentence in the territory of one State Party whose presence in another State Par-

ty is requested for purposes of testimony, identification or otherwise helping in obtaining indication for prosecutions, investigations or judicial proceedings in relation to Offenses covered by this Convention may be transferred if the following conditions are met:

- The person freely gives his or her informed consent;
- The competent authorities of both States Parties agree, subject to such conditions as those States Parties may deem appropriate.

7. Central authority has the power and it is responsible to receive requests for mutual legal assistance and each state party should appoint a central authority. Central authorities shall ensure the immediate and proper execution or transmission of the requests received. The requests for mutual legal assistance and any communication related thereto shall be transmitted to the central authorities designated by the States Parties.
8. Requests shall be made in writing or, where possible, by any means capable of producing a written record, in a language acceptable to the requested State Party, under conditions allowing that State Party to establish authenticity.
9. The Secretary-General of the United Nations should be informed of the language and the languages is accepted by each State Party at the time it deposits its instrument of acceptance, ratification or approval of or accession to this Convention. In urgent circumstances requests are made orally and are agreed by state parties but later the requests should be in writing.
10. A request for mutual legal assistance is made to contain the identity of the authority to which the requests relate and the name and functions of the authority conducting the prosecution, investigations or judicial proceedings. It also contains the summary of the relevant facts, except in relation to requests of judicial documents.

The main purpose of these requests is to get the details of any procedure that the requesting party wishes to be followed. The information, evidence or action is required by the state parties, and the parties are also concerned with the identity, nationality, and the location of any person.

11. It is necessary for the requested state parties to have more information for the execution in accordance with its domestic law or when it can enable such execution.
12. A request is completed by the state parties in accordance with

its domestic law where the procedures are stated in the request.

13. The fundamental principles of domestic law states that when an individual is in the region of a State Party and has to be heard as an expert or witness by the judicial authorities of another State Party, the first State Party may, at the request of the other, permit the hearing to take place by video conference and in case, if it is not possible to get connect with the individual than the State Parties may agree for the hearing which is conducted by a judicial authority of the requesting State Party.

14. The requesting State Party are not allowed to use information or communicate, or evidence furnished by the requested State Party for investigations, prosecutions or judicial proceedings other than those stated in the request without the prior consent of the requested State Party. Nothing in this paragraph shall prevent the requesting State Party from disclosing in its proceedings information or evidence that is exculpatory to an accused person.

In the latter case, the requesting State Party should also inform the requested State Party about the use of information prior to the disclosure. If, in an exceptional case, notice is not possible for the requesting State Party and should inform the requested State Party that not to disclose the additional information.

15. The requesting State Party need that the requested State Party can keep the confidential information, except to the level, necessary to execute the request. If the requested State Party cannot fulfill with the requirement of confidentiality, it should inform t the requesting State Party on time.

Article 19: Joint Investigations

States Parties shall consider concluding bilateral or multilateral agreements or arrangements that are the subject of prosecutions, investigations judicial proceedings in one or more than one States, the competent authorities are afraid to joint investigative bodies. In the absence of these agreements or arrangements, joint investigations may be assumed by agreement on a case-by-case basis. The States Parties are fully involved in the investigation and make sure that the power of the State Party in their area where the investigation is going to take place is fully appreciated.

Article 20: Special Investigative Techniques

1. If allowed by the basic principles of its domestic legal system,

each State Party should take the necessary measures to agree for the proper use of controlled delivery and, where it believes appropriate, for the use of other special investigative techniques, such as electronic or other forms of surveillance and undercover operations, by its competent authorities in its area for effectively fighting organized crime.

2. The main purpose of investigating the crimes covered by this Convention is that the states parties are encouraged to achieve bilateral or multilateral agreements or arrangements for using such special investigative techniques in the context of cooperation at the international level. Such arrangements or agreements shall be carried out strictly in accordance with the terms of those arrangements or agreements. It can also be implemented in full compliance with the principle of sovereign equality of States.
3. In the absence of an agreement or arrangement, decisions to use such special investigative techniques at the international level which is made on a case-by-case basis and may take into reflection or consideration financial understanding and arrangements with respect to the exercise of jurisdiction by the States Parties concerned.
4. On an International level, decisions are made for controlling the delivery with the consent of the state parties concerned, include various methods such as interrupting and allowing the goods to continue replaced, intact or be removed in whole or in part.

Article 21: Transfer of Criminal Proceedings

Transfer of proceedings can be an option when extradition for an Offense has not been possible, and the state parties reflects the possibility of transferring to one another proceedings for the examination of an Offense covered by this Convention.

Article 22: Establishment of Criminal Record

Each State Party may adopt such legislative or other measures as may be necessary to take into consideration, under such terms as and for the purpose that it deems appropriate, any previous conviction in another State of an alleged offender for the purpose of using such information in criminal proceedings relating to an Offense covered by this Convention.

Article 23: Criminalization of Obstruction of Justice

Each State Party must have the power to make law and adopt such legislative measures as may be necessary to establish as criminal Offenses when committed intentionally:

- The use of physical threats, force, or promise or intimidation, offering or giving of an unnecessary advantage to make false evidence or to interfere in the giving of evidence or the production of evidence in a proceeding in relation to the commission of Offenses covered by this Convention;
- The use of physical force, threats or intimidation to interfere with the exercise of official duties by a justice or law enforcement official in relation to the commission of Offenses covered by this Convention. Nothing in this subparagraph shall prejudice the right of States Parties to have legislation that protects other categories of public officials.

Article 24: Protection of Witnesses

1. Each State Party is responsible for the witness protection program and witness protection laws and provides effective protection from potential retaliation or intimidation for witnesses in criminal proceedings who give evidence concerning Offenses covered by this Convention.
2. States Parties are making deals and arrangements or agreements with other States for the transfer of persons.
3. The provisions of this article apply to the people who have suffered because they are the witnesses.

Article 25: Assistance to and protection of victims

1. In this article, each state party takes suitable measures to help and protect the persons from doing the crime covered by this convention.
2. Each state party has the right to found suitable procedures to provide access to restitution and compensation for victims of Offenses covered by this convention.
3. Each state party with its domestic law, enable views and concerns of victims to be considered and presented at various stages of criminal proceedings.

Article 26: Measures to enhance cooperation with law enforcement authorities

1. Each State Party should take suitable measures to inspire or encourage persons who want to participate or who have already participated in organized criminal groups:
2. The competent authorities need useful information for investigative and evidentiary purposes on such matters as:
- The nature, location, identity, structure, composition or activities and the links including international links of organized criminal groups;
- Offenses that organized criminal groups have committed or may commit;
- To provide historical, concrete help to competent authorities that are contributing to depriving organized criminal groups of their resources or of the proceeds of crime.
3. Each state party with fundamental principles of its domestic law to look for the possibility of granting protection from prosecution to a person who provides substantial cooperation in the prosecution or investigation of an Offense covered by this convention.

Article 27: Law Enforcement Cooperation

1. States Parties collaborate closely with one another, consistent with their respective domestic legal and administrative systems, to improve the effectiveness of law enforcement action to combat the Offenses covered by this Convention. Each State Party should adopt some effective measures:
- It is necessary to improve and establish channels of communication between their agencies, services, and competent authorities to facilitate the protected and rapid exchange of information concerning all aspects of the crimes covered by this Convention.
2. It is necessary in conducting investigations for crimes with other states parties covered by this convention concerning:
3. The location, situation, position, and activities of persons suspected of involvement in such crimes or the location of other persons concerned;
- The movement of proceeds of crime or property derived from the commission of such Offenses;

- The movement of equipment, property or other instrumentalities are used in the commission of such Offenses;
- To provide necessary items or quantities of substances for analytical or investigative purposes;
- To facilitate effective coordination between their agencies, competent authorities and services and to promote the exchange of personnel and other experts, including, subject to bilateral agreements or arrangements between the States Parties concerned, the posting of liaison officers;

4. With a view to giving effect to this Convention, states parties entered into bilateral or multilateral agreements or arrangements on direct cooperation between their law enforcement agencies and to improve the agreements or arrangements which are already exists. The state parties may consider this Convention as the basis for mutual law enforcement cooperation in respect of the Offenses in the absence of such agreements or arrangements covered by this Convention. Whenever appropriate, States Parties should make full use of agreements or arrangements by including international or regional organizations, to order to improve the cooperation between their law enforcement agencies.
5. States parties should respond to TOC by using the modern technology.

Article 28: Collection, Exchange, and Analysis of Information on the Nature of Organized Crime

1. Each state party should analyze and make discussion with the scientific and academic communities for the movements in organized crime in its region. In some situations, the organized crime works where the technologies and professional groups are involved.
2. States parties shall consider developing and sharing analytical expertise concerning organized criminal activities with each other and through international and regional organizations. For that purpose, common definitions, standards, and methodologies should be developed and applied as appropriate.
3. Each state party shall consider monitoring its policies and actual measures to fight organized crime and making calculations of their effectiveness and efficiency.

Article 29: Training and technical assistance

1. It is necessary for each state party to develop, initiate or improve specific training program for its law enforcement employees, including investigating magistrates, prosecutors, and customs personnel, and other employees charged with the detection, control, and prevention of the Offenses covered by this Convention. These kinds of program may include secondments and exchanges of staff. Such programs shall deal, and to the extent permitted by domestic law, with the following:

- There are various methods which are used in the prevention, detection, and control of the Offenses;
- The modern technology and routes are used by persons suspected of involvement in Offense.
- Monitoring of the movement of contraband;
- Monitoring and detecting the movements of property, proceeds of crime, equipment or other instrumentalities and the methods which are used for the transfer, concealment or disguise of such proceeds, equipment, property or other instrumentalities, as well as technical methods which are used in combating money-laundering and other financial crimes;
- Collection of evidence;
- Control techniques in free trade zones and free ports;
- Modern law enforcement techniques and equipment, including electronic surveillance, controlled deliveries, and undercover operations;
- The technology and methods are used in the protection of victims and witnesses and combating TOC committed with computers, telecommunications networks or other forms of modern technology;

2. States Parties support one another in planning, executing, and implementing research and training programs which are designed to share expertise in the areas, and the parties use regional and international conferences and seminars to promote cooperation and to stimulate discussion on problems of mutual concern, including the special problems and needs of transit states.
3. States Parties helps in promoting training and technical assistance that will facilitate extradition and mutual legal assistance. Such trainings and technical assistance may include language

training, secondments, and exchanges between peoples in central authorities or agencies with relevant responsibilities.

4. State parties could make efforts to maximize operational and training activities within international and regional organizations and within other relevant bilateral and multilateral agreements or arrangements.

Article 30: Other Measures: Implementation of the Convention Through Economic Development and Technical Assistance

1. States Parties should take measures which is helpful to the optimal implementation of this Convention through international cooperation, considering the negative effects of organized crime on society in general, on sustainable development.
2. States Parties shall make concrete efforts to the extent possible and in coordination with each other, as well as with international and regional organizations:

- To help and improve their cooperation at various levels with developing countries, with a view to strengthening the capacity of the latter to prevent and combat TOC;
- To support the efforts of developing countries and enhance financial and material assistance to support the efforts of developing countries to fight TOC effectively and to help them implement this Convention successfully;
- To provide technical assistance to developing countries and countries with economies in transition to assist them in meeting their needs for the implementation of this Convention. To that end, States Parties shall endeavor to make adequate and regular voluntary contributions to an account specifically designated for that purpose in a United Nations funding mechanism. States Parties may also give special consideration, in accordance with their domestic law and the provisions of this Convention, to contributing to the account a percentage of the money or of the corresponding value of proceeds of crime or property confiscated in accordance with the provisions of this Convention;
- To provide more training programs and modern equipment for the development of the countries and inspire, encourage, and persuade other States and financial institutions to support them in achieving the objectives of this Convention.

3. To the extent possible, these measures shall be without prejudice

to existing foreign assistance commitments or to other financial cooperation arrangements at the bilateral, regional or international level.

4. States Parties complete the bilateral or multilateral agreements or arrangements on material and logistical assistance which are taken into consideration for the financial arrangements which is necessary for the means of international cooperation which is provided to be effective and for the prevention, detection, and control of TOC.

Article 31: Prevention

1. States Parties make the effort to develop and evaluate national projects and promote best practices and policies which are expected at the prevention of TOC.
2. States Parties with their domestic law may reduce the existing or future opportunities for organized criminal groups to participate in lawful markets with proceeds of crime, through appropriate legislative, administrative or other measures. These measures should focus on:

- The strengthening of cooperation between law enforcement agencies or prosecutors and relevant private entities, including industry;
- The prevention of the misuse by organized criminal groups of tender procedures conducted by public authorities and of subsidies and licenses granted by public authorities for commercial activity;

3. States Parties try to promote the reintegration into society of persons convicted of Offenses covered by this Convention.
4. States Parties try to evaluate sometimes which is related to legal instruments and administrative practices with a view to detecting their weakness and cannot be misused by organized criminal groups.
5. States Parties try to promote public awareness about the causes, gravity, and existence, and the threat posed by TOC. Information may be distributed through the mass media and include measures to promote the participation of public in preventing and fighting such crime.
6. Each State Party must inform the Secretary-General of the United Nations regarding the name and address of the authority or

authorities to support other States Parties in developing measures to prevent TOC.

7. States Parties should able to collaborate with each other and relevant international and regional organizations in promoting and developing the measures referred to in this article. This program includes participation in international projects designed for the prevention of TOC.

Article 32: Conference of the Parties to the Convention

1. The meeting or discussion of the parties is held to improve the capacity of States Parties to fight with the TOC and to promote and review the implementation of this Convention.
2. The Secretary-General of the United Nations should assemble the Conference of the Parties within one year and not later than one year by following the entry into force of this Convention.
3. The Conference of the Parties is agreeing upon instruments or mechanisms for achieving the objectives mentioned in paragraph 1 of this article, including:

- Helping in the exchange of information among States Parties on patterns and trends in TOC and on successful practices for combating it;
- Cooperating with relevant international and regional organizations and non-governmental organizations;
- Reviewing periodically the implementation of this Convention;
- Making recommendations to improve this Convention and its implementation.

4. Each State Party shall provide the Conference of the Parties with information on its programs, plans, and practices, as well as legislative and administrative measures to implement this Convention, as required by the Conference of the Parties.

Article 33: Secretariat

1. The Secretary-General of the United Nations should provide the necessary secretariat services to the Conference of the Parties to the Convention.
2. The secretariat shall:

- To support the Conference of the Parties in carrying out the activities set forth in article 32 of this Convention and provide the necessary services for the sessions of the Conference of the

Parties;

- Ensure the necessary coordination with the secretariats of relevant international and regional organizations.

Article 34: Implementation of the Convention

1. Each State Party should take legislative and administrative measures according to fundamental principles of its domestic law to ensure that the responsibilities or duties are completed on time.
2. Each State Party should adopt more strict or severe measures than those provided for by this Convention for stopping or preventing the TOC.

Article 35: Settlement of Disputes

1. States Parties should try to settle the disputes regarding the interpretation or application of this Convention through negotiation.
2. Any kind of disagreements between two or more States Parties regarding the understanding or application of this Convention cannot be settled through negotiation within a reasonable time, and by requesting of one of those State Parties can be negotiated. The requests which is made for settlement after the date of six months is not relevant and are unable to agree on the organization for the negotiation as it results that any of the state parties may argue in the international court of justice.
3. Each State Party at the time of acceptance, signature, ratification or approval of or accession to this Convention should announce that it does not consider itself bound by paragraph 2 of this article. The other States Parties shall not be bound by paragraph 2 of this article with respect to any State Party that has made such a reservation.
4. This implies that any State Party that has made a reservation in accordance with paragraph 3 of this article can withdraw that reservation at any time by giving notice to the Secretary-General of the United Nations.

Article 36: Signature, Ratification, Acceptance, Approval, and Accession

1. This Convention is open to all states for signature from 12 to 15 December 2000 in Palermo, Italy, and thereafter at United Nations Headquarters in New York until 12 December 2002.

2. This Convention is open for signature by regional economic integration organizations to provide that at least one member state of such organization has signed this Convention in accordance with paragraph 1 of this article.
3. This Convention is focused to the approval, acceptance or ratification. Instruments of ratification, acceptance or approval shall be deposited with the Secretary-General of the United Nations. A regional economic integration organization may deposit its instrument of ratification, acceptance or approval if at least one of its member States has done likewise.

The organization should declare the instrument of ratification, acceptance or approval to the extent of its capability with respect to the matters governed by this Convention. The organization shall also inform the depositary of any relevant variation in the extent of its competence.

4. This Convention is open for agreement by any regional economic integration organization of which at least one member State is a Party to this Convention. Instruments of accession shall be deposited with the Secretary-General of the United Nations. At the time of its agreement, a regional economic integration organization shall declare the extent of its competence with respect to matters governed by this Convention. The organization shall also inform the depositary of any relevant modification in the extent of its competence.

Article 37: Relation with Protocols

1. This Convention may be enhanced by one or more protocols that will reflect the culture and norms of the organization.
2. Regional economic integration organization or a state in this convention can become a Party in relation with the protocols.
3. Any protocol to this Convention shall be understood together with this Convention, considering the purpose of that protocol.

Article 38: Entry into Force

This Convention shall enter into force on the ninetieth day after the date of deposit of the fortieth instrument of ratification, acceptance, approval or accession. For this paragraph, any instrument deposited by a regional economic integration organization shall not be counted as additional to those deposited by member States of such organization.

Article 39: Amendment

1. After the expiry of five years from the entry into force of this Convention, a state party may suggest some change and file it with the Secretary-General of the United Nations, who shall immediately communicate the proposed amendment to the States Parties and to the Conference of the Parties. This purpose of this Convention for considering and deciding on the proposal.

The Conference of the Parties shall make every effort to achieve consensus on each amendment. If all efforts at consensus have been exhausted and no agreement has been reached, the amendment shall, as a last resort, require for its adoption a two-thirds majority vote of the States Parties present and voting at the meeting of the Conference of the Parties.

2. Under this article, the regional economic integration organizations shall exercise their right to vote with several votes which is equal to the number of their member states that are Parties to this convention. Such organizations shall not exercise their right to vote if their member States exercise theirs and vice versa.
3. An amendment adopted in accordance with paragraph 1 of this article is focus to acceptance, ratification or approval by the States Parties.
4. An amendment adopted in accordance with paragraph 1 of this article will enter into the force in respect of a state party within the ninety days after the date of the deposit with the Secretary-General of the United Nations of an instrument of ratification, acceptance or approval of such amendment.
5. When an amendment enters into force, it becomes necessary on those states parties which have expressed their agreement to be bound by it while the other states parties are still bound by the provisions of this Convention and any earlier amendments that they have ratified, accepted or approved.

Article 40: Denunciation

1. A State Party may denounce this Convention by giving notice to the Secretary-General of the United Nations in written. Such denunciation has become active for one year after the date of receipt of the notification by the Secretary-General.
2. When all the member of the states has denounced than the regional economic integration organization shall end to be a party to this convention.

3. Denunciation of this Convention in accordance with paragraph 1 of this article to need the denunciation of any protocols thereto.

Article 41: Depositary and Languages

1. The Secretary-General of the United Nations is designated depositary of this Convention.
2. The original of this Convention is that the languages such as Arabic, Chinese, English, French, Russian, and Spanish texts are so authentic, and it is deposited with the Secretary-General of the United Nations. In witness whereof, the undersigned ministers, being duly authorized thereto by their respective Governments who have signed this Convention.

5.4. OBLIGATIONS UNDER THE TRANSNATIONAL ORGANIZED CRIME (TOC) CONVENTION

From the Attorney-General's Department, Ms. Blackburn stated the major obligations in the Convention of TOC as:

- To outlaw Offenses committed by organized crime groups, including corporate or company Offenses and corruption.
- To defend witnesses appearing against criminal groups.
- To deal with money laundering and empower the proceeds of crime to be attached.
- To accelerate and extend the reaches of extradition.
- To constrict cooperation to seek out and accuse suspects.
- To increase prevention of organized crime at the national and international levels.

According to the observation of Ms. Blackburn, the Attorney-General's Department, obligations of Australia under the Convention would be met by prevailing Commonwealth, state, and territory legislation and new guidelines under the Mutual Assistance in Criminal Matters Act and the Extradition Act. The Committee perceived that most of the obligations of the Convention are already covered in domestic legislation related to cooperation elements and Offenses.

5.5. CONCLUSION

The concept of TOC has drastically changed in various ways due to new opportunities, modern technologies and mainly due to the discerning activities of law enforcement. In the meantime, the evolution of global terrorism has provided with an additional issue to its dimension.

Anyhow, the theoretical uncertainties of characterizing terrorism and organized crime, the group of terrorists appear to be involved in criminal activities to acquire access to funding, and modern working relationships are establishing among terrorists, political insurgents, and crime networks. The knowledge regarding these kinds of developments is remained as incomplete because of very few and conflicting reports of intelligence.

The United Nations UNTOC plays an uncertain role in terms of the international response to organized crime. From few of the commentators, there was an element related to optimism that the convention might have had a slow beginning, but there are also few signs of hope that it is being accelerated with time.

Many others were not that certain, stating that the scope of convention is very limited and it is very slow to adapt the ever-changing nature of the problems. Assessing what has been done till now seems a dynamic task, so far questionably the procedure for doing so remains unclear.

It is not that enough to measure the execution of the convention; the main challenge is in forming the connection between real-world variations in the harm produced by organized crime and the convention. Furthermore, it is valuable noting that the mandate to take on such tough and debated evaluations may be hard to gain from the member states of the Palermo Convention.

REFERENCES

1. Calderoni, F., (2016). *U.N. Convention Against Transnational Organized Crime.* [online] Available at: https://www.researchgate.net/publication/267625139_UN_Convention_Against_Transnational_Organized_Crime (Accessed on 12 April 2019).
2. Pereira, P., (2013). *The UN Convention Against Transnational Organized Crime and its Ambiguities.* [online] E-International relations. Available at: https://www.e-ir.info/2013/10/25/the-un-convention-against-transnational-organized-crime-and-its-ambiguities/ (Accessed on 12 April 2019).
3. Standing, A., (2010). *Transnational Organized Crime and the Palermo Convention: A Reality Check.* [eBook] Available at: https://www.ipinst.org/wp-content/uploads/publications/e_pub_palermo_convention.pdf (Accessed on 12 April 2019).
4. *Together Against Trafficking in Human Beings*, (2000). The United Nations convention against transnational organized crime - together against trafficking in human beings - European Commission. [online] Available at: https://ec.europa.eu/anti-trafficking/legislation-and-case-law-international-legislation-united-nations/united-nations-convention-against_en (Accessed on 12 April 2019).
5. Treaties.un.org., (2018). *UNTC.* [online] Available at: https://treaties.un.org/pages/viewdetails.aspx?src=ind&mtdsg_no=xviii-12&chapter=18&lang=en (Accessed on 12 April 2019).
6. *United Nations Convention Against Transnational Organized Crime and the Protocols Thereto*, (2004). [eBook] Available at: https://www.unodc.org/documents/middleeastandnorthafrica/organised-crime/UNITED_NATIONS_CONVENTION_AGAINST_TRANSNATIONAL_ORGANIZED_CRIME_AND_THE_PROTOCOLS_THERETO.pdf (Accessed on 12 April 2019).
7. Unodc.org., (2018). *United Nations Convention Against Transnational Organized Crime.* [online] Available at: https://www.unodc.org/unodc/en/organized-crime/intro/UNTOC.html (Accessed on 12 April 2019).

6

Corruption, Anti Money Laundering, and Transnational Organized Crime

CONTENTS

There are, in general, four concepts including the transitional crime, money laundering, the organized crime and the corruption one, along with the domestic as well as the international profile being related to the increment in the magnitude. In terms of all of the four concepts, various countries are being considered to be under the pressure to be able to respond in a manner being uniform, taking into account the several numbers of the agreements on an international level, the various conventions, as well as the guidelines being present. In this, one out of the provided cases performs the issue which generally tends to possess the inclusion of the definitions which has been fretted over. Instead, being more of fundamental, it does have the inclusion or the involvement of the debate regarding the nature of the various pertaining entities which all have been subsumed staying under this particular concept.

6.1. INTRODUCTION

The transnational organized crime (TOC) become of utter importance in relation with the subject matter in the practice of the state, after getting or facing much of the disregard by the legal doctrine at an international level for a very long period of time.

In accordance with the provided fact, the categorized TOC, as well as the terrorism on an international level, has been considered as the novel danger or threat to the peace all across the globe.

It generally tends to possess the capability to sabotage not only the institutions which are democratic but also the rule of the pertaining law, but also the development or the growth of sustainability and the stability or poise within the various pertaining regions (Figure 6.1).

It generally created the requirement or the need to reach out to this particular subject in a way or the manner which is much more comprehensive in relation to having a simple watching out only for the contents of the various treaties at an international level and the various initiatives which basically tend to provide them with the compliment.

During the last ten years and within the globalization of the various states belonging to the TOC, they have incorporated a framework at an international level which generally tends to have a great impact or the influence in virtual terms related to all of the corners of the various societies, be it in the sense of the optimism or the pessimism.

Figure 6.1: Transnational organized crime (TOC).

Source: https://www.slideserve.com/garrett-sharpe/transnational-organised-crime

Thus, to attain or acquire a better or sound understanding regarding this, there persists a requirement of having insights into the basic concepts and the various existing controversies which have already surrounded many of the documents that in turn helps in defining the particular area of the study.

The requirement or the importance of having an analysis regarding the effectiveness of the provided instruments has been an implication.

In addition to it, many of the lawyers at a global level, possess the background of the conservatives in the law related to the public as well as the administrative and thus, it has only the knowledge in the terms of rudimentary related to the various fundamental concepts regarding the debate on the TOC and the various manifestations being transnational.

6.2. CORRUPTION

The dictionary of the etymology provides the explanation regarding the term corruption, which got utilized for the first time in the 14th century. Much of the meaning and the definition has been provided related to corruption and has been utilized in the literature. The one which is actually very well known or a popular one provides the explanation regarding corruption as the behavior, which generally tends to deviate from the responsibilities related to the role of the public, be it the elective one or the appointive one.

This all happens due to the privacy, which is being related to the private clique, the wealth belonging to one's family, and the personal wealth or the gains within the status.

In today's time, various institutions like the Transparency International, the international monetary as well as the world bank, have the utilized the standard definition which has already been set related to the corruption as for the purpose of having gains or profits in the private sector, abusing the office of the public sector.

In contrast, many researchers recognize or identify it as the process of arranging which generally tend to possess the involvement of the exchanges that have been taking place among the two parties, the ones who demands and the ones who supplies, which:

(i) Possess the impact or the effect on the process of allocating the various pertaining resources either on the spot or later in the future; and

(ii) Possession of the utilization or the abuse of the public or the collaborative responsibility or the duty of the various people for the ends being private.

6.2.1. Forms of Corruption

Having corruption in business is considered to be a common element or the component in today's time. Many of the forms or the types of the corruption are being accepted at a much normal or involuntary way. Thus, these are being dealt similar to the price of performing or continuing the business.

It has been said that the cost which usually incurs for the corruption is generally being passed on to the customers or the consumers, due to which the competition becomes choking, which in turn causes the free market to get unstable.

In addition to it, it has been admitted or accepted that it is not very simple to have a proper estimation or the assessment of the pertaining levels of the corruption which has already been suffered or experienced by all of the organizations or the enterprises pertaining within the country, in totality.

The center related to the infrastructure of the campaign of the anti-corruption at a global level, each, and every type of the corruption have been acknowledged as the criminal Offense in case of the most jurisdiction.

- **Bribery:** The process of bribing someone has been considered as one of the most widely spread form of the corruption in case of the business.

It generally occurs in case of the corporate or the private sector and is basically having an inclusion of the payments which are being made by the individuals or the organizations to the officials of the public sector so as to have an impact or the effect on the decisions which are being made by the administrative in accordance with their responsibility.

Having a comparison to the gift, the bribe is being acknowledged as the payment which has been made for a specific service that usually remains a secret and not to be disclosed to anyone as it is not legal.

Anything which tends to exceed a particular value is generally being considered as the offense being made internally against the ethics or the ethical standard procedure.

Figure 6.2: Bribery – corruption at international level.

Source: https://www.publicdomainpictures.net/pictures/170000/nahled/hands-in-handcuffs-1462607673XzB.jpg

The understanding related to the bribery generally provides with the explanation of it as the most dishonest behavior, which is because of the transgression of the trust with the bureaucrats, the relationships within the business and the politicians (Figure 6.2).

The possession of the temptation of selling off things which are being restricted offers with the basis for the process of bribing someone as anything and everything has a price in today's world.

Therefore, at times, it is being referred to as the money which has been used to "grease" the palms of others.

Thus, in spite of that, the trust or the belief amongst the various people who are making people corrupt and the people who are the ones being corrupt at the first place, does not generally build up a great alliance.

In the various countries across the world, wherein there is an absence of the enforcement which are being legal or the efficient institutions, generally, tend to get facilitated by the various relationships being personalized.

- **Extortion:** The process of extortion has been provided the definition which stated that it is an act or the process of threatening the other people in terms of causing harm to them, so that they could be able to acquire much of the benefits to which people does not possess a legal right or hold.

Figure 6.3: Extortion – business getting adversely affected due to blackmailing.

Source: https://cdn.pixabay.com/photo/2013/07/13/13/52/lobbying-161689_960_720.png

The dictionary which is considered to be the legal one provides with the description of extortion as the process of attaining the property from the other person by the utilization of wrong ways or by the threatened force, the fear or the violence, or staying within the color of the right which has been legal or official (Figure 6.3).

Under the standard law which is common for all, the term extortion is being considered as the misdemeanor which has the inclusion or the involvement of the various activities being unlawful which consists of taking up of the money from the officer working for the government.

Thus, four basic ways are existing under which the officers, working for the general public, tends to commit the process of extortion:

a) The process of extortion generally takes place when the officer working for the government takes up the fee which is bei9ng considered as higher than the standard fee which has been set by the law;

b) The officers working for the general public, which is actually higher than the implied fee which has been permitted by the law only;

c) When the officer working for the public starts asking up for the fee prior of it being due; and

d) When the officer asks for the fee for the services which has never been performed in real.

1. **Patronage:** Patronage is generally being considered as the support in financial terms which has been provided to the various organizations or the various activities being provided by the provider of patronage, which are generally known as the patron.

In much of the countries, the groups providing patronage have created or formed up the hierarchy wherein all the payoffs are being shared from the ranks starting up from the lower to the higher one and the otherwise.

Additionally, possession of the personal intact or the connection generally tend to play an essential role in the process of the patronage and many of the relationships of the private business generally tend to depend or rely on the belief or the trust as well as the goodwill, in order to be assured of the quality being related to the performance.

Generally, patronage is being determined or focused on the interests of the big- businesses, similar to that of the in the organizations which has been owned by the state, wherein the state is being acknowledged as the major customer of that particular sector.

And, in this specific case, the contracts which are being related to the procurement by the government are being allotted to the various companies or the organizations which have already been specified without the possession of any of the competition.

2. **Embezzlement:** A definition has been provided by the Investopedia for the term embezzlement, which states that it is a type of the white- collar crime wherein the person generally tends to swindle the assets which has been entrusted to him or her.

In accordance with this particular type of the frauds, all the assets are generally being taken with the permit of the law, and the various embezzlers possess the right to have them, but afterward, all those assets are being utilized for the wrong intentions or purposes.

This is considered to a usual problem which is quite common, and thus, might possess a serious impact or the effect which is negative, on the running business which is being seen as falling victim to those negative effects.

The manner in which the process of embezzlement possesses an impact on the business has been explained by many of the researchers and is being provided below:

a) There is a possibility that the businesses might have to suffer from the great losses because of the dearth of the money or the various other assets. Thus, being specific, the various novel or the small businesses are being greatly affected by it the most;

b) Charging the customers overtly so that they could be able to get much of the resources belonging to the company, which tend to make the appearance of the business as incompetent; and

c) The secretary which has been needed or required for the process of the embezzlement generally tends to avert the various honest as well as the relationships related to the open working business.

There pertains many of the ways which provides with the suggestion as to how to make one's business secured from the embezzlement.

6.2.2. Measuring Corruption

The index for the perception of the corruption as well as holding or controlling the corruption are the two indices which are considered to be two of the most greatly established as well as greatly used indices for the corruption.

They generally tend to trust or believe the data which is subjective, wherein the instruments which are based on the various experiences and are being devoted to the perception of the people or the experts who have already been surveyed related to the corruption within the various sectors, be it the private one or the public one.

However, the system of the management or the perfect index which possess the ability to precisely account for the various real levels of the corruption for having a comparison at the cross-national still does not exist yet.

Thus, in accordance with this, not even a single indicator possesses the capability of capturing the whole of the complexity of the phenomenon which is being related to the corruption. And, as an outcome of this, it is being acknowledged as much more valuable for the purpose of utilization of the combination of the various tools instead of the pertaining single indicators.

- **Corruption Perception Index (CPI):** The index of the perception being related to the corruption is considered to be the index which is based on the survey of the annual corruption which has been getting compiled since the year 1995 with the help of the Transparency International.

It is being seen as the most greatly utilized indicator of the occurrence of the corruption for the purpose of the cross-section of the various countries.

Much of the countries have now been covered by the index or the perception related to the corruption, and the number must be around 170, which is being considered as way too small in the earlier time.

According to the TI, the index of the perception related to the corruption is being considered as the amalgamation of the various surveys as well as the assessments belonging to the corruption, which have been collected by the various types of the institutions which are actually reputed.

In much of the studies or the researches, the meaning of the index of the perspectives being related to the corruption as the on the spot or the impromptu measure belonging to the corruption, which generally possess the target or the aim of providing the data on the various perceptions which are being extensive, being related to the corruption within the various countries.

The index of the perspectives related to the various countries; generally tend to make an apt utilization of the various sources of the data from the institutions or the organizations, which are independent as well as specialized in the process of the governance and in performing the analysis related to the climate of the business.

- **Worldwide Governance Indicators: Control of Corruption (CC):** The simple or the basic approach for the index of the perception related to the corruption got improved by the various researchers who all were present at the World Bank for the project which was related to the indicators of the worldwide governance.

The main target of the WGI, taking into consideration the WB, is basically to make up or create the various instruments which will prove to be of great use for the purpose of the establishment of the various instruments, which possess much more efficiency or the efficacy, related to the assistance being provided by the government.

The project of WGI generally tend to report the various indicators related to the government, be it the aggregate one or the individual one, for approximately 200 countries as well as the territories for the pertaining six dimensions set in by the government.

In addition to it, both the indicators CPI as well as the CC, which are totally based on the various perceptions being provided, could not be considered as wholly be trustworthy or reliable and are generally being frequently criticized, which possess the impact or the influence on the occurrence of the assessment or the estimation of this particular thesis.

Thus, the major critics have been provided below:

- This might not be much clear that what the two provided indicators: CPI, as well as CC, is being measuring as the main sources belonging to the occurrence of the corruption, have been averaged collectively.
- Because of the fact that the various sources, which are being utilized in the process of the construction of the pertaining indices, tend to change or transform over a specific period of time, all naturally, the description being provided regarding both the indices, also changes.
- The indices being related to the perceptions does not take into

account the sufferings or the experience of the people who are poor or disenfranchised.

Also, the fact, that many of the people are being biased towards the opposition or towards the government, is being ignored.

The two indicators: CPI, as well as CC, is being provided with the advice that it is better to get used instead of the complementary information.

6.2.3. Causes of Corruption

In accordance with the TI, i.e., the Transparency International, the corruption is being considered as one of the greatest problems all across the world and is being threatening the growth of the economy for the countries, the one which has already been developed or the one which is still developing.

Thus, in general terminology, the literature of the economics has observed many of the groups of the factors which might possess a great impact, directly on the corruption, which are: the political one, the economic one, social, historical as well as the cultural one.

Thus, many of the studies possess the analysis which has been performed extensively on the various probable drivers being related to the corruption.

However, the pertaining causes of the corruption have been taken into consideration and are being compared with the outcomes coming out from the literature belonging to the economics. The result of the relativeness or the comparison has been provided in the form of the hypothesis.

- **Judicial system:** The various entrepreneurs or the businessmen provides with the claim that they are not comfortable on trusting the judiciary of the court or they cannot rely on it due to the judgment which has been provided by the court and is often being performed in the support of the various officials working for the public.

Thus, it generally makes it quite an impossible thing for any of the organization or the companies to make their rights evident in the court even in case the actions of the various organizations have been quite consistent with the provided legislation.

In addition to it, the higher level of relying or the dependency of the system of the judicial on the various politicians generally tend to lead to the possessiveness or the insecurity in the forming of the various decisions which are totally related to the business.

- **Salaries and GDP:** Corruption in the various countries tend spreads quite easily also because of the low salaries of the various officials working for the general public in case of the various local bodies of the various administrative for example the system of the health, the traffic police, system of providing education or related to academics and the administration working on the taxes.

The various other important or the key factors has been examined as that they could be able to know about the relationship or the connection pertaining amongst the lower rate of the corruption as well as the higher level of the growth.

The estimations or the assessments which is empirical provides with the two results:

- The growth of the economy generally tends to decrement the various amounts of the bribe which has been paid to the various officials who are working for the government.
- The decrement in the level of the corruption which has been caused by the growth of the economy is relatively larger for the various enterprises or the organizations possessing higher capability of doing the relocation.
- **Centralized governance:** The other essential point which helps in driving the corruption in the various countries is governance which has already been centralized, and puts a limit on the process of the making up of the decision in case of the local government.

The government which has been located in the respective capital does not possess the capability of solving or sorting up of the several pertaining issues being local and therefore, because of the disturbance which concerns the problem of the various regions, never tend to perform which much efficacy or efficiency on the domestic level.

A great amount of the fiscal revenues has been collected from the local ones and is transferred to the budget of the central, and thus, accordingly, the governments on the local level are considered to be wholly dependent on the process of the funding which has been collected by the parliament.

- **Competition among local governments:** The process of the decentralization of the various power related to the politics, is also being looked up to as the way of mitigating the corruption and to encourage greater level of the development of the growth.

The hold or the control over the various countries, on a complete note, was always being considered as the ones amongst the various politicians and their respective relatives.

The existing history related to the competition within the politics was never ever been clear or visible.

According to many of the researchers, many of the politicians tend to make the utilization of the physical force against the opponents standing in the elections, the others might use the various means of the anti-democratic things or things which are actually not legal, so that they could be able to stay in the power at the time when the positions they are holding starts to weaken (Figure 6.4).

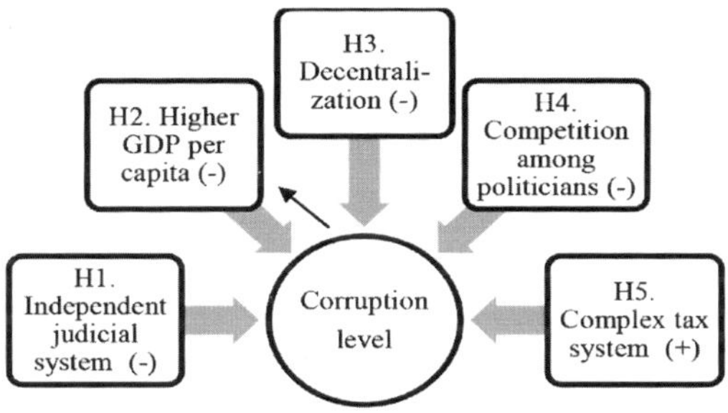

Figure 6.4: Levels of corruption.

Source: http://tampub.uta.fi/bitstream/handle/10024/98100/GRADU-1446032677.pdf;sequence=1

6.2.4. Effects of Corruption

The summarization of the several repercussions of the corruption has been provided below:

- Lower level of the investment having the involvement of the foreign direct investment.
- Decrement in the growth or the development of the economy.
- The slide or the movement in the composition of the spending of the government from the various activities being productive to the ones which are less productive.
- Greater level of the discrepancy as well as the higher level of the incidence being related to the poverty.
- Possession of the reduction in the efficacy or the efficiency of the assistance being provided.
- Exposition of the country to the crisis going on within the country.

6.2.5. Combating Strategies

To reach out to the question regarding how to fight with the corruption, it would certainly be considered to be of great worth providing with the framework which helps in bringing the various factors at one place, be it the economic ones or the non- economic ones.

- The approach related to the economy in order to avert or at least put on a limit on the repercussions of the corruption by providing with the response to the causes, pertaining in the economic terminology, of the corruption.
- The description which has been provided related to the corruption has to be first clarified, having an inclusion of its forms or the types, the various components it possesses and the association of the various legal penalties with it.
- Setting up of the priorities in the process of handling the corruption in accordance with the cost incurred in the corruption and the payoff too, which has been intended for the process of induction.

6.3. ANTI MONEY LAUNDERING

The process of the money laundering has been acknowledged as the attempt or the try for the process of concealing or disguises the location, the nature, various sources, ownership or the persistence of the control of the money, which has been obtained using the various illegal means (Figure 6.5).

The process of laundering of the money is actually illegal everywhere. Thus, there are in all three stages of this process:

- Placement;
- Layering; and
- Integration.
- The funds which have been derived from the various activities involving crime are being utilized for the purpose of the transferring of the legit money, is being considered to be the Placement.
- Creation of the series of the great transactions in order to conceal the first transaction is being referred to as the process of Layering.
- Getting the return of the funds so that they could be able to make the activities legit is known as the process of Integration.

- Placement generally tends to possess much greater degree of the risk to the respective business:
- The various transactions are required to get designed or structured so that they could be able to ignore the process of recordkeeping or the reporting of the various thresholds.
- The wrong or the false recognition or the presentation of the wrong or the fallacious information.

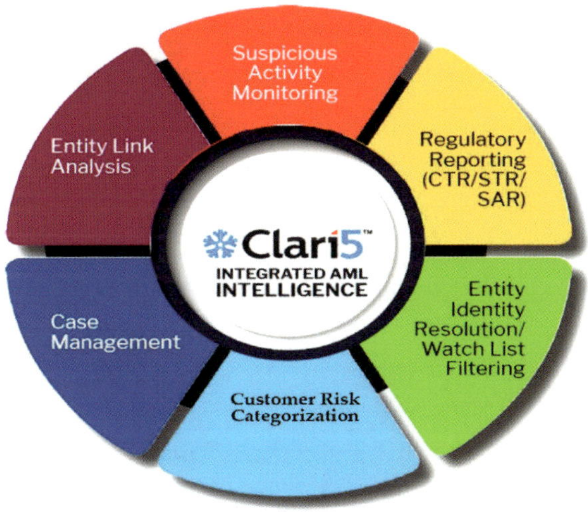

Figure 6.5: Anti-money laundering solutions.

Source: https://financialit.net/products/anti-money-laundering-aml/clari5-anti-money-laundering-solution

6.3.1. MSB Registration

As one engages in the activities or the tasks related to MSB, he or she is being required to get registered with authority of the supervisory of the country or the local ones, being the MSB only.

The MSB are required to keep up with the Xerox or the copy of their respective form of the registration, in case the MSB is not being required or needed to get registered or get licensed under the standard rules and regulations within a particular country and it is a mandate to document as to why are they needing or required to get themselves registered as the MSB. Due to process of selling up of the transfer of the money, one is subjected to the various laws related to the AML of the respective country, wherein they are being located or belong, and to their particular obligations of the process of reporting as well as keeping up of the record.

The various existing businesses are all required to follow the several strict rules which have been set up so that they could be able to avert the laundering of the money and the occurrence of the various activities which are being related to the financing of the terrorists.

6.3.2. Anti-Money Laundering (AML) Compliance Program

It has been required that all the pertaining agents within a country must adopt the compliance program related to the AML, being in the written form, which has been structured or designed reasonable to get a proper assurance regarding the process of reporting or recordkeeping related to the various transactions, and to avert the business from getting utilized for the process of laundering of the money.

Thus, the compliance program related to AML has to have at least the following:

A. The process of adopting the compliance program being related to AML, present in the written form, along with the various internal policies, the controls as well as the provided procedures for:

- Checking or verification of the identity being provided by the customer.
- Filing of the various reports which are being needed or required by the regulations which has been made locally.
- Creation or the retention of the various provided records.
- Providing a response to the requests being made by the law enforcement.
- Requirements or the need for the license.
- Having a compliance with the requirements or the needs or the local regulatory.
- Providing training related to the employee as well as the compliance officer.

B. The position or the designation related to the compliance officer who is actually being responsible for the process of ensuring that:

- The various standard policies or the procedures which has been set are being followed.

- As per the needs, the procedures being set get updated timely.
- Providing with the education as well as the required training.

C. The current program for providing training to the employees that:

- Providing explanation regarding all the policies or the procedures set.
- Provides with the clear understanding regarding identification of the activities being suspicious.

6.3.3. Recordkeeping

- **Recordkeeping Requirements for Money Transfers:** In this it is being required that the agents, be it the sending one or the one who is receiving, are supposed to acquire and record the various particular information for the process of the transfer of money at the amounts in terms of dollars, without taking into consideration the way or the method of making payment, prior to the completion of the specific transaction.

Thus, the various regulations being set locally might be requiring acquiring or attaining the information at the thresholds which are lower or might be needing or requiring one to achieve the information, being an addition to the requirement.

- **Money Gram Money Transfer Form/Receipt:** It is a must or a mandate for everyone to record or keep up with information regarding the transfer of the money through the form of the money transfer or the receipts which are being provided after the transaction gets completed or within a particular system, any of the time the customer might want to send the transfer of the money or receive it.

Thus, the forms are always required to get completed as per the instructions being provided on the available form before the completion of any of the transaction.

- It is required to attain all the necessary information prior to the competition of any of the transaction.
- Recording the most valid information related to the process of identification for the senders or the receivers.
- In case a third party has been involved in this particular process, then it is required to have a record of information for the process

recognition or identification and the various other details for the sender, the receiver and the third party which has been involved.

6.3.4. High Currency Amount Transaction Reporting

One might require filing the various reports belonging to the amount having higher currency along with the government which is entirely based on the regulations being made locally.

The process of reporting is being required for the transactions, be it the individual or the multiple one, which generally tend to exceed a particular threshold of money and might also possess the requirement or the need over the distinct time period.

Thus, one is required to get a proper assurance regarding the compliance with the various regulations being made locally, the process of recognition or identification and knowing the requirements of their respective customers for the transaction of the amount having higher currency.

6.3.5. Structuring

Much of the people who do the laundering of the money are being familiar with the threshold of the dollars which might possess the requirement to do the reporting or keeping up with the records.

Thus, in case one wants to stay anonymous and avert with the detection of the various officials working for the process of enforcement of the law, he or she is required to design or structure their specific transactions so that the requirements or the needs or the reporting, as well as the keeping up of the record, does not get triggered.

The process of designing or structuring is considered to be the act of breaking a larger transaction which is actually potential, into various small parts of those particular transactions.

Similarly, it is being acknowledged as illegal for any of the organization or their respective employees to provide with the assistance or aid to anyone in the process of structuring up the transactions so that they could be able to avoid the requirements of the keeping up of the record or reporting.

Thus, it is needed to be present on the lookout for the process of designing or structuring so that they could be able to avert it from happening.

6.3.6. Suspicious Transaction Reporting

The activities which are suspicious is being understand as the very complex or difficult concept in terms of defining as it can vary widely from one particular transaction to the other on the basis of all the situations or the circumstances, which generally tend to surround the provided transaction or the whole group of the transactions.

The rules or the regulations which has been set by the government might be requiring anyone to file a report related to the transaction being suspicious for any of the presented transaction or the whole of the pattern or the trend of the transactions, which have already been attempted for any of the provided amount one knows, is being skeptical or possess a reason for being dubious:

- **Filing Requirements for Suspicious Transaction Reports:** The requirements or the needs of the reports related to the transactions being suspicious generally tend to vary widely from one country to another.

However, at this time, much of the countries are being required to possess a report based on the transactions being suspicious.

- **Recordkeeping of Suspicious Transaction Reports:** People are required to keep up with the Xerox or the copy of the specific report and all the documents which provides with the assistance for minimum of five years since the date it has been filled.

The regulations which have been made locally might be requiring that the copy should be kept for the period which is quite long for the future prospects.

6.3.7. Fraud Prevention for Money Transfers

All the agents are basically responsible on the financial terms for the occurrence of any of the losses to their respective business due to the fraudulent activity. Thus, the assistance of people is essentially required to prevent such activities from occurring.

In order to present oneself from such fraudulent activities, the following steps are required to follow:

- Protection of one's PIN.
  - Changing the PIN number every time any of the employees leaves the company.
  - Having the PIN changed on a regular basis.

- One should never state their PIN number or the agent number in front of any of the respective customers.
    - Posting of one's PIN number should not be there in any of the stores or in the view of the customer.

6.3.8. Terrorism Financing Prevention

The process of laundering the money is generally being present in the association with the process of dealing up with the drugs as well as the version of the tax.

However, the various other people, usually the terrorists, might make an attempt to transfer or launder the money so that they could be able to hide their respective identities or fund their functions or the operations.

- The process of movement or the transfer of the funds from either with the help of the country which has been designated by the various agencies as being 'non- cooperative,' by a person who has been recognized as the particularly designated or positioned national.
- Various transactions which has been conducted with the help of the group of the nationals from many of the countries which are being associated or involved in the activities of the terrorists.
- All the individuals who are acting or performing on the behalf of the other businesses who are doing the transmission of the business so that they could be able to transfer the finances or the funds to the various provided locations.

6.4. TRANSNATIONAL ORGANIZED CRIME (TOC)

The terminology of the organized crime has greatly emerged since the year 1919, and this term tend to still maintain the undertones of the gangs of bootlegging, which are being widely spread at that time.

But this phenomenon relating to the criminal activity being organized which are far from the prelates of this specific coinage and also the manifestations it possesses have grown or developed at a considerable rate since that particular time period.

Thus, the reliability or the dependency on the description being provided, the various Offenses being done which could have been classified as a crime which has been organized have always been there with it, but now in today's time, the various nations or the countries have started to make a comparison of the notes and have a collaboration on the response being provided in collaboration (Figure 6.6).

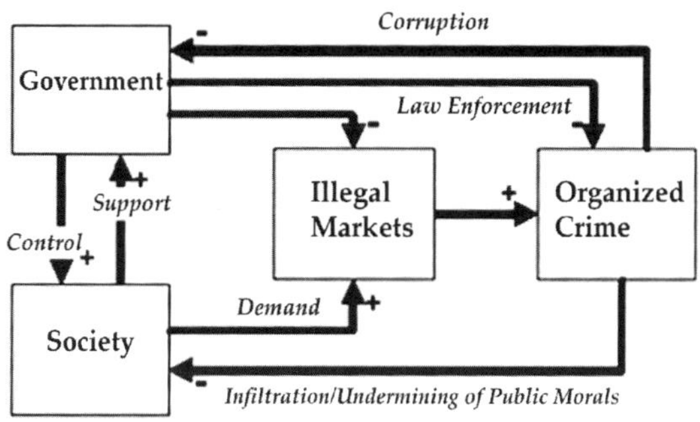

Figure 6.6: Main activity fields of transnational organized crime.

Source: https://link.springer.com/chapter/10.1007/978-3-319-15027-7_7

Thus, within this particular convention, the group of the criminals which has been organized is:

- A group consisting of three or more people which has not been formed or created on a random basis;
- Having an existence for a specific time period;
- Performing or acting in a concert possessing the target or aim of doing minimum of one crime which has a punishment of at least four years of imprisonment.

6.4.1. Changes in Global Situation

Many of the people might seem to possess a natural tendency of self-organizing, and performing it quite promptly whilst none of the authority at a higher designation presents with of the orders.

Many of the people and the activists who all fails in regulating or managing, might tend to get under the hold or control of the various actors being local, who afterward may tend to defend for their power quite vigorously from the again attainment by any of the state of the country.

6.4.2. Factors Influencing the Evolution of Organized Crime Threats

The transitional crime which has been very well organized has grown or evolves over the years. The epidemics of drugs have been into existence and left and then resurfaced into the novel environs.

This particular report does not have much effect on the prediction, but it does finds out or experiences various pertaining factors of risk that might possess an influence or impact on the way the transitional crime which has been very well organized has evolved since many of these years.

- **The enhanced movement of everything:** The terminology having almost as much meanings as the users are present, wherein the term globalization has been referred to as the process of developing or growing the interconnection amongst the various countries or nations across the world, which tend to follow the process of liberalization of the trade at a global level, every time at end of the cold war.
- **Grey and black markets:** Many definitions or the descriptions regarding the crime which has been organized generally tend to provide with the specification related to its nature which is driven by the profits or the gains, and the businesses which are like licit, and all the enterprises do the criminal which are being subjected to the various vagaries of the economic climate at an international level.

Besides the process of opening of the way to the globalization which has already been discussed, the quick or the fast changes which has been taken place in the various countries or the nations and tend to generate with much accuracy the type of the gaps present within the government which is in general, making the organized crime to rise.

6.5. USING ANTI-MONEY LAUNDERING (AML) MEASURES IN THE FINANCIAL WORLD TO COMBAT ORGANIZED CRIME

6.5.1. The Concept of Money Laundering

The first and the foremost reason for the engagement of many of the groups or the individuals in the activities which are not legitimate is to earn as much money as they can.

In today's time, because of the considerate growth and the development in the systems providing information related to finance and also the communication being online, and also the money might get transferred or laundered on the spot anywhere and at any time across the world possessing great speed as well as the anonymity (Figure 6.7).

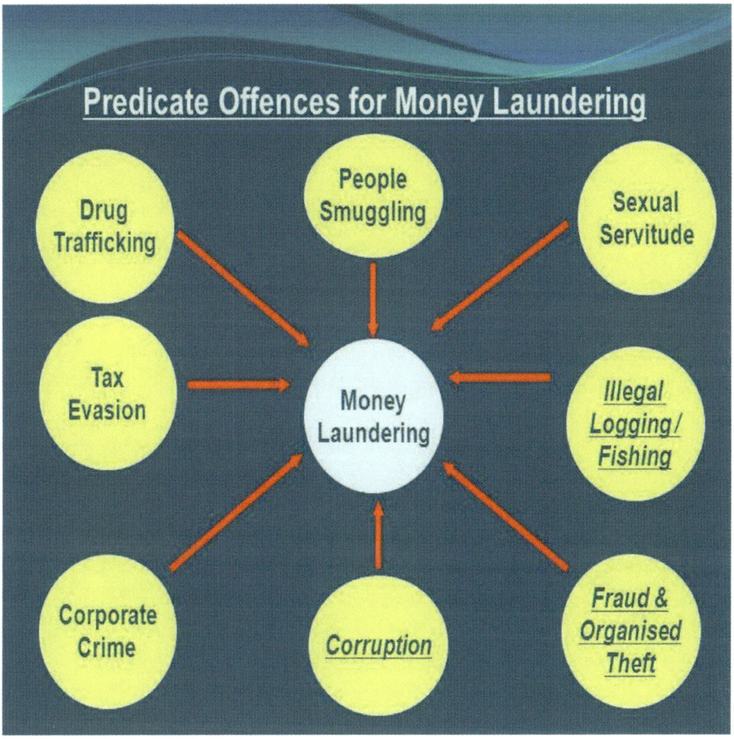

Figure 6.7: Predicate offenses for money laundering.

Source: https://slideplayer.com/slide/10264691/

The people who do the laundering of the money tend to seek the novel ways or the routes to conceal and also the make their funds legal or legitimate. The economies of the nation along with the expansion or the development or growth in the financial hubs, but with the possession of the insufficient hold or the control.

These are being vulnerable dominantly, whereas the economies which have been established financially tend to execute or implement comprehensive systems related to the anti-laundering of the money.

6.5.2. Assessing the Scale of Money Laundering

When the case is of having a measurement of the range or the extent of the process of the laundering of money, there persist no way or the method which could be considered as usual that the various researchers thinks of delivering the figures which precise and unambiguous.

Similarly, the process of segregation or the classification and also the description of the predicate of the laundering or the movement of the money, which might tend vary widely on the basis of the authority of the jurisdiction (Figure 6.8).

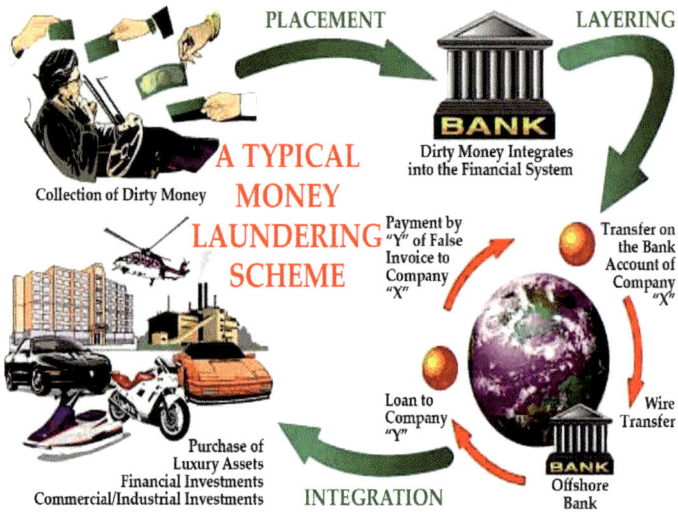

Figure 6.8: Money laundering cycle.

Source: http://www.inquiriesjournal.com/articles/1268/using-anti-money-laundering-measures-in-the-financial-world-to-combat-organized-crime

6.5.3. Costs of Financial Crime to Government and Society

All the risks or the vulnerabilities pertaining for the government, all the financial organization or the institution and the society which has been stemming or rising from the flows of the money being illegitimate are the mainly rooted in the various activities relating to the elementary crime which helps in providing with the funds to those flows. The process of trafficking in the drugs, the people or the various medicines being counterfeit possess a considerate impact on the various sectors, be it public or the private ones.

6.6. CONCLUSIONS AND RECOMMENDATIONS

The point of the beginning of this was to provide with the description of the various positions being related to the member states on the corruption as well as the organized crime which are totally based on the data, being in the quantitative format, already have been available, i.e., indicators of the crime, social as well as the corruption.

The major hypothesis related to the working for the process of causality is generally the organized crime making a complete utilization of the corruption, making it a tool, so that they could be able to achieve the required target or aim.

The application of the analysis related to the regression as well as the correlation does not tend to determine only the existence or the persistence of a relationship but also the various factors which all possess a great statistical impact or the influence on the various pertaining levels of the corruption, along with the strength of that impact as well as its direction.

Various other important factors generally tend to determine or understand the impact or the influence of the crime which has been organized on the police as well as the various officers involved in the process of probing, is considered to efficacy of the units of the internal affairs.

The provided data presents with the suggestion regarding the growth or the development of the strong IAUs which has led to a sharp decrement in the corruption amongst the police in the period of the 1980s, in spite of the persistence of the market having such great criminality.

Thus, such company might be able to facilitate the white- collar crime as well as the process of money laundering. Many of the techniques have been applied to it which involves:

Corruption of the various employees, generally in the corporate sector or the private sector which tend to operate or function in a way, which is almost similar to that of the various other public institutions, possession of the agreement with the management of the various senior officers and the owners of the company.

6.7. CASE STUDY: CORRUPTION, ORGANIZED CRIME, AND MONEY LAUNDERING

The relationship between private wealth and public power frames the discussion of corruption and embraces not only explicit quid pro quo deals but also lobbying, campaign donations, and other forms of pressure exerted by both private individuals and businesses.

Some use the term "corruption" to cover all the ways that concentrated wealth influences political choice. I am sympathetic to such concerns, but I am not convinced that extending the corruption label to all these issues is the most productive route to understanding and reform.

Some forms of corruption are well studied, and reasonable reform proposals can constrain the underlying incentives for corruption. These include low-level payoffs by households and small businesses to obtain scarce government benefits, to qualify for benefits or licenses, and to lower the costs of taxes and fines.

Abstracting from the overall problem of corruption and governance, this essay concentrates on the interface between corruption, organized crime, and money laundering.

6.7.1. Organized Crime

Corruption and organized crime often go together. Organized crime dominates illegal businesses, but it may also control legal businesses to gain monopoly profits and exclude competitors.

Large-scale illegal businesses or Mafia infiltration of legal activities are both likely to have a corrupting influence on government, especially law enforcement and border control. Corrupt rulers and illegal businessmen feed on each other.

Bribes reduce the cost of illegal business ventures and help them raise capital, fueling their growth and generating more corrupt arrangements. If a strong symbiotic relationship exists, anti-corruption policy needs explicitly to target organized crime. Otherwise, it will ignore one key root of the problem.

Although organized criminal groups operate on the margin of formal markets and outside legal norms, they behave very much like business firms, often operating like franchises loosely linked to a central organization.

They produce where costs are lowest and sell where the return is highest. Instead of paying taxes, they make direct payments to government representatives in the form of bribes.

They tend to be organized hierarchically, although horizontal networks have started to develop (Center for the Study of Democracy, 2010), and frequently, those in the lower ranks cannot identify their superiors.

They face competition, but their methods are often based on threats of violence, rather than on advertising and creative marketing.

Organized crime also corrupts private businesses into facilitating their illicit production or smuggling operations. Alternatively, OCGs may take advantage of other widely-accepted illegal activities.

For example, in Colombia, drug trafficking organizations used existing contraband networks to launder their drug proceeds. As private businesses cross the line into illegitimate activity, and the public welcomes access to these goods (low-cost contraband or new psychotropic substances, for example), the law, in general, becomes less relevant.

OCGs commonly use bribery, threats of violence, and blackmail to corrupt the police, customs officials, judges, politicians, and military in order to gain not only prosecutorial immunity but outright cooperation and assistance, especially in smuggling operations.

As some parts of government become corrupt, transparency becomes increasingly difficult, thus enabling more corruption in other sectors and feeding a vicious spiral.

When organized crime has a strong foothold many of the standard reform proposals outlined above will have only minor effects. Deeper changes are needed.

6.7.2. Money Laundering

Most corrupt proceeds eventually end up in the legitimate global economy, either deposited in financial institutions or invested in real estate or business ventures. Much of it flows across national borders into assets and financial institutions located in money centers in wealthy countries or in so-called "financial paradises."

Hence, the international control of money laundering and of investment vehicles with opaque ownership could make corruption more expensive and troublesome even if domestic law enforcement is weak.

The large commercial banks of the United States and Europe are also involved in money laundering. Indeed, many critics in developing countries argue that the OECD countries are responsible for both generating bribes and laundering the funds.

For example, ill-gotten funds deposited in a subsidiary in Mexico can be moved to an account in New York. Conversely, funds could be deposited in the United States, and then transferred to accounts in Mexico to pay for drugs delivered.

In the wake of a major money-laundering scandal involving London bank HSBC in Mexico (HBMX), it was alleged that HBMX was responsible for 60–70% of laundered funds in Mexico.

Between 2005 and 2007, U.S. bank Wachovia reportedly transferred US$14 billion in cash from Mexico to U.S. branches on behalf of foreign exchange houses "and other foreign correspondent bulk cash customers"; HSBC's Mexican subsidiary laundered $881 million or more from Mexican and Colombian drug cartels.

The state may need to make more direct efforts to reduce the excess profits available to criminal entrepreneurs in legitimate business. One way to do that is to promote the entry of well-capitalized legitimate businesses that, with some state help on the law enforcement side, can compete with mob-dominated firms.

The corruption generated by the illegal drug trade is one argument in favor of legalization to produce a more competitive and less corrupt market.

6.7.3. Conclusion

One of the greatest dangers of corruption is a vicious spiral that enables organized crime to get a foothold and propagate.

Once some of the police, legislators, court clerks, and judges are identified as "for sale," members of organized criminal groups will take advantage of this weakness in the rule of law, and such activity will escalate.

Some of their most lucrative businesses will be illegal—such as trafficking of drugs and people. Others may be legal with high profits (running casinos or "winning" public tenders) or opportunities to launder ill-begotten gains.

The danger is that, rather than being a stage of development that will wither away over time, criminal activity may become so intertwined with politics and legitimate business, that it is difficult to tell them apart.

The goals of international aid and lending organizations should be to improve the lives of people living on the margins and to enhance the functioning of their government so that they benefit their populations.

If these goals can be achieved, fewer people will predictably be drawn into both organized crime and violence—both for motivational reasons and because the polity is better able to provide security.

REFERENCES

1. Anon, (n.d.). [online] Available at: https://www.jstor.org/stable/10.3138/9781442670242 (Accessed on 12 April 2019).
2. *Anti-Money Laundering Compliance Guide,* (2018). [eBook] p. 37. Available at: http://corporate.moneygram.com/Documents/Corp%20site%20docs/Compliance/LatAm%20and%20Caribbean/aml_lacaml0908_eng.pdf (Accessed on 12 April 2019).
3. *Anti-Money Laundering Compliance Program*, (n.d.). [eBook] p. 66. Available at: http://files.acams.org/pdfs/English_Study_Guide/Chapter_4.pdf (Accessed on 12 April 2019).
4. Chêne, M., (2018). *Organized Crime and Corruption.* [eBook] p. 11. Available at: http://file:///C:/Users/acer/Downloads/expert-helpdesk-171.pdf (Accessed on 12 April 2019).
5. *Examining the Links Between Organized Crime and Corruption*, (n.d.). [eBook] p. 335. Available at: https://ec.europa.eu/home-affairs/sites/homeaffairs/files/doc_centre/crime/docs/study_on_links_between_organised_crime_and_corruption_en.pdf (Accessed on 12 April 2019).
6. Hauck, P., & Peterke, S., (2016). *International Law and Transnational Organized Crime*, p. 609.
7. M.G, Gorai., (2018). *Foundational Understanding of Corruption.* [eBook] p. 34. Available at: http://chs.uonbi.ac.ke/sites/default/files/chs/chs/CHS%20-%2017–06–2016%20-CONCEPT%20OF%20CORRUPTION.pdf (Accessed on 12 April 2019).
8. Stankiewicz, N., (2018). *Using Anti-Money Laundering Measures in the Financial World to Combat Organized Crime.* [online] Inquiries journal. Available at: http://www.inquiriesjournal.com/articles/1268/using-anti-money-laundering-measures-in-the-financial-world-to-combat-organized-crime (Accessed on 12 April 2019).
9. Tanzi, V., (1998). *Corruption Around the World.* [eBook] p. 39. Available at: https://www.imf.org/external/pubs/ft/wp/wp9863.pdf (Accessed on 12 April 2019).
10. *The Threat of Transnational Organized Crime*, (n.d.). [eBook] p. 14. Available at: https://www.unodc.org/documents/data-and-analysis/tocta/1.The-threat-transnational-organized-crime.pdf (Accessed on 12 April 2019).
11. *Transnational Organized Crime (TOC),* (n.d.). [eBook] p. 1. Available

at: https://www.dni.gov/files/documents/NIC_toc_foldout.pdf (Accessed on 12 April 2019).

12. *Transnational Organized Crime and the Impact on the Private Sector*, (2017). [eBook] p. 78. Available at: http://globalinitiative.net/wp-content/uploads/2017/12/GITOC_TOCPrivateSector_web.pdf (Accessed on 12 April 2019).
13. Utorontopress.com., (n.d.). *Critical Reflections on Transnational Organized Crime, Money Laundering, and Corruption*. [online] Available at: https://utorontopress.com/ca/critical-reflections-on-transnational-organized-crime-money-laundering-and-corruption-3 (Accessed on 12 April 2019).

7

Human Rights, International Humanitarian Law, and Transnational Organized Crime

CONTENTS

Countries are facing the threat of organized crimes, for example, human trafficking, drug, and arms, cybercrime, terrorism, oil bunkering, and advanced-fee fraud for many years. The aim of this chapter is to identify the implications of criminal activities on human rights. This chapter contends that transnational crimes disturb the image of a country in a negative aspect. The phenomena arise due to economic and political situations such as bad governance, weak state institutions, greater international mobility and economic crisis in the globalized world. The chapter depends on secondary data which is crucially examined. The conclusions reveal that oil bunkering and, human drugs and arms trafficking are very hard to control as they are very profitable businesses situated in developing countries. The chapter concludes that the incapability of the government to cater for the citizens has donated to increasing incidence of transnational crime.

7.1. INTRODUCTION

Human rights and crimes are two different concepts which reflect the position and legal characteristic of an individual in a State. There is a huge relationship between Human Rights, criminal laws and transnational organized crime (TOC). Human Rights are defined as moral principles or norms that describe certain standards of human behavior and are regularly protected as accepted and lawful rights in municipal and international law.

International humanitarian law (IHL) is also known as the law of armed conflict. This particular law has been framed to help people get rid of all those sufferings that they go through during the time of war. It is that branch of international law which is required for regulating the conduct of the war, and it seeks to limit the effects of armed conflict by protecting people.

TOC can be defined as organized crime which coordinates across two different countries involving groups or networks of individuals, national borders which are working in more than one country to design and implement illegal business ventures.

There are various criminal groups that use systematic ferocity and exploitation in order to achieve their goals. It reflects on 'crimes' and 'human rights' so that to enter into the different abstract and normative traditions in (international) legal scholarship with respect to the state authority and responsibility for the position of natural and legal persons.

Criminal Law is that kind of law that regularly turns around the idea of the state as the (collective) victim, and every individual in the organization as the criminal which help human rights law to focus on the state as the offender and every individual in the organization as the target.

That traditional distinction, however, is increasingly blurring as—on one hand—the pursuit and prosecution of criminal organizations is subjected to a growing set of human rights. There are few activities of a variation of 'non-state actors' have 'horizontalized' human rights, i.e., human rights violations can be official to such non-state actors as non-governmental organizations, and indeed organizations that are rightfully or wrongfully considered as 'criminal,' such as terrorist organizations, mafias, bikers, and gangs.

IHL is the law of armed conflict, and the main aim is to moderate human sorrow at the time of war. It involves various principles and rules specifically planned to keep persons who do not or who no longer directly participate in the conflicts, above all, the civil population and fighters, i.e., those who are injured, marooned, sick, or detained (*hors de combat*). In addition, IHL unfolds its civilizing effects through barring and limiting certain methods and means of war.

7.2. TRANSNATIONAL ORGANIZED CRIME (TOC) AND ITS DISCONNECTION WITH HUMAN RIGHTS

7.2.1. Impact of Transnational Organized Crime (TOC) on Policies and Law

The most imposing and legal international document is the United Nations Convention against Transnational Organized Crime (UNTOC). It basically focuses on the issue of TOC and comprises an excellent beginning point for inspecting the stance of international community on the relationship between human rights and TOC.

The major conclusion which can be drawn after reading the United Nations UNTOC is that there is no discussion of human rights in it. Regarding human rights, all the articles of the convention are practically silent.

Human rights are slightly mentioned in the Preamble and Articles 2(b), 10(2), and 14(1) of the Protocol to Prevent, Suppress, and Punish Trafficking in Persons, Especially Women and Children, and Article 19 of the Protocol against the Smuggling of Migrants by Land, Sea, and Air.

The addition of human rights in the convention secures that nothing in this protocol will affect other obligations, rights, and responsibilities of individuals and states under international law, comprising international human rights law and IHL. This does not perform any substantial function.

In 2013, a thematic paper on the topic ‘Exploitation and abuse of international migrants, particularly those in an irregular situation: a human rights approach’ was published by the Global Migration Group. This paper gave a better understanding of the relationship between violations or abuses of human rights and criminal organizations or crimes.

The exploitation concept provided the best example, but its definition is still unclear and therefore lacks a legal international definition. Law against the trafficking in persons was modeled by the United Nations Office on Drugs and Crime (UNODC), which on the other hand recognizes exploitation as situation of work which is not consistent with human dignity.

This may be further explained by the fact that the Trafficking in Persons Protocol does not criminalize exploitation in and of itself. It is a kind of exploitation which describes whether exploitation would be the violation of human rights or a criminal act or both. The three major examples of exploitative acts which are not covered by criminal law but by human rights are exploitation en route, exploitative labor, and exploitative traditional practices.

Courts clearly differ like authority and subject matter at an international level, which are determined predominantly by their statues. The distinction between international criminal courts (ICC) and human rights courts at the international level is very important for the current discussion.

Clapham exactly states that the problem is not whether organizations can involve in transnational activities which are otherwise labeled as criminal or violate international criminal laws, but whether these organizations can be the matter of suitable international adjudication. The answer to the former question tends not to be positive.

Human right courts, committees, and international criminal tribunals are basically prohibited from involving cases in which organizations act as the ‘defendant.’ Under national law, these organizations at least have a legal status. Generally, the organizations having intentions of crime do not have explicit legal status.

Many of the identified organizations with crime intent would not have that explicit legal personality which would make able courts and prosecutors to move against the organizations instead of their members (Figure 7.1).

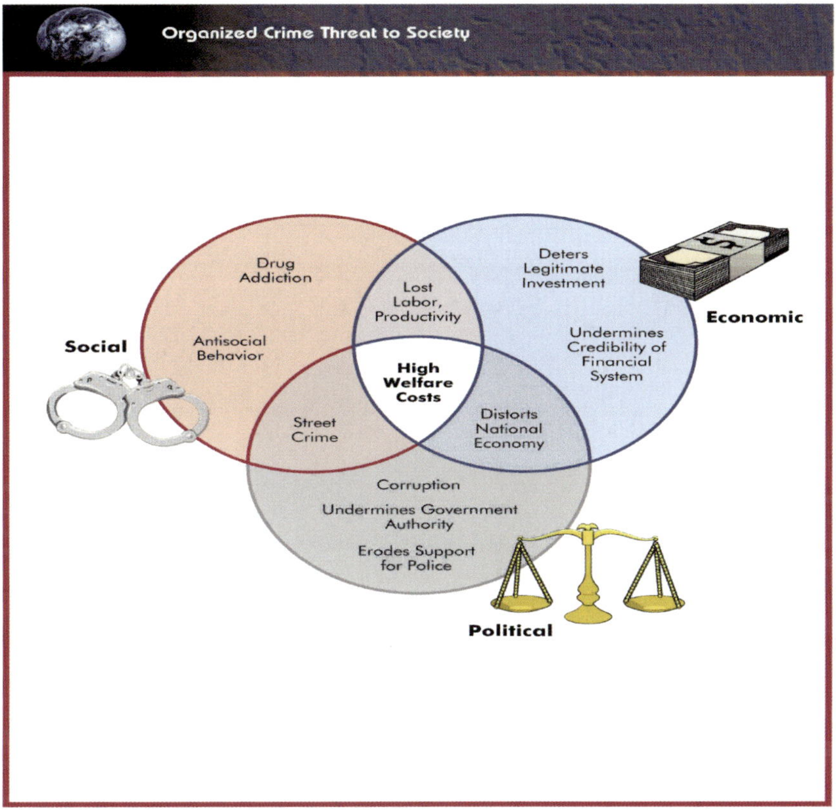

Figure 7.1: International crime threat assessment.

Source: https://fas.org/irp/threat/pub45270chap4.html

7.2.2. Crimes Related to Human Rights and TOC

The survey done by Hauck and Peterke concluded that it is very tough to reach consent on the suitable meaning and use of the term 'organized crime.' The UNTOC, the principal international instrument itself provides no definition of TOC, but a variety of criteria under which it would fall.

Examples which could come under the convention would involve people and drug trafficking, money laundering, the illegal arms trade, piracy, and potential terrorism which depend upon the nature of transborder and structure of organization (Figure 7.2).

Figure 7.2: Human trafficking.

Source: http://kathmandupost.ekantipur.com/news/2017-07-30/the-fight-against-trafficking-in-persons.html

Criminal behavior is inherent in all these examples which influences the individual human rights affected, directly or indirectly. Under international laws, domestic law of sender states, transfer states or destination states, few of the criminal behavior may be prohibited in part or in whole.

This would ultimately criminalize the underlying acts which combine to effect in a TOC, and a major motivation of the Palermo Convention was to encourage state party's cooperation to reduce and contest TOC more efficiently by mutual legal, national criminalization and joint investigations, preventative policies and technical assistance.

The human trafficking law of UK would be a good example as it states that a person does a crime if the person facilitates or arranges another person's travel with an opinion to exploit that other person. The above-mentioned TOC amount to stand-alone crimes under law of international crime is not clear. While there is evidently a probable overlap with crimes against humanity that is CAH, for example the extensive trafficking of girls and women within conflict for sexual exploitation purposes and the systematic attack by a terrorist killing a huge number of civilians and the International Criminal Tribunal for the former Yugoslavia (ICTY) has identified that international crimes are not required to be committed by state actors, and there is kind of argument within academic literature as to whether TOC can be understood so far to fall under the category of CAH.

7.3. HUMAN RIGHTS, TRANSNATIONAL ORGANIZED CRIME AND TRAFFICKING IN PERSONS

To be specific, the alarming trend in human trafficking, human smuggling and TOC calls for global cooperation to address them. Though, it is relevant for stakeholders to recognize the difference between the two crimes so that at the point of detection, one will not be mistaken for the other.

This will make the governments enable and lawmakers to comprise significant legislation which will restrict the crime. Criminal groups destabilize the authority of a state and the law rule by compromising elections, hurting the legitimate economy and fueling corruption.

In every case, money, and criminal influence are having substantial impact on the quality and livelihoods of life of citizens, mainly the women, poor, and children. In the Declaration of the High-Level Meeting on the Rule of Law, Member States strained the status of reinforced international cooperation to pull apart the illegal networks, counter the problem of drugs around the globe and TOC together with trafficking in persons, money-laundering, trafficking in arms and other kinds of organized crime, which impend national security and destabilize sustainable development and the rule of law.

Member states are assisted by the United Nations system in their struggle against TOC. The UN UNTOC and its protocols and various other international conventions on drug control, migrant smuggling, human trafficking and trafficking of firearms along with the UN Convention against Corruption establish the main framework for strategic response.

The protector of international conventions is the UNODC. The diction of human trafficking as a discrete crime problem demanding enforcement of transnational law is clearly personified in the 2000 UN UNTOC and its supplementary Trafficking Protocol. Anyhow, its reference to measures 'to protect the victims,' the UN Trafficking Protocol has been structured primarily as a law enforcement instrument for the 'prevention, suppression, and punishment of trafficking in persons' ('Preamble,' UN Trafficking Protocol).

The implementation of the Protocol to Prevent, Suppress, and Punish the Trafficking in Persons, particularly children and women, accompanying the United Nations UNTOC in 2000 was a breakthrough which provided the first globally agreed definition of "trafficking in persons": "the recruitment, transportation, transfer, harboring or receipt of persons, by means of the risk or use of force or other forms of coercion, of abduction, of fraud, of deception, of the abuse of power or of a position of vulnerability or of the giving or receiving of payments or benefits to achieve the consent of a person having control over another person, for the purpose of exploitation" (Figure 7.3).

Figure 7.3: High time to combat human trafficking.

Source: https://media.defense.gov/2016/ Jan/27/2001769871/780/780/0/150724-F-XX000-001.JPG

Exploitation intends to comprise, the exploitation of the prostitution of others or other forms of sexual exploitation, slavery or practices similar to slavery, forced labor or services, servitude or the removal of organs at a minimum."

Despite the existence of an inclusive international legal framework, loads of men, women, and children, continue to be smuggled each year, in all regions and in many countries of the world. Victims may be smuggled within a country or across the border for many purposes, comprising forced and exploitative labor in farms, factories, and private households, forced marriage, sexual exploitation and removal of organs.

Quantification of the phenomenon becomes very difficult due to the clandestine nature of trafficking. As per the Walk Free Foundation and ILO Global Estimates, 25 million people were exposed to sexual exploitation and forced labor in 2016 globally. UNODC's 2016 Global Report (PDF) on recognized victims shows that 51% of victims are women, 21% men, 20%

girls, and 8% boys. Among those victims, 38% for forced labor and 45% have been trafficked for sexual exploitation. In current years, trafficking has also prospered amongst populations living in or absconding conflict situations.

While the connection between human trafficking and human rights is relatively clear, it does not essentially follow that human rights will be at the middle of responses to trafficking. The approach based on human rights places the victim at the center of any operative and reliable action.

It also outspreads the attention to the root causes which motivate trafficking, preserve impunity for traffickers, and contradict justice to victims, for example, unjust distribution of power, patterns of discrimination, demand for goods and services which are derived from exploitation and involvement of the public sector.

The approach based upon human rights also recognizes that governments are responsible for promoting and protecting the rights of all persons within their authority, including non-citizens, and hence have a legal responsibility to work towards removing trafficking and related exploitation.

The UN Human Rights Office is leading the efforts to encourage a human rights-based approach to trafficking in persons. Recommended Principles and Guidelines have developed by the office on Human Rights and Human Trafficking and its extensive Commentary which intent to the people who are engaged in anti-trafficking efforts to completely assimilate human rights into their analysis and responses to trafficking.

The following core areas are addressed in the document which comprises seventeen recommended principles:

- The primacy of human rights;
- Protection and assistance;
- Preventing trafficking;
- Criminalization, punishment, and redress.

7.4. ORGANIZED CRIME AND GANG VIOLENCE IN PUBLIC INTERNATIONAL LAW

Organized crime and gang violence have progressively become subject to international regulation. After the end of the cold war, the states became increasingly attentive of the transnational dimensions of organized crime as a side-effect of globalization. They consequently adopted an international framework to contain 'organized criminal groups' and their most harmful activities.

The following analysis will start by clearing up the evolution and significance of the legal regime. IHL and International Criminal Law both address violence by 'organized armed groups. The question arises whether armed criminal groups may become party to an armed conflict and the question whether armed criminal groups may become party to an armed conflict and, if so, under which specific preconditions.

They are responsible for the international crimes and their qualification as an 'organized armed group' would then let for their members. International framework is allowed to fight with the organized crime. Co-operation in criminal matters is a very sensitive issue.

Its success often depends on the confidential exchange of information and a common interest in the success of an operation. In the beginning of the cold war, the mutual confidence was slightly limited in the state communities. Organized crime was also supposed as actuality primarily a domestic problem.

The absence of common interests and mutual confidence, and the slowly developing awareness of the transnational dimensions of organized crime, explain only in part why states have been unwilling to establish a legally binding multilateral framework designed to encourage and promote international co-operation for the defeat of organized crime.

As transnational offending – truly a catch-all term understood to mean different behavior at a level of criminality that by its very nature essentially involves either transcending state borders, violating the laws of several states, or escaping a state's authority by not being attributable to a certain state territory.

There are many forms of organized crime which have a habit of to be subject to so-called defeat treaties, that is, multilateral agreements between the parties of the state to fight deviance successfully from an international perspective.

To look a little further back in history which shows that states themselves have regularly tried to make profit from markets and in future, it become illegal and after it was supplied by the criminal organizations. This holds especially correct for drug and human trafficking, which are today considered to be the world's most harmful and illegal activities in order to make profit.

Human trafficking is basically a modern form of slave trade that involves practices related to sexual exploitation, forced labor, slavery, and similar practices. Due to economic reasons, governments hesitated until the nineteenth century to distinguish in their constitutional instruments that the fundamental right of each and every person is not to be held in slavery or servitude and not to be operated as a commodity.

During the year 1861–1865, a civil war was clashed in the US to enable this basic human right to prevail over the economically driven interest of the south. In other states, its recognition came about quietly, but even later.

It was not until after the Second World War that it was universally recognized and subsequently became normal international law with the status of jus cogens, from which obligations erga omnes derive. European states had adopted the statement on the abolition of the Slave Trade in 1815, yet it took more than a hundred years to reach an international consensus on a relatively narrow definition of slavery, slavery-like institutions and practices, and the slave trade.

In 1904, International agreement was made for the defeat of the white slave traffic and telling documents for addressing shameful issues. The slavery, slave-related practices, and forced labor became familiar as international crimes before the adoption of the 1988 Rome Statute of the ICC. It was not until the year 2000 that states adopted the Protocol to Stop, Overpower, and Punish Trafficking in Persons, especially Women and Children, supplementing the United Nations UNTOC.

Great Britain fought the Opium Wars (1839–1842, 1856–1860) to force China to accept free trade in that drug and to open its domestic market. In 1909, the process of international suppression of drugs has started with the Shanghai Opium Conference.

It led to the first international anti-drug treaty, the 1912 International Opium Convention, which is connected to the trade in cocaine and heroin and illustrious between legal and illegal drugs. There are many other anti-drug instruments have been accepted since then, successively banning all kinds of drugs and their production, trading, and consumption.

In 1936, convention for the Suppression of the Illicit Traffic in Dangerous Drugs, and there are75 states parties who were enjoined to make the necessary legislative provisions for severely punishing acts such as 'possession, offering (for sale), distribution, purchase, sale, delivery, brokerage, communication (in transit), transport, importation, and exportation of narcotic drugs.

As the power, effect, and transnationality of criminal groups involved in these markets became more obvious in the 1980s, the international efforts to fight them ended in the 1988. United Nations agreement against Illicit Traffic in Narcotic Drugs and psychotropic substances, which today enjoys quasi-universal character.

This is the time when it only covers one specific illegal market and does not address organized crime in a more comprehensive way. These agreements have mainly focused on international consent and co-operation, rather than on establishing international or even universal authority over the crimes concerned.

It is safe to say that group or organized criminal conduct strength be regulated by them. The criminalization of those crimes, however, rests with national jurisdictions and not with supranational authorities but it is hard to link the concept of transnational criminal to gang violence and organized crime whenever the unconventionality does not cross borders.

7.4.1. Organized Crime and Gang Violence as Subject Matter of the Rome Statute

On the face of it, and like terrorism, Organized crime or gang behavior do not in themselves usually in the amount to crime of killing according to the Rome Statute and they take place with the specific ('genocidal') 'resolved to destroy, in entire or in part, a national, ethnical, racial or religious group.'

For example, in remote places such as the Amazon rainforest where criminal collectives engage in all kinds of illegal trafficking activities, they may deliberately eject or eliminate groups such as indigenous peoples defending their territory against the interlopers.

According to Article 7(1) of the Rome Statute, to find a crime against humanity, 'there are following acts which are committed as a part of a widespread or systematic attack directed against any civilian population.' This kind of acts include several crimes typically also committed by criminal organizations such as murder, termination, addiction, lack of physical liberty, torture, rape, and so forth.

The term "enslavement" is defined by the Rome Statute as 'the exercise of any or all of the powers assigning to the right of ownership over a person and includes the exercise of such power in the course of trafficking in persons for specific women and children.'

The Article 7(2) of the convention states for the purpose of paragraph 1, that an attack which is focused against any civilian population defines a course of conduct comprising the multiple commission of acts which referred in paragraph 1 against any civilian population, in accordance with law in furtherance of a State or organizational policy to perform such kind of attack.

The provision explains that crimes which are against humanity can be devoted by non-state entities. Though the meaning of an organization under Article 7(2) is very much disputable. The tendency is not to signify the criteria which spread over to 'armed organized groups' but to utilize different ones, like power and use of force comparable to those of state institutions.

Under the Article 8(2) (f) of the Rome Statute, additional serious violations of the laws and customs related to armed conflicts not of an international character, that are committed in the territory of state when there is prolonged armed conflict between organized armed groups and governmental authorities, constitute war crimes.

7.5. HUMAN RIGHTS AND THE UNITED NATIONS

Although the effort to declare the Human rights of humans as universal is new, Human Rights are not new in Britain as they are as old as Magna Carta known today human rights and these individuals are not new depending on the culture of the people (Figure 7.4).

Figure 7.4: The United Nations and its logo.

Source: https://cdn.pixabay.com/photo/2016/02/07/05/01/united-nations-1184119_960_720.jpg

They are the first written Rights Charter in the world, and also different peoples and cultures of the world have at one time or the other, attempted, and/or made certain declaration on the rights of her citizens. In the meantime, due to killings of the Second World War, there was a need to declare the basic rights of individuals as universal.

Thus, the UN Commission on Human Rights under the leadership of Mrs. Eleanor Roosevelt was charged with the responsibility of drafting a universal declaration of human rights. After every day the crash between champions of the Western and Soviet concepts of fundamental human freedom, the Commission submitted its report to the General assembly of the United Nations for support.

The assembly stated it as a common standard of achievement for all peoples and all nations so that the every individual and every organ of society will keep this declaration always in mind, so that try to teach and educate the peoples and to promote respect for these rights and freedoms by progressive measures, national, and international, to secure their universal and effective recognition and observance both among the peoples of member states themselves and among the peoples of territories under their influence.

On December-10-1948 the approval was made, with total votes from 48 to 0, so that it can participate with six nations of the Soviet bloc, Saudi Arabia, and the Union of South Africa abstaining (Palmer and Perkins, 2001).

The UDHR involves 30 articles which contain an inclusive listing of key civil, economic, political, social, and cultural rights. Articles 3 through 21 outlines political and civil rights, which involve the right against suffering, the right to an operative therapy for the violations of human rights, and the right to take part in government.

Articles 22 through 27 detail social, economic, and cultural rights, for example, the right to work, the right to form and to join trade unions, and the right to take part without any restrictions in the cultural life of the community (United Nations, 2007) (Figure 7.5).

Figure 7.5: The universal declaration of human rights.

Source: https://c1.staticflickr.com/1/416/31456212961_1864ea91fa_b.jpg

However, the statement is just a statement of principles, not a legally binding instrument (Palmer and Perkins, 2001). The nonbinding status of UDHR would appear to be one of its major shortcomings. But authoritarian states are required to protect themselves against what they considered interfering in their internal affairs, approved of this feature of the declaration, and even some democratic countries firstly concerned about the potentially intrusive nature of the obligations that a legally binding document would carry out.

It was said that the nonbinding status is one of the major advantages it has. Its flexibility has offered enough room for new strategies to promote human rights and has become a factor providing opportunity for the development of numerous legislative initiatives in international human rights law.

These are the developments that make someone runway with the idea that, despite its nonbinding status, its provisions have achieved a juridical status like that of norms of customary international law. Some of the people still believe it would give the idea when the universal declaration of Human Rights was under the auspices of the UN.

As a result, Universalists, and cultural relativists have mismatched over the validity and applicability of human rights outside the west. Some argue that the Western Political Philosophy upon which the Universal Declaration of Human Rights is based provides only one interpretation of human rights and that these western notions may not be successfully applicable to non-western areas due to ideological and cultural differences or religious traditions (Goodhart, 2003).

The differences of opinions notwithstanding, one factor contributing to the UDHR's moral authority is precisely that it transcends positive international law. Indeed, it pronounces general moral principles applicable to everyone, thus universalizing the notion of a fundamental baseline of human well-being.

Despite its shortcomings, the UDHR was and remains the key reference point for international human rights address. For example, during the hateful apartheid era in South Africa, several organs of the United Nations based their condemnation of the racial judgment on Universal Declaration of Human Rights.

Again, protestors throughout the Eastern bloc held on these provisions to demand greater political freedom and established local committees to fight for government compliance (Whiteclay, 1999). Even during outright war, the law of war grants fundamental defense to persons and objects other than combatants and military objective. The fundamental protection granted applies to all persons and objects in the power of the aggressive party or the neutral state.

It agrees to basic humanitarian principle and human rights. Universal Declaration of Human Rights has the authority to make idea of human rights so that it can be accepted by the universe. The idea of human rights has proven to be a highly energetic one.

Be it in the constant development of certain aspects of already existing rights, the birth of new ones, or the progressive improvement of the protection mechanism in the human rights field (Sora, 2010). Again, because the Charter of the United Nations is indefinite and/or uncertain issues of human rights, there was need for a covenant that would give a clear meaning to those rights in the UDHR. The effects on armed conflicts occur because of the divide opinions of democratic human rights and IHL. Since 1945, 71 nations and the communist nations have participated to create human rights, and the UDHR was completely failed to save support the universe as it deserves.

To find the solutions of the problem there are two contracts to study the opinions of the two parties and different opinions and to find a common ground to assume. On that day, the Universal Declaration of Human Rights was adopted by the General Assembly, and it requested as a matter of priority, an agreement of human rights and draft measure of execution.

The commission is prepared to complete the two drafts of ninth and tenth sessions in the year of 1953 and 1954. But it was not until 1966 that the General Assembly adopted the covenants (United Nations, 2007).

7.6. TRANSNATIONAL ARMED CONFLICTS AND INTERNATIONAL HUMANITARIAN LAW (IHL)

Transnational conflict is a neutral and descriptive term which incorporates all battles with a transboundary character which comprise non-State actors and therefore apparently outflow the classic division of international and non-international armed conflict (Figure 7.6).

These conflicts can be illustrated through the assistance of the following model in a better way. Reasonably, armed hostilities can include States and non-State actors and can happen within a single State or cross boundaries. Depending on these premises, armed conflicts can be divided into eight categories:

- Conflict between two or more States;
- State fighting against non-State actors completely within the State;
- Non-State actor conflicting with non-State actor completely within the State;
- State fighting on its own territory against a domestic non-State actor which operates from abroad;
- State fighting on its own territory against foreign non-State actor(s);
- State fighting against foreign non-State actors on the territory of

another State with the consent of the State;

- State fighting against foreign non-State actors on the territory of another State without the consent of that State; and
- Non-State actors from different countries fighting against each other crossing border.

Figure 7.6: International humanitarian law (IHL).

Source: http://study-aids.co.uk/dissertation-blog/international-humanitarian-law/

Conflicts categories from no. 4 to 8 belong to the category of transnational conflicts. They do not fit easily in the outdated dichotomy of the separation of international and non-international armed conflicts. Although they include international, cross-border elements and the existence of non-State actors also make these conflicts analogous to non-international armed conflicts. In a huge number of conflicts, these scenarios really take place at the same time.

The outdated dichotomy of international and non-international armed conflict is based on the principle that these bodies work in different contexts. Though, in an increasing number of conflicts, transboundary hostilities take place without the involving States on both sides. These conflicts apparently challenge the impermeable separation of international and non-international armed conflicts as fundamentals of both bodies are present cross-border armed violence and the participation of non-State armed groups.

7.7. INTERNATIONAL HUMANITARIAN LAW (IHL) AS IT AFFECT ARMED CONFLICTS

The international human rights law and the national law successfully address the issue of human rights. There is a law when these rights are violated, and it remains a challenge for the students to study international human rights law. The methodological problems that exist in IHL also exist in international human rights.

For example, it has been said that the destruction of IHL was not due to lack of its rule but rather from unwillingness to respect the rules, from inadequate means to apply them, from worries as to their application in some circumstances and a lack of alertness of them on the part of political leaders, commanders, combatants, and the public (Henckaerts, 2005).

Everybody questions that there must be an agreed common cause for outside action on behalf of human rights and it is regularly said that injustices can hurt somebody's feelings and it is important to have human ethics and cry out for corrective action.

Even though it is widely recognized that human rights are unchallengeable. Yet human condition is affected by widespread misuses, exploitations, and related inter-communal conflict, political oppressive rules, and deeply set prejudgments within and across different societies and culture (Viotti and Kauppi, 2009).

It has been stated that nowhere in the declaration was it instructed that a member state had the right to interfere in another country's affair to stop human right abuses. The principle of this idea is the 'Responsibility to Protect,' and this idea states that the government have a duty to safeguard their citizens from mass killings and this idea has been outdated by the Brahimi report which led to the UN adopting in 2005, so that the international community has a duty to interfere if a state fails in this responsibility.

IHL strikes a balance between humanity and military requirement, and it limits the use of violence in armed conflict to spare those who do not or who no longer directly participate in hostilities, while at the same time decline the military potential of the enemy.

Both in limiting the violence and in regulating the treatment of persons affected by armed conflict in other respects, IHL strikes a balance between humanity and military requirement. Article 2 common to the Geneva Conventions states that: In addition to the provisions which shall be implemented in peacetime, the present Convention shall apply to all cases of declared war or of any other armed conflict which may arise between two or more of the high contracting parties, even if the state of war is not recognized by one of them.

The convention shall also apply to all cases of partial or total occupation of the territory of the High Contracting Party, even if the said occupation meets with no armed resistance (UNOHC, 2011). Although it is said that traditionally, international human right law is seen as imposing obligations on states only, while IHL is quite unique in international law in that it is binding not only on sates, but also on non-state armed groups (ICRC, 2007).

On the contrary, even though Geneva Conventions and Protocols specify the type of situation, they would apply but have failed in giving a clear definition of armed conflict. In today's generation, many armed conflicts are non-international in nature. They take place within the borders of states and are paid between a state and organized non-state armed group(s) or among such groups themselves (ICRC, 2008).

7.7.1. Human Rights, International Humanitarian Law, and Conflict

When faced with widespread human rights violations in situations of conflict, it is often expected that what is needed is more effective implementation of human rights law and principles. It may be that the legal framework for the safety of human rights in conflict situations needs to be retreating to provide an effective basis on which to act or to advocate.

The importance of IHL in terms of protecting human rights and increasing merging between the bodies of law as attempts are made to bridge the protection gap in conflict-related crises. These are the following sections to discover the applicability of human rights law to situations of conflict.

Human rights law and conflict Human rights are official in the international system through a range of legal and diplomatic instruments, and they are both moral and a legal construct. These kinds of instruments develop their authority directly from the voluntary agreement of sovereign states.

It is accepted that only the UN Convention on the rights of the child has been approved generally and the agreements are not compulsory on those states which are not participants. The human rights legal framework changed as a means of limiting the arbitrary or excessive power of the state against the individual which causes the transformation in the nature of war and the state in the post-Cold War world to presents substantial challenges.

Particularly since the 1990s, the most acute threats may stop from lack of protection afforded by weak, failed or broken states, and the illogical or unnecessary use of force by non-state actors. It is necessary for the states to develop an effective agenda of international law that can be applied generally - across contexts and across the increasingly blurred divide between peace and war.

This agenda will be followed not only in all states but also by the non-state actors. The major concern of the International human rights law is to develop a strong relationship between the individual and the state in times of peace; its direct application to situations of armed conflict or violent insecurity is limited.

The states which follow the humanitarian law are permitted to derogate from certain civil and political rights under conditions of 'public emergency' and except for a certain core of fundamental rights laid down in each treaty, including the right to life, the prohibition on torture and inhuman punishment or treatment, the prohibition on slavery, and the principle of non-discrimination.

However, it could be argued that even fundamental, inalienable rights, such as the right to life, are certainly violated by war. Since human rights are not based on a particular context, determining what constitutes arbitrary deprivation of life requires a greater level of detail than the provisions of human rights law provide.

7.7.2. Humanitarian Law and Conflict

In the Year 1949, it announced that the IHL is alive in the Geneva agreements, nearly universally ratified, and their additional protocols of 1977. The second additional Protocol applies to situations of non-international conflict and builds on the provisions of Common Article 3 of the 1949 Geneva Conventions.

Some of the Protocol's provisions constitute principles of customary law and so are binding on all parties to a civil war. Common Article 3 itself has customary legal status and provides a core minimum set of protective provisions for those who take no direct part in hostilities. To protect the human rights, humanitarian law is designed specifically for situations of armed conflict, and it happens because of two main reasons;

- Firstly, it is applied to specific categories of people (prisoners of war, the wounded and sick, non-combatants, and civilians), by their protected status under the law but it does not apply to all humans by quality of their humanity; and
- Secondly, human rights have never successfully been surrounded within the legal duties of humanitarian law.

The Rights which are discussed by IHL are derived from the duties which the law executes. The focus is on the obligations of duty-bearers but not on the rights of the individuals.

The scope of IHL is much finer than human rights, and humanitarian law does not offer individual redress or compensation to individuals based on rights, and it does not address many of the human rights protected in the agreements.

Even so, it is founded that IHL is better than human rights law to realize basic rights in conflict. There are some examples of IHL such as ban on starvation as a weapon of war, and a duty on those in control of a territory both to provide for a population's needs and to permit external relief.

7.7.3. Toward a Convergence between Human Rights and Humanitarian Law

The both IHL and human rights law have failed to provide a suitable legal framework for the safety of human rights conflict. In recognition of this, agencies, and advocates day by day increasingly draw on both bodies of law to find the best legal means available.

IHL is used to interpret the meaning of human rights provisions during conflict and requirements on the indiscriminate use of landmines, or the use of chemical weapons have been used to understand the human rights prohibition against the arbitrary deprivation of life. In this sense, IHL has been understood as a complement to human rights law.

In recent years, the importance of IHL was also accepted by the human rights organizations. In 1996, Amnesty International used IHL to judge a government military action for the first time in southern Lebanon. Since that time, much of the advocacy work of international human rights and humanitarian agencies has highlighted a meeting between the two bodies of law, and it cannot be seen as a major difference between IHL and Human Rights Law.

7.8. CASE STUDY

7.8.1. Addressing Human Trafficking and Child Labor in West African Cocoa

- **Organization:** International Cocoa Initiative (ICI);
- **Sector:** Agriculture;
- **Commodity:** Cocoa;
- **Location:** Ghana, Ivory Coast.

7.8.1.1. Background

Established in 2002, the ICI is a multi-stakeholder partnership that brings together major chocolate brands, cocoa processors, labor unions and NGOs in an effort to eliminate child and forced labor in cocoa growing. Corporate members include ADM, Barry Callebaut, Cargill, Cadbury Schweppes, Ferrero, Ferrara Pan Candy, Hershey Foods, Kraft Foods, ICA, Mars Incorporated, Nestlé, and Toms.

7.8.1.2. The Issue

In the recent past, there have been cases of child trafficking and adult forced labor reported in the West African cocoa sector. These have occurred in the context of well-established and complex social and cultural relationships.

7.8.1.3. Responses and Results

The ICI takes a multi-stakeholder approach to tackling the problems of child and forced labor, and human trafficking in the cocoa sector. It works at national, industry, and community levels with business, unions, and civil society groups to raise awareness, develop effective and sustainable policies, build local capacity and change attitudes.

It also helps support groups that provide social protection to victims of exploitation. With a community-based focus, ICI sensitizes cocoa-growing communities about abusive labor practices such as trafficking, child labor, and forced labor, and helps them plan how best to ensure these practices are eliminated.

ICI draws on the support of others to invest in the community and to improve farming, infrastructure, and other needs. As part of this approach, the organization provides training not only to global buyers and local farmers, but also to cocoa boards, key government agencies, cooperatives, local NGOs, and the media.

The following are among the key responses and results of engagement by ICI and its implementing partners:

- Over 7,000 community mobilization meetings have been organized on the issue of child labor, including trafficking. This outreach has sensitized over 250,000 community members.
- 1,625 key people in the public, private, and civil society sectors have been trained on child and forced labor through almost 70 training programs.
- Local communities have implemented 476 initiatives to reduce the vulnerability of children to child labor and trafficking, including new by-laws, school rehabilitation and recruitment of teachers.
- Local authorities have supported communities with 220 new initiatives to support the implementation of Community Plans of Action.
- New or rehabilitated school blocks have become available in 129 communities, representing an additional 329 classrooms and benefiting 16,450 pupils.

7.8.2. Mobilizing Business in the Fight against Human Trafficking

- **Company:** Manpower Inc.;
- **Sector:** Employment services;
- **Location:** Colombia.

7.8.2.1. Background

With the financial support of the Embassy of Belgium in Colombia, IOM developed a project in 2007 and 2008 to prevent human trafficking amongst internally displaced persons (IDP) in Medellín, Colombia's second largest city. The project focused on preventing sexual exploitation of women and the forced recruitment of children by illegal armed groups by enhancing training and employment opportunities for potential victims.

Manpower, Inc. – the global workforce solutions company – was the first company to sign the Athens Ethical Principles, which articulate a "zero tolerance" policy towards trafficking in human beings. In October 2007, the company signed an "Expression of interest for the implementation of joint actions aimed at the prevention of human trafficking" with IOM Colombia.

At that time, Workforce joined IOM to support the anti-trafficking project in Medellín. This engagement was part of a larger program initiated by Manpower Colombia called JóvenesVisionarios (Visionary Young People), in which over 250 youths have participated since 2007.

7.8.2.2. The Issue

IDP in Colombia – a group mainly composed of women and young people – are disproportionately affected by unemployment, discrimination, and lack of access to training opportunities to enter the labor market; they are therefore among the groups in the country that are most vulnerable to human trafficking.

7.8.2.3. Responses and Results

Workforce, as part of its overall corporate responsibility strategy, has developed program to help disadvantaged groups such as IDPs gain access to training and employment opportunities. Its Jóvenes Visionaries program targets different groups of endangered and isolated youth, including orphans, young people in foster care and, beginning in 2010, deportees from other countries who have been returned to Colombia.

The common thread that unites these groups is Manpower's effort to assist young people who are approaching the age of 18 and must transition from government support to legal independence. Building on its prior engagement, Manpower, and IOM joined forces to provide training to 30 youth vulnerable to human trafficking to enhance their skills, education, and employability.

Workforce provided the necessary training facilities, equipment, technology, and trainers, while IOM identified the group of trainees, assisted in training, and contributed to the economic and material resources required by trainees. Program participants received:

- A vocational assessment and appropriate guidance on choosing a career;
- Online training relevant to the chosen career path;
- Access to an online library of more than 5000 courses in areas like business skills and professional development;

- IT training, including computer and desktop software literacy.

Participants also received counseling from a professional psychologist on the transition to independence and the adjustment to work; training in social skills appropriate for the workplace; guidance on job search strategies, including job interview techniques; and direct job placement assistance, linking program participants with vacant positions at Manpower's clients.

Manpower and IOM conducted follow-up with each participant of the program to track his or her progress after the course; and, although the period of intensive service is generally about 8 months, program experience has shown that candidates benefit from the support relationship for as long as 5 years. Of the 19 candidates for which information is currently available, 12 are employed, with 8 having been placed in jobs directly through Workforce; 3 are unemployed, and 4 are continuing with further training and education.

REFERENCES

1. Hauck, P., & Peterke, S., (2010). *Organized Crime and Gang Violence in National and International law*. [eBook] International review of the Red Cross, p. 30. Available at: https://pdfs.semanticscholar.org/4e46/0ba56e9b66aad093d2921bd73528b07ade90.pdf (Accessed on 12 April 2019).
2. *Human Trafficking and Business: Good Practices to Prevent and Combat Human Trafficking*, (2010). [eBook] p. 68. Available at: https://www.ilo.org/wcmsp5/groups/public/---ed_norm/---declaration/documents/publication/wcms_142722.pdf (Accessed on 12 April 2019).
3. Humanrights.gov.au., (n.d.). *Submission - Impact of Organized Crime,* (2007). Australian Human Rights Commission. [online] Available at: https://www.humanrights.gov.au/submission-impact-organised-crime-2007 (Accessed on 12 April 2019).
4. *International Humanitarian Law and the Challenges of Contemporary Armed Conflicts*, (2004). [eBook] p. 32. Available at: https://www.icrc.org/eng/assets/files/other/irrc_853_fd_ihl_challenge.pdf (Accessed on 12 April 2019).
5. Lee, M., (n.d.). *SAGE Books - Trafficking and Transnational Organized Crime*. [online] Sk.sagepub.com. Available at: http://sk.sagepub.com/books/trafficking-and-global-crime-control/n5.xml (Accessed on 12 April 2019).
6. Ohchr.org., (n.d.). *OHCHR | Human Rights and Trafficking in Persons*. [online] Available at: https://www.ohchr.org/EN/Issues/Trafficking/TiP/Pages/Index.aspx (Accessed on 12 April 2019).
7. Sassòli, M., (2006). *Transnational Armed Groups and International Humanitarian Law*. [eBook] occasional paper series, p.50. Available at: https://www.uio.no/studier/emner/jus/humanrights/HUMR5503/h09/undervisningsmateriale/sassoli_transnational_armed_groups_and_ihl.pdf (Accessed on 12 April 2019).
8. Truong, T., (2001). *Human Trafficking and Organized Crime*. [eBook] p. 30. Available at: https://www.researchgate.net/profile/Thanh_Dam_Truong/publication/5130620_Human_trafficking_and_organised_crime/links/0a85e5319a6b767c1c000000/Human-trafficking-and-organised-crime.pdf?origin=publication_detail (Accessed on 12 April 2019).

9. Unodc.org., (n.d.). *United Nations Convention Against Transnational Organized Crime*. [online] Available at: http://www.unodc.org/unodc/en/organized-crime/intro/UNTOC.html (Accessed on 12 April 2019).

8

The International Perspective on Policing Transnational Organized Crime

CONTENTS

In this chapter Globalized illegal economy and hidden cost to society with respect to Transnational Organized Crime (TOC) are very well explained. Different Forms of TOC like Drug Trafficking, Human Trafficking, Smuggling of Migrants, Illicit Trading in Firearms, Sale of Fraudulent Medicines, and Cybercrime are briefly explained form international point of view. This Chapter describes key U.S. programs, initiatives, and legislation to combat transnational crime. It provides additional information on the five criminal areas. Priority actions and strategy to combat TOC are explicitly described in this chapter.

8.1. THE GLOBALIZED ILLEGAL ECONOMY

The falsely depicted picture of organized crime is far from the truth. The truth is less as shown in Hollywood, and far more about fluid organized criminal networks which makes money from the sale of illegal goods everyplace there is a demand. At present, there are more complex and anonymous international illegal markets than ever, and each year make earning in billions of dollars.

TOC is large business. In 2009 it was estimated to generate $870 billion which is approximately equal to the 1.5 per cent of global GDP (United Nations office on drugs and crime, estimating illicit financial flows resulting from drug trafficking and other transnational organized crimes: Research report, 2011), which accounts to more than 6 times the amount of official development assistance in the year 2009, and approximately equivalent to 7% of the world's exports of goods.

8.2. HIDDEN COST TO SOCIETY

TOC includes nearly all serious profit-motivated criminal actions of significant global nature where more than one country is involved. There are many activities that can be characterized as TOC (Figure 8.1), including:

- Drug trafficking;
- Money-laundering;
- Smuggling of migrants;
- Human trafficking;
- Wildlife and cultural property;

- Counterfeit goods;
- Trafficking in firearms;
- Some aspects of cybercrime.

These activities result in following:

- Threatens peace and human security;
- Leads to human rights being violated;
- Weakens the political, economic, social, cultural, and civil development of societies around the world.

Figure 8.1: Secret service and DEA agents investigate major drug trafficking conspiracies.

Source: http://coastguard.dodlive.mil/2012/08/california-crackdown-takes-seizures-over-50-ton-mark/

The enormous amount of money involved can compromise legitimate economies and have a straight influence on governance, such as through corruption and the "buying" of elections. Every year, due to organized crime countless lives are lost (Figure 8.2), which encompasses:

- Drug-related health problems and violence;
- Firearm deaths;
- Unscrupulous methods and motives of human traffickers;

- Migrant smugglers.

Figure 8.2: Human smuggling through waterways.

Source: http://coastguard.dodlive.mil/files/2011/03/Haitian-migrant-interdiction.jpg

Millions of victims are affected every year because of the activities of organized crime groups.

8.3. DIFFERENT FORMS OF TRANSNATIONAL ORGANIZED CRIME (TOC)

TOC is not stagnant, but is an ever-changing industry, adapting to markets and creating new forms of crime. In short, it is an illicit business that transcends cultural, social, linguistic, and geographical boundaries and one that knows no borders or rules.

8.3.1. Drug Trafficking

The most lucrative form of business for criminals is drug trafficking, with an estimated annual value of $320 billion. In 2009, United Nations Office on Drugs and Crime (UNODC) placed the estimated annual worth of the global cocaine and opiate markets alone at $85 billion and $68 billion, respectively (World Drug Report, 2011) (Figure 8.3).

Figure 8.3: Drug trafficking.

Source: https://upload.wikimedia.org/wikipedia/commons/1/1b/US_Navy_040101-N-2295R-006_Over_2%2C800_pounds_of_narcotics%2C_believed_to_be_hashish_was_seized.jpg

8.3.2. Human Trafficking

Human trafficking is an international crime where men, women, and children are used as products for labor-based or sexual exploitation. International Labor Organization (ILO) in 2005 has made an estimate which indicates the number of victims of trafficking at any given time to be around 2.4 million, with annual profits of about $32 billion.[1] Recent studies on general forced labor trends, however, would signifies that the scope of the problem is much bigger.[2]

As stated by UNODC in Europe, the trafficking of mostly women and children for sexual exploitation alone brings in $3 billion annually and involves 140,000 victims at any one time, with an annual flow of 70,000 victims (United Nations Office on Drugs and Crime, 2010).

1 www.ilo.org/wcmsp5/ groups/public/@ed_

2 http://www.ilo.org/sapfl/Informationresources/ILOPublications/WCMS_182004/lang--en/index.htm

8.3.3. Smuggling of Migrants

Smuggling of migrants is a well-organized business moving people around the globe through criminal groups, networks, and routes. Organized crime groups offer migrants a "smuggling package," and corresponding to the price migrants pay to the smugglers and accordingly they get their treatment along the route. In the process of being smuggled, migrants' rights are generally breached, and they can get robbed, raped, beaten, held for money or even left to die in many cases, when the risks get too high for the smugglers (Figure 8.4).

Figure 8.4: Smuggling of migrants.

Source: http://coastguard.dodlive.mil/files/2011/11/100422-G-0000A-001.jpg

Many smugglers do not care if migrants drown in the sea, die of dehydration in a desert or suffocate in a container. Every year this trade is valued at billions of dollars. In 2009 some $6.6 billion was generated through the illegal smuggling of 3 million migrants from Latin America to North America (The Globalization of Crime: A Transnational Organized Crime Threat Assessment, 2010), while the previous year 55,000 migrants were smuggled from Africa into Europe for a sum of $150 million.

8.3.4. Illicit Trading in Firearms

According to UNODC, illegal trading of weapons makes around $170 million to $320 million yearly and supply firearms and assault rifles to criminals and mobs. To count the victims of these illegal weapons is hard, but in some regions like the America, there is a strong correlation between homicide rates and the percentage of homicides by firearms (United Nations Office on Drugs and Crime, 2011) (Figure 8.5).

Figure 8.5: Illicit trading in firearms.

Source: https://upload.wikimedia.org/wikipedia/commons/5/50/Norway%27s_WW2_Resistance_Museum%2C_Oslo_%28Hjemmefrontmuseet%29._Illegal_handmade_arms_-_Stengun_%28detail_from_exhibition%29._Photo_2017-11-30_b.jpg

Natural resources trafficking comprise the trafficking of raw materials like diamonds and rare metals (often from conflict zones). In South-East Asia, the trafficking of timber makes annual revenue of $3.5 billion (The globalization of crime: A transnational organized crime threat assessment). In addition to the funding criminal groups, this strand of criminal activity leads to:

- Deforestation;
- Climate change;
- Rural poverty.

Another lucrative business for organized criminal groups is the illegal trade in wildlife, poachers aiming for skins and body parts of wild animal for the purpose of exporting them to foreign markets. Trafficking in elephant ivory, rhino horn and tiger parts from Africa and South-East Asia to Asia produces $75 million in criminal profits each year and threatens the existence of some species.

Organized crime groups also deal in live and rare animal species and plant species and threatening their very existence to meet demand from collectors or unwitting consumers. According to the World Wildlife Fund (WWF), traffickers illegally move over 440,000 tons of medicinal plants, 100 million tons of fish and 1.5 million live birds and per year.[3]

8.3.5. Sale of Fraudulent Medicines

The most worrying business is the sale of fraudulent medicines, as it denotes a possible deadly trade for consumers. In pharmaceutical industries, piggybacking is on the rising legitimate trade from Asia to other emerging nations, criminals' traffic fraudulent medicines from Asia, in particular to South-East Asia and Africa to the value of $1.6 billion (Globalization of crime: A transnational organized crime threat assessment).

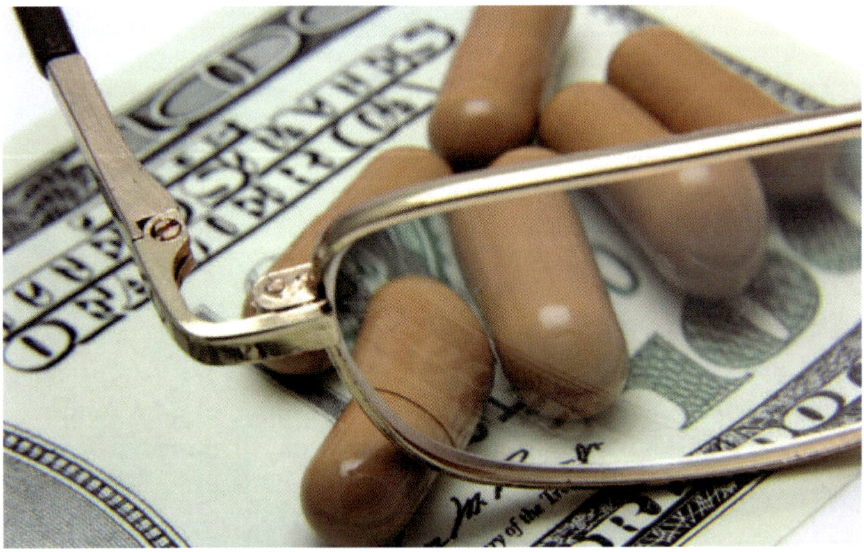

Figure 8.6: Sale of fraudulent medicines.

Source: https://torange.biz/photo/19/IMAGE/money-medicament-sale-medicines-19330.jpg

3 http://wwf.panda.org/about_our_earth/species/problems/illegal_ trade/

Instead of curing people, these activities can outcome in death or cause resistance to drugs which are used to cure deadly infectious diseases like tuberculosis and malaria. Criminals continue to build a lucrative online trade in fraudulent medicines in addition to conventional trafficking methods, targeting both developing and developed nations alike that lead to health allegations for consumers (Figure 8.6).

8.3.6. Cybercrime

Cybercrime includes several areas, but identity theft is one of the most profitable for criminals, which account for around $1 billion each year. Criminals are increasingly exploiting the Internet to steal private data, access bank accounts and fraudulently attain payment card details (Figure 8.7).

Figure 8.7: Cybercrime.

Source: https://cdn.pixabay.com/photo/2017/10/24/07/12/hacker-2883632_960_720.jpg

8.4. GLOBAL THREATS AND LOCAL EFFECTS

Although TOC is an international threat, but its effects are suffered locally. As soon as organized crime expands its root it can threaten countries and entire regions, thus decrease development assistance in these areas. Organized crime groups can also work with local criminals, leading to an increase in:

- Corruption;
- Racketeering and violence;
- Extortion; and
- Range of other more sophisticated crimes at the local level.

Violent gangs can also change inner cities into dangerous areas and place citizens' lives at risk.

In the developing and the developed world's organized crime affects people. Through banking systems money is being laundered. Individuals are become victims of identity theft, around 1.5 million people each year being caught out. In many developed nations, criminal groups traffic women and use them for sexual exploitation and children for purposes of:

- Forced begging;
- Burglary;
- Pickpocketing.

Car stealing is also considered as an organized business, with vehicles stolen to order and transport abroad. Fraudulent food products and medicines are supplied to the licit market, and this not only defraud the public but places their lives and health in danger. Added to this is the trade in fake products, which deprives countries of tax revenues. This makes an impact on legitimate firms when illegally make goods displace sales of original products, which in turn harms employer earnings.

Organized crime makes public to increase their spending for security and policing which weakens the very human rights standards that many nations try to preserve, mainly activities such as human trafficking in human beings, extortion, and kidnapping are taken into consideration. This also leads to increase in local crime, which in turn increase cost of insurance premiums and adds to the general level of criminality and insecurity in society.

8.4.1. Ways in Which Money is Laundered

The profits of most crimes are made in cash, and for criminals, this is very risky due to following reasons:

- Cash is difficult to hide;
- Cash increases the probability of exposure;
- Theft by rival criminals or can be seizure by the police.

Cash when enters to the legitimate economy, it is mainly susceptible to identification and law enforcement intervention. As an outcome, criminals move to prevent cash from attracting suspicion. For illustration, criminals may move their money to abroad, or might use cash to buy other assets or attempt to turn their cash into the legitimate economy by the means of businesses that have a high turnover in cash.

As an integral part of TOC, it is estimated that some 70 percent of illegal profits are likely to have been laundered through the financial system. Yet less than 1 percent of those laundered proceeds money is captured and confiscated (United Nations office on drugs and crime, estimating illicit financial flows resulting from drug trafficking).

8.4.2. Putting Organized Crime Out of Business

Partnerships are required at all levels for combating a worldwide phenomenon such as TOC. Everyone has to participate against organized crime including Governments, businesses, civil society, international organizations and people present in all corners of the world. In fighting organized crime some aspects are very important, which includes:

- **Coordination:** Integrated action at the international level is crucial in identifying, investigating, and prosecuting the people and groups behind these crimes.
- **Education and awareness-raising:** Ordinary citizens should learn more about organized crime and how it affects everyday lives. Express your concerns to policy and decision makers so that this truly global threat is considered by politicians to be a top priority among the public's major concerns.
- **Consumers also have a key role to play:** Know what you are purchasing, do so ethically and make sure that you do not fuel organized crime.
- **Intelligence and technology:** Criminal justice systems and conventional law enforcement methods are often no match for powerful criminal networks. Better intelligence methods need to be developed through the training of more specialized law enforcement units, which should be equipped with state-of-the-art technology.
- **Assistance:** Emerging nations requires assistance in developing their capacity to counter these threats. United Nations Convention against Transnational Organized Crime (UNTOC) is an essential tool that can help, United Nations UNTOC has been ratified

by 170 parties[4] and offers a universal legal framework to help recognize, prevent, and dismantle organized criminal groups.

In October 2012, United Nations UNTOC was held in Vienna, the sixth session of the Conference of the Parties. These types of biennial series of meetings brings Governments from across the world together to encourage and examine the execution of the Convention to make sure better implementation in undertaking this international issue.

At a practical level, UNODC helps in reinforce the capacity of States to avoid and track money-laundering with training and technical assistance for following the money trail. These measures can help to reduce the profits generated through criminal activities.

8.5. COMBATING TRANSNATIONAL ORGANIZED CRIME THROUGH BETTER INTERNATIONAL CO-OPERATION

There is a need to strengthen international cooperation due to the globalization of criminal activities. The investigation, prosecution, and control of crime cannot be limited within national boundaries. To keep pace with contemporary forms of crime, including TOC, corruption, and terrorism, there is a need to improve and streamline mechanisms.

More concerted efforts are needed in:

- Extradition;
- Mutual legal assistance;
- Transfer of sentenced persons;
- Transfer of criminal proceedings;
- International cooperation for purposes of confiscation;
- Including asset recovery;
- International law enforcement cooperation.

4 http://treaties.un.org/Pages/ViewDetails.spx?src=TREATY&mtdsg_no=XVIII–12&chapter=18&lang=en

8.6. THE ROLE OF UNITED NATIONS CONVENTIONS

United Nations multilateral instruments help in harmonizing international cooperation standards. The United Nations UNTOC and its additional Protocols and the United Nations Convention against Corruption were implemented following the precedent of the 1988 Drug Trafficking Convention (the United Nations Convention against Illicit Traffic in Narcotic Drugs and Psychotropic Substances), to establish rules, institutions, and shared responsibility to combat transnational crime.

They play a key role in harmonizing responsibilities and addressing legal gaps in global cooperation in criminal matters. For illustration, these instruments offer a foundation for extradition and mutual legal assistance. There is almost universal adherence to the three crime-related conventions. As of 5 December 2014, the 1988 Drug Trafficking Convention had 189 parties, the United Nations UNTOC 183 parties and the United Nations Convention against Corruption 174 parties.

8.7. UNITED NATIONS MULTILATERAL INSTRUMENTS AS CATALYSTS FOR FURTHER INTERNATIONAL COOPERATION

To increase the effectiveness of international cooperation, the universal crime-related conventions boost States parties to conclude bilateral and multilateral agreements. The ultimate objective is to improve international cooperation through broadening the range of legal bases on which States can rely through a combined use of multilateral and bilateral agreements. The model treaties developed through the United Nations Crime Congresses have offered guidance towards convergence of related treaty provisions. The Model Treaty on Extradition and the Model Treaty on Mutual Assistance in Criminal Matters, in particular, are valuable tools for the development of bilateral and multilateral arrangements in the area of judicial cooperation.

The UNODC has also developed tools that promote and support international cooperation in criminal matters, including the Directory of Competent Authorities, the Mutual Legal Assistance Request Writer Tool and, most recently, the knowledge management portal known as SHERLOC (Sharing Electronic Resources and Laws against Crime). UNODC also runs the Counter-Terrorism Online Learning Platform, which provides a gateway to practitioners (mostly criminal justice and law enforcement) for networking, exchanging information and sharing best practices.

8.8. THE REGIONAL PERSPECTIVE

The second half of the 20th century saw the arrival of regional agreements and schemes, mainly between States of the same region or those sharing common legal traditions. For illustration, the European Union Member States have decided, subject to specified grounds for refusal, to identify and implement European evidence and arrest warrants without any additional regulations. The Caribbean Community (CARICOM) also has an arrest warrant treaty.

8.8.1. Central and Competent National Authorities

The ability to timely request and responds to worldwide cooperation requests is most important, provided the serious nature of the Offenses and their transnational nature. Under the crime-related conventions, States parties elect central and capable authorities to enable international cooperation in the matters of criminal. The sending, receiving, and processing of requests are coordinated by these authorities. The most commonly designated central authorities for mutual legal assistance are:

- Ministries of justice;
- Offices of the attorney-general;
- Ministries of foreign affairs.

States have extensively shown their experiences of effective central authorities, such as:

- The importance of around-the-clock availability;
- Their competence for mutual legal assistance purposes under different treaties;
- Quality control of requests.

The extent to which central authorities are able to perform an effective coordination role is also dependent upon the availability of:

- Infrastructure;
- Staffing;
- Training opportunities.

UNODC has offered technical assistance to Member States to improve their capacity to deal rapidly and efficiently with mutual legal assistance requests and enable international cooperation.

8.8.2. Regional Cooperation Networks

International cooperation can be enhanced through regional networks. UNODC supports Member States in setting up networks of prosecutors and central authorities, such as:

- The Central American Network of Prosecutors against Organized Crime (REFCO);
- Prosecutors against Organized Crime (WACAP);
- The Network of West African Central Authorities.

8.8.3. Enhancing International Cooperation

The Thirteenth Crime Congress will consider further opportunities to broaden the range of legal bases on which Member States can rely for international cooperation in criminal matters, to build on the existing framework of international conventions and regional treaties.

8.9. U.S. EFFORTS AGAINST TRANSNATIONAL ORGANIZED CRIME: AGENCY ROLES AND CONGRESSIONAL ACTION

8.9.1. Weapon of Mass Destruction (WMD) Smuggling

U.S. anti-nuclear smuggling efforts are coordinated by the Departments of (Figure 8.8):

- State and defense departments;
- Energy departments;
- Homeland security departments;
- Commerce departments.

Figure 8.8: Smuggling of weapon of mass destruction (WMD).

Source: https://upload.wikimedia.org/wikipedia/commons/7/7e/US_Navy_030323-N-4142G-042_Bunker_Buster_bombs_are_staged_in_the_hangar_bay_aboard_USS_Constellation_%28CV_64%29.jpg

8.9.2. State and Defense Departments

These agencies lead coordination of the Proliferation Security Initiative. Announced by United State of America President in May 2003, it builds international agreements and partnerships to permit the United States and its allies to search planes and ships suspected of carrying nuclear material or technologies.

In addition, the United States Department of Defense managed Cooperative Threat Reduction program works to destroy nuclear weapons, especially in the former Soviet Union. The State Department also funds the International Science and Technology Centers in Russia and Ukraine to help employ scientists with non-weapons related projects.

8.9.3. Energy Department

United States Department of Energy runs several programs to secure nuclear weapons and weapons-usable nuclear materials.

The International Materials Protection, Control, and Accounting program works in the former Soviet Union and other countries. Its activities include upgrading security at nuclear sites, consolidating material into more secure locations, and improving nuclear smuggling detection capabilities at borders. The President's Financial Year 2007 budget requests about $1.12 billion for Energy, State, and Defense Department programs that provide nonproliferation and threat reduction assistance to Russia and other former Soviet states.

This compares to about $1.02 billion appropriated in Financial Year 2006. The Financial Year 2007 request includes $372.1 million for United States Department of Defense's Cooperative Threat Reduction programs, down from $415.5 million in Financial Year 2006. The request includes $675 million for Energy Department WMD threat-reduction efforts, up from $530 in Financial Year 2006. It also calls for $75 million in comparable State Department funding, up from $71 million in Financial Year 2006 (CRS Report RL31957).

8.9.4. Homeland Security Department

The goal of the Container Security Initiative launched in January 2002 by the former U.S. Customs Service (now part of DHS) is to increase inspection of the approximately seven million shipping containers entering the U.S. annually. DHS's Customs and Border Protection (CBP) is generally charged with protecting U.S. borders from incoming nuclear material. Its efforts include border patrols, seaport security, and customs inspections. DHS also leads interagency efforts to develop technology to protect the United States from WMD threats.

8.9.5. Commerce Department

Commerce's Bureau of Industry and Security (BIS) is responsible for safeguarding U.S. national security and for promoting its foreign policy and economic interests by implementing U.S. export-control policy on dual-use commodities, software, and technology. As part of the State Department's Export Control and Related Border Security Assistance Program (EXBS), BIS helps other countries develop and enforce effective export controls through workshops, training, and other activities.

8.9.5.1. Legislative Activity

Several nuclear black market-related proposals are contained in the Foreign Relations Authorization Act for Financial Year 2006 and Financial Year 2007. Title VIII, the Nuclear Black-Market Elimination Act, has four basic components. These are:

- Sanctions;
- Penalties for corporate entities associated with proliferation activities;
- Incentives for proliferation-interdiction cooperation; and
- Nonproliferation conditions required to receive United States assistance.

Another H.R. 2601 section calls for the U.S. government to ask Pakistan for direct access to A.Q. Khan in order to further investigate his nuclear smuggling activities.

8.9.5.2. Drug Trafficking

A number of United States agencies, coordinated mainly by the State Department's Bureau of International Narcotics and Law Enforcement Affairs (INL), run anti-drug programs and initiatives. United State anti-narcotics efforts center mainly on global narcotics interdiction and foreign crop eradication. The State Department and other agencies help eradicate crops by providing foreign countries with equipment and supplies.

8.9.5.3. State Department

The State Department's Bureau of INL Enforcement Affairs manages the Andean Counterdrug Initiative (ACI), the primary U.S. program supporting counternarcotics and economic development in the Andean region. ACI funding from Financial Year 2000 through Financial Year 2004 totals about $3.5 billion. Congress appropriated $731 million for Airports Council International in Financial Year 2005; $734.5 million was approved for Financial Year 2006. The White House is requesting $721.5 million for Financial Year 2007.

INL also leads other agencies in training and assisting foreign law enforcement, managing interagency coordination of programs such as the International Law Enforcement Academies (ILEAs). ILEAs train foreign personnel and promote international legal cooperation. They have trained over 13,000 officials from 68 countries in Africa, Asia, Europe, and Latin

America. The U.S. Agency for International Development (AID) also funds a variety of anti-narcotics programs. Many promote education, institutional development, and alternative employment for people involved in drug production. AID also provides balance of payments support to compensate countries (especially Andean) forgoing drug export revenue.

8.9.5.4. Justice Department

Drug Enforcement Agency (DEA) agents cooperate with law enforcement agencies in 58 countries in activities such as bilateral investigations, institution building, and training. In the Justice-led Southwest Border Initiative (SWBI), several federal agencies work to combat Mexico- and Colombia based trafficking groups operating along the Southwest Border.

Working in concert, the DEA, the FBI, the U.S. Customs Service, and U.S. Attorneys' offices around the country conduct wiretaps aimed at tracking drug movements and identifying traffickers. DEA and other Justice Department officials play a central role in bringing smugglers to face justice in the United States through extradition, a significant judicial tool in combating narcotics.

8.9.6. Defense Department

United States Department of Defense responsibilities include heading federal efforts to detect aerial and maritime drug trafficking toward the United States. United States Department of Defense analysts also work with DEA and other United State agents to execute anti-narcotics actions in key drug production and transit countries.

8.9.6.1. Legislative Activity

The Financial Year 2006 Foreign Operations Appropriations Act authorizes $734.5 million for ACI in Financial Year 2006. In addition, the Financial Year 2006 National Defense Authorization Act, signed by the President on January 6, 2006, approves $901.7 million for Defense Department global drug interdiction. Unlike the Financial Year 2005 authorization, it did not involve provisions concerning to Colombia or the ACI.

8.9.6.2. Trafficking in Persons

Interagency anti-trafficking efforts are led by the State Department. Other agencies also play key roles including:

- The Departments of Justice;
- Health and Human Services;
- Homeland Security;
- Labor.

8.9.6.3. State Department

The Victims of Trafficking and Violence Protection Act of 2000, signed into law October 28, 2000, contained several key anti-trafficking provisions. One established an annual State Department Trafficking in Persons Report. First issued in July 2001, it reviews anti-trafficking trends and rates countries' anti-trafficking efforts.

P.L. 106–386 also authorizes the President to impose sanctions, under the International Emergency Economic Powers Act (P.L. 95–223), against countries that do not meet anti-trafficking "minimum standards" (Trafficking and Violence Protection Act of 2000 and the Trafficking Victims Protection Reauthorization Act of 2003). Also authorized was the Interagency Task Force to Monitor and Combat Trafficking in Persons. Created in 2002, it includes the Secretary of State, the Attorney General, the Secretary of Labor, and other top officials. It receives assistance from the State Department Office to Monitor and Combat Trafficking in Persons.

8.9.6.4. Justice Department

The Trafficking in Persons and Worker Exploitation Task Force, established by the Justice and Labor Departments, is charged with coordinating anti-trafficking investigations and prosecutions. On January 24, 2002, the Attorney General announced the implementation of a special "T" visa, authorized under P.L. 106–386, to assist trafficking victims cooperating with law enforcement officials. Victims facing significant retribution or other risks upon returning abroad may be granted permission to remain in the United States and are eligible to apply for permanent residency after three years.

8.9.7. Legislative Activity in the 109th Congress

On October 7, 2005, the Senate ratified the United Nations Protocol to Prevent, Suppress, and Punish Trafficking in Persons (United Nations, protocol to prevent, suppress, and punish trafficking in persons), to which the United States became a party on December 3, 2005. Currently, 113 countries have signed the Protocol, with 94 countries party to the agreement. On January 10, 2006, the President signed the Trafficking Victims Protection Reauthorization Act of 2005 (P.L. 109–164). Among other things, the bill aims to assist foreign trafficking victims in the United States, address the needs of child victims, and develop anti-trafficking programs in post-conflict situations and foreign humanitarian emergencies. It authorizes $188 million in 2006 and $173 million in 2007 to combat human trafficking.

8.9.8. Intellectual Property (IP) Crimes

The Office of the United States Trade Representative (USTR) leads other agencies including the Departments of Commerce, State, Justice, and Homeland Security in combating IP violations.

8.9.9. USTR

A centerpiece of U.S. efforts to strengthen IP enforcement is the annual USTR-led "Special 301 process," (Omnibus Trade and Competitiveness Act) which seeks to identify countries lacking adequate intellectual property (IP) protection. If a trading partner is identified as a Priority Foreign Country (PFC), the USTR has 30 days to decide whether to investigate the countries' questionable policies. Such an investigation can lead to separate IP agreements with the PFC or to U.S. trade sanctions. USTR also manages several tariff preference programs, such as the Generalized System of Preferences (Trade and Tariff Act, 1984).

Many U.S. anti-piracy initiatives involve forging international agreements, often through the World Trade Organization (WTO). Through the WTO, the USTR can initiate dispute settlement proceedings against foreign governments and institutions; a stringent WTO membership application process also promotes tougher IP laws. Free trade agreements (FTA) help, too; FTA partner nations must bring their enforcement regimes up to U.S. legal standards, as mandated by the Bipartisan Trade Promotion Act of 2002 (P.L. 107–210).

In October 2004 the Administration launched the interagency Strategy Targeting Organized Piracy (STOP!), which aims to strengthen existing anti-piracy efforts and includes new actions such as the creation of a government IP complaint hotline.

8.9.10. Homeland Security Department

DHS's efforts include seizing pirated goods at U.S. borders and ports. According to the agency, it made more than 7,200 seizures valued at nearly $140 million in FY2004. Chinese goods comprised almost 70% of this value. DHS is developing a risk-assessment computer model to help target suspected shipments.

8.9.11. Legislative Activity

The 109th Congress has seen a number of legislative actions related to trade and IP violations. The United States Trade Rights Enforcement Act (H.R. 3283), for example, would boost funding and increase enforcement through several federal agencies. Among other things, it would authorize an additional $6 million for the USTR beyond the President's budget request for FY2006 and FY2007, for a total of $44.78 million and $47.02 million, respectively. H.R. 3283 passed on July 27, 2005. A similar bill, S. 1421, has been introduced in the Senate.

Another bill, H.R. 4186, would create a Chief Trade Prosecutor to ensure compliance with trade agreements. Separate legislation, S. 2317, would require the USTR to identify trade enforcement priorities, act with respect to PFC trade practices, and establish within the USTR's office a Chief Enforcement Officer and a Trade Enforcement Working Group (CRS Issue Brief IB91121).

8.9.12. Money Laundering

U.S. anti-money laundering (AML) efforts are coordinated by the Departments of Treasury, Justice, Homeland Security, and other agencies.

8.9.13. Department of Treasury

The Office of Terrorism and Financial Intelligence (TFI) and it's subsidiary bureaus safeguard domestic and foreign financial systems through financial sanctions, financial regulation and supervision, international initiatives, private sector outreach, law enforcement support, and other methods. TFI offices such as the Financial Crimes Enforcement Network (FinCEN) support U.S. law enforcement agencies in international financial crime investigations and provide U.S. policymakers with global money laundering analyses. FinCEN and other Treasury affiliates cooperate with 32 foreign government institutions to improve international money laundering standards through the Financial Action Task Force (FATF). FinCEN also participates in global AML networks. The Egmont Group is comprised of FinCEN and 100 similar international agencies. Egmont works to expand, systematize, and secure information sharing among its members.

8.9.14. Department of Justice (DOJ)

The Asset Forfeiture and Money Laundering Section guide's law enforcement agencies on money laundering-related investigations and prosecutions. It also coordinates multi-district investigations and prosecutions, develops regulatory and legislative initiatives, and ensures uniform application of forfeiture and money laundering statutes.

8.9.15. Homeland Security Department

U.S. Immigration and Customs Enforcement (ICE) manage a handful of money laundering programs and initiatives. It's Financial Investigative Program investigates money laundering crimes involving drugs, human smuggling, telemarketing fraud, and counterfeit goods trafficking. ICE's domestic and international money laundering operations are coordinated through its Money Laundering Coordination Center.

8.9.16. Legislative Activity

The USA PATRIOT Improvement and Reauthorization Act (P.L. 109–177, H.R. 3199), contains significant language on money laundering. Signed by President Bush on March 9, 2006, it will, among other things, increase penalties for financing terrorist activities and place greater restrictions on certain money-transferring businesses (CRS Report RS22400).

8.10. SHARED RESPONSIBILITY FOR TRANSNATIONAL ORGANIZED CRIME

- Reduce the demand for illicit drugs in the United States, thereby denying funding to illicit trafficking organizations.
- Continue to attack drug trafficking and distribution networks and their enabling means within the United States to reduce the availability of illicit drugs.
- Sever the illicit flow across U.S. borders of people, weapons,

currency, and other illicit finance through investigations and prosecutions of key TOC leadership, as well as through the targeting of TOC networks' enabling means and infrastructure.

- Identify and act against corporate and governmental corruption.
- Work with Congress to secure ratification of the Inter American Convention against the Illicit Manufacturing of and Trafficking in Firearms, Ammunition, Explosives, and Other Related Materials.
- Seek accession to the Protocol against the Illicit Manufacturing of and Trafficking in Firearms, their Parts and Components, and Ammunition, supplementing the UN UNTOC.

8.11. ENHANCE INTELLIGENCE AND INFORMATION SHARING

- Enhance U.S. intelligence collection, analysis, and counterintelligence on TOC entities that pose the greatest threat to national security.
- Develop greater synergies between intelligence analysts, collectors, and counterintelligence personnel; ensure their efforts directly support operational law enforcement needs and screening requirements.
- Strengthen ties among U.S. intelligence and counterintelligence, law enforcement, and military entities, while strengthening cooperation with international intelligence and law enforcement partners.
- Develop and foster stronger law enforcement and Intelligence Community relationships among Federal, State, local, tribal, and territorial authorities.
- Support multilateral senior law enforcement exchanges to promote the sharing of criminal intelligence and enhance cooperation, such as the "Quintet of Attorneys-General" and the "Strategic Alliance Group" for established with the United Kingdom, Canada, New Zealand, and Australia.
- Update the National Intelligence Priorities Framework to ensure that it is aligned with current TOC threats.
- Enhance support to Intelligence Community analysis of TOC by

the Office of the Director of National Intelligence, specifically by the National Intelligence Council and the National Intelligence Managers.

- The National Counterproliferation Center shall develop a plan that assesses the links between TOC and WMD proliferators.
- Create a comprehensive and proactive information-sharing mechanism to identify TOC actors and exclude them from the United States or uncover them within the United States.

8.12. PROTECT THE FINANCIAL SYSTEM AND STRATEGIC MARKETS AGAINST TRANSNATIONAL ORGANIZED CRIME

- Implement a new Executive Order to prohibit the transactions and block the assets under U.S. jurisdiction of TOC networks and their associates that threaten critical U.S. interests.
- Prevent or disrupt criminal involvement in emerging and strategic markets.
- Increase awareness and provide incentives and alternatives for the private sector to reduce facilitation of TOC.
- Develop a mechanism that would make unclassified data on TOC available to private sector partners.
- Implement the Administration's joint strategic plan on IP enforcement to target, investigate, and prosecute IP crimes committed by TOC.
- Enhance domestic and foreign capabilities to combat the increasing involvement of TOC networks in cybercrime and build international capacity to forensically exploit and judicially process digital evidence.
- Use authorities under the USA PATRIOT Act to designate foreign jurisdictions, institutions, or classes of transactions as "primary money-laundering concerns," allowing for the introduction of various restrictive measures on financial dealings by U.S. persons with those entities.
- Identify foreign kleptocrats who have corrupt relationships with TOC networks and target their assets for freezing, forfeiture, and

repatriation to victimized governments.

- Work with Congress to enact legislation to require disclosure of beneficial ownership information of legal entities at the time of company formation in order to enhance transparency for law enforcement and other purposes.
- Support the work of the FATF, which sets and enforces global standards to combat both money laundering and the financing of terrorism.

8.13. STRENGTHEN INTERDICTION, INVESTIGATIONS, AND PROSECUTIONS

- Work with Congress to enhance U.S. authorities to identify, investigate, interdict, and prosecute top transnational criminal networks.
- Utilize rewards programs to assist in gathering information leading to the arrest or conviction of top transnational criminals.
- Issue a new Presidential Proclamation under the Immigration and Nationality Act to refuse visas/ deny entry to TOC-affiliated aliens, corrupt foreign officials, and other persons designated for financial sanctions pursuant to the International Emergency Economic Powers Act.
- Develop a strategy that denies TOC networks and individuals in the United States access to their infrastructure and their enabling means.
- Deny visas to TOC members and associates and capture top TOC figures who take refuge in the United States or partner countries.
- Fully integrate financial, weapons, and TOC-related corruption investigations into comprehensive organizational attack activities and operations.
- Strengthen cooperation with international police organizations, such as Interpol, Europol, Ameripol, and the International Association of Chiefs of Police (IACP), to facilitate cross-border police cooperation.
- Strengthen efforts to interdict illicit trafficking in the air and maritime domains.

- Develop and implement a whole-of-government plan to counter kidnapping for ransom in order to disrupt the funding for terrorists, pirates, and other bad actors.
- Deny TOC access to secure facilities and locations.

8.14. DISRUPT DRUG TRAFFICKING AND ITS FACILITATION OF OTHER TRANSNATIONAL THREATS

- Work with international partners to reduce the global supply of and demand for illegal drugs and thereby deny funding to TOC networks.
- Sever the links between the international illicit drug and arms trades, especially in strategic regions that are at risk of being destabilized by these interconnected threats.
- Sustain pressure to disrupt Consolidated Priority Organization Targets, as they often have a particularly corrupting influence or provide support to terrorism.
- Maximize use of the Kingpin Act to pursue transnational drug organizations.
- Develop a comprehensive approach to dismantle DTOs with connections to terrorist organizations.
- Work with international partners to shut down emerging drug transit routes and associated corruption in West Africa.
- Coordinate with international partners to prevent synthetic drug production, trafficking, and precursor chemical diversion.

8.15. BUILD INTERNATIONAL CAPACITY, COOPERATION, AND PARTNERSHIPS

- Raise international awareness of TOC and build multilateral cooperation against it.
- Partner with countries able to contribute key law enforcement resources, other donors, and the United Nations to launch a new International Police Peacekeeping Operations Support Program to enhance policing and law enforcement capacity in ungoverned

spaces.

- Leverage assets to enhance foreign capabilities, including counterterrorism capacity building, foreign law enforcement cooperation, military cooperation, and the strengthening of justice and interior ministries.
- Implement a public diplomacy strategy to reduce the demand for illicit goods and services that fuels TOC.
- Implement the Central American Citizen Security Partnership to strengthen courts, civil society groups, and institutions that uphold the rule of law in the region.
- Implement the State Department's West Africa Citizen Security Initiative to combat transnational criminal threats in the region.
- Initiate new dialogue in multilateral for a to combat corruption and illicit trade, to include, as part of the Administration's IP enforcement strategy, stemming the flow of dangerous counterfeit products.
- Build partnerships with other donors, private sector experts, nongovernmental organizations, civil society groups, the media, and academia that focus on supporting political will for criminal justice reform.
- Increase international scientific research, data collection, and analysis to assess the scope and impact of TOC and the most effective means to combat it.
- Institutionalize the U.S.-UK Organized Crime Contact Group to deepen bilateral cooperation and galvanize multilateral collaboration against TOC.
- Finalize the U.S.-Mexico 21st Century Border Action Plan agreements on law enforcement cooperation.
- Expand cooperation with the United Nations to promote implementation of the United Nations UNTOC, including through the development of an appropriate review mechanism.
- Strengthen capacities for program management, internal controls, and contract administration to prevent the diversion or improper use of foreign assistance in countries threatened by TOC-related corruption.
- Increase collaboration with international partners to improve their capacity to support immigration, customs, transportation, and

critical infrastructure screening requirements and to harmonize their standards for screening and identification.

8.16. CASE STUDY: THE IMPACT OF DRUG ENFORCEMENT POLICIES ON TRANSNATIONAL ORGANIZED CRIME IN LATIN AMERICA

"For illicit drugs, organized crime is sine qua non. In other words, organized crime can exist without drug trafficking, but illicit drugs cannot live without organized crime." This quote illustrates the long-standing and infamously mutually beneficial relationship between organized crime and illicit drug trafficking. While the public threat of this relationship is long recognized and well understood, the solution is far less clear-cut. While the majority of the international community has stood with the consensus of prohibition and enforcement, in recent years, countries have begun to reexamine this approach for a variety of reasons.

Proponents of replacing prohibition with regulation have cited a variety of social issues to support their arguments, such as limiting violence from criminal organization and reducing illicit drug use. This article will briefly survey the relationship between drug trafficking and modern organized crime and the modern controlling international law on illicit drugs. Then, the article will examine the effect, if any, of two different styles of drug laws on combating organized crime through Uruguay's landmark policy of marijuana decriminalization and Mexico's hard-line approach to drug enforcement and organized crime.

8.16.1. Modern Organized Crime and the Illicit Drug Market

The United Nations UNTOC defines organized crime, as "a structured group of three or more persons, existing for a period of time and acting in concert with the aim of committing one or more serious crimes or Offenses established in accordance with this Convention, in order to obtain, directly or indirectly, a financial or other material benefit…"

The very nature of transnational illicit drug trafficking, which typically involves multiple actors committing drug trafficking offenses over a period, motivated by financial gain, results in most drug trafficking groups fitting into the U.N.'s definition of organized crime. Given the profit-driven focus of most drug traffickers, the illicit drug trade is often seen as the most lucrative activity. This high profitability is attributed largely to the nature of drug consumption; unlike firearms, gems, or even human beings, drugs are constantly consumed and are hence in need of continuous supply renewal. In fact, in 2014, between one third to one-fifth of all revenue attributed to TOC groups was estimated to have been from drug sales.

Modern organized crime has continued to evolve and shift in form and function to both survive increased efforts by law enforcement while harnessing new technology to expand drug markets and increase trafficking efficiency.

Recent statistics show that many criminal organizations have started to move away from the traditional rigid hierarchical organizational model, to looser "horizontal" networks, in response to efforts of law enforcement to remove key individuals and disrupt the organizational hierarchy. This reorganization has allowed these groups to quickly restructure when individuals have been detained. The adaptation has continued to increase across organizations.

Currently, thirty to forty percent of criminal organizations identified in 2017 were made up of loose criminal networks. Furthermore, transnational criminal organizations have utilized advances in communication technology, transportation, and even the dark web to expand their ability to smuggle larger quantities of illegal drugs, making it more difficult for law enforcement to detect and disrupt these activities.

8.16.2. Current International Drug Laws

For over 100 years, the international community has formally recognized and condemned the use of certain drugs. The 1912 Hague International Opium Convention became the first official international effort to control drug use and illicit drug trade. Since then, several multilateral treaties have taken this idea and expanded its scope well beyond opium. The 1988 Convention against Illicit Traffic in Narcotic Drugs and Psychotropic Substances, which currently includes 189 parties and eighty-seven signatories, focuses primarily on developing a strategy to combat TOC by creating mandates for member states to mitigate and disrupt the international drug trade.

The Convention requires signatories to take steps to eliminate demand within their respective countries for illegal drugs and other psychotropic substances. To fulfill these objectives, the treaty maintains that member states should take steps to implement domestic criminal laws outlawing "possession, purchase or cultivation of narcotic drugs or psychotropic substances for personal consumption."

8.16.3. Mexico: A Policy of Prohibition

Mexico first outlawed marijuana use in 1920, seventeen years before the United States. Over the last few decades, Mexico, in response to the well-published rise in organized crime, has taken several different approaches towards marijuana and drug trafficking to curb cartel operations. During the reign of President Felipe Calderon, from 2009–2012, the Mexican government took a strong approach to prohibition enforcement, targeting high-level organization members, increasing drug interdiction at the U.S./Mexico border, and utilizing the Mexican army to combat criminal activities.

This led to an explosion in drug-related killings, from 1,080 in 2001 to 6,587 in 2009. Some experts attribute this spike to the increased interdiction efforts, saying that removing powerful organizational leaders creates a power vacuum that results in infighting, encroachment by rival organizations, and organizational splintering.

In response to this spike in gang-related violence, Mexico has taken surprising steps towards relaxing their drug laws and reforming their criminal justice system. In 2009, Mexico passed a law legalizing the possession of small amounts of drugs, including 5 grams of marijuana. This appears to have had minimal immediate effect on the illegal drug trade; in 2010 the FBI reported Mexico as the number one importer of marijuana into the U.S. In 2015, the Mexican Supreme Court handed down a landmark decision in marijuana legalization, ruling that it is the right of individuals to grow and use cannabis for personal recreational use.

While this has not overruled the black letter law of the country, it is seen by many as a significant step towards legalization. In April 2016, in response to both the 2015 supreme court ruling and increasing disenchantment of the population towards the ongoing violence from the cartel wars, President Enrique Pena Nieto sent a proposal to the Mexican Congress calling for an increase to the allowance of personal possession of marijuana from 5 grams to 28 grams.

While these measures seemed promising, with homicide rates declining from 2013–2014, the homicide rate again exploded. 2016 saw an estimated 7,000–11,000 homicides (25–40% of the nationwide total) attributed to organized crime. The steps taken towards marijuana legalization were named as a reason for this upswing, due in part to organized crime changing their focus from trafficking marijuana to harder drugs such as cocaine and heroin.

8.16.4. Uruguay: Leading Latin America towards Marijuana Legalization

On December 24, 2013, Uruguay passed a law legalizing the purchase, possession, and growing of small to moderate quantities of marijuana. The law allows registered users to buy up to 40 grams of marijuana a month from licensed dealers, registered growers to keep up to six plants; and "cannabis clubs" of up to 45 members to cultivate as many as 99 plants. When the bill was first introduced in 2012, supporters of the bill cited both promotion of public health and reduction of organized crime among the top reasons for the supporting of the initiative.

This law has been met with limited success since its inception. The price for legal marijuana undercuts its illegal counterpart sold on the street, resulting in the drastic drop in price of "black market" marijuana. As of 2011, 66% of all marijuana users reported they were still purchasing their marijuana from illegal dealers. Despite assurances from independent sources and officials that the illegal drug market will subside over time, there has been a recent increase in organized crime activity in the county.

In the past several years, the number of foreign organized crime group members arrested in Uruguay rose. Officials believe that this is because of recent intensified international efforts to limit Pacific drug smuggling routes, which shifted these routes to the Atlantic. This triggered fear among Uruguayan officials that the country would subsequently then be used as a primary "springboard" for drug trafficking from the Americas to Europe. Recent statistics seem to support this fear. In 1999, only ten kilograms of illegal cocaine were seized in the country; in 2013, this exploded into over one ton of the drug being seized.

The annual homicide rate for Uruguay, which historically has been astonishingly low at around 180 homicides per year, nearly doubled to 289 in 2015. Finally, officials have reported that the style of killings has likewise changed drastically, with the majority of the recent murders bearing the signature of organized crime: daylight assassinations and execution-style killings.

8.16.5. Conclusion & Recommendations

The evidence discussed here supports a variety of conclusions and recommendations. First, due to the evolving nature of organized crime via loose organizational structures, advanced technologies, diversified drug trade, and global markets, legalization of only one drug within one country has a minimal impact on TOC. Additionally, policies of pure prohibition backed by hard-lined enforcement techniques do little except increase violence amongst organized criminal groups.

This evidence suggests that to be effective, decriminalization needs to be on a global scale followed up with targeted enforcement. Decriminalization not only limits income sources to drug traffickers, it also frees up valuable law enforcement resources to concentrate on combating other profit sources for organized crime.

Finally, the requirements in the 1988 Convention against Illicit Traffic in Narcotic Drugs and Psychotropic Substances should be adjusted to allow for member states to include legalization and decriminalization policies as part of their plan to eliminate the demand for illegal drugs. Implementing these lessons learned from Uruguay and Mexico will allow nations across the world to take a collective step at eliminating transnational criminal organizations.

REFERENCES

1. Amy, F. W., (1957). *CRS Report RL31957, Nonproliferation, and Threat Reduction Assistance: U.S. Programs in the Former Soviet Union*. Available at: https://fas.org/sgp/crs/nuke/RL31957.pdf
2. Barbera, C., (2017). The impact of drug enforcement policies on transnational organized crime in Latin America: A case study. [online] *Denver Journal of International Law and Policy*. Available at: http://djilp.org/7036/the-impact-of-drug-enforcement-policies-on-transnational-organized-crime-in-latin-america-a-case-study/ (Accessed on 12 April 2019).
3. CRS Issue Brief IB91121, China-U.S. Trade Issues, by Wayne M. Morrison (2014), and CRS Report 98–928, The World Trade Organization: Background and Issues, by Ian F. Fergusson. Available at: https://fortunedotcom.files.wordpress.com/2014/03/rl33536.pdf
4. Doyle, C. (2008). *Money laundering*. New York: Nova Science Publishers.
5. Obamawhitehouse.archives.gov., (2011). *Strategy to Combat Transnational Organized Crime*. [online] Available at: https://obamawhitehouse.archives.gov/sites/default/files/Strategy_to_Combat_Transnational_Organized_Crime_July_2011.pdf (Accessed on 12 April 2019).
6. *The Globalization of Crime: A Transnational Organized Crime Threat Assessment*, (2010). United Nations publication, Sales No. E.10.IV.6.2010. Available from: www.unodc.org/documents/data-and-analysis/tocta/TOCTA_Report_2010_low_res.pdf (Accessed on 13 April 2019).
7. Un.Org., (2015). *Combating Transnational Organized Crime Through Better International Cooperation*. [online] Available at: http://www.un.org/en/events/crimecongress2015/pdf/Factsheet_4_International_cooperation_EN.pdf (Accessed on 12 April 2019).
8. United Nations office on drugs and crime, (2010). "*Trafficking in Persons to Europe for Sexual Exploitation*." Available from: www.unodc.org/documents/publications/TiP_Europe_EN_LORES.pdf (Accessed on 13 April 2019).
9. United Nations office on drugs and crime, (2011). *Global Study on Homicide: Trends, Contexts, Data*. Available from: www.unodc.org/documents/data-and-analysis/statistics/Homicide/Globa_study_on_

homicide_2011_web.pdf (Accessed on 13 April 2019).

10. United Nations Office on Drugs and Crime, *Estimating Illicit Financial Flows Resulting from Drug Trafficking and Other Transnational Organized Crimes: Research Report,* (Vienna, October 2011). Available from: www.unodc.org/documents/data-and-analysis/Studies/Illicit_financial_flows_2011_web.pdf (Accessed on 13 April 2019).
11. *United Nations's Protocol to Prevent, Suppress, and Punish Trafficking in Persons*. http://www.unodc.org/unodc/en/trafficking_protocol.html (Accessed on 13 April 2019).
12. Unodc.org., (n.d.). *Transnational Organized Crime – The Globalized Illegal Economy*. [online] Available at: https://www.unodc.org/documents/toc/factsheets/TOC12_fs_general_EN_HIRES.pdf (Accessed on 12 April 2019).
13. Wagley, J. R., (2006). *Transnational Organized Crime: Principal Threats and U.S. Responses*. [online] Fas.org. Available at: https://fas.org/sgp/crs/natsec/RL33335.pdf (Accessed on 12 April 2019).
14. World Drug Report, (2011).

INDEX

H

I

J

K

L

M

N

O

P

Q

R

W